Making Sense
of Human Rights

Making Sense
of Human Rights

Philosophical Reflections on the
Universal Declaration of Human Rights

James W. Nickel

University of California Press

Berkeley / Los Angeles / London

University of California Press
Berkeley and Los Angeles, California

University of California Press, Ltd.
London, England

© 1987 by
The Regents of the University of California

Library of Congress Cataloging-in-Publication Data

Nickel, James W.
   Making sense of human rights.
   Includes index.
   1. Civil rights.   2. United Nations. General
Assembly. Universal Declaration of Human Rights.
I. Title.
JC571.N49 1987   341.4'81   86–11306
ISBN 0–520–05688–4 (alk. paper)
ISBN 0–520–05994–8 (ppb.)
Printed in the United States of America
1 2 3 4 5 6 7 8 9

To Regi

Contents

Preface

Shaky governments facing severe problems often try to preserve their power by jailing, torturing, and murdering those who oppose their rule. When cases of this sort come to our attention, we are now likely to describe them as violations of human rights—instead of simply saying that they are unjust, immoral, or barbaric. If pressed to be more specific, we may add that such actions violate rights to freedom from arbitrary arrest, to due process, to freedom from torture, and to life. These rights are internationally recognized in the Universal Declaration of Human Rights and other human rights documents.

Appealing to human rights in order to describe and criticize the actions of repressive governments is relatively new as a popular phenomenon. Talk of natural or human rights has long been common among philosophers and lawyers, but in the past few decades the idea of human rights has become part of the vocabulary of the general public in large parts of the world. Violations of human rights are now often recognized and reported as such, and the public has come to have some new categories of thought and appraisal and—one hopes—some new sensitivities in regard to repressive governments.

The formulation by the United Nations in 1948 of the Universal Declaration of Human Rights made possible the subsequent flourishing of the idea of human rights. The Declaration was an attempt to provide an authoritative international list of human rights that would give some fixed meaning to the idea, and this attempt was successful to a substantial degree. Its progeny, such as the European Convention on Human Rights and the International Covenants of 1966, refined the formulations of these rights and gave them the status of international law.[1]

1. The texts of the Universal Declaration of Human Rights, the European Convention on Human Rights, the International Covenant on Civil and Political Rights

This book is an extended philosophical reflection on these documents. It examines and evaluates many of their key concepts and norms. Reflective people often find the idea of human rights perplexing and may raise questions about the analysis, content, or justification of these rights. Analytical questions pertain to the nature of human rights; here one might ask for an analysis of the concept of a right or for an exploration of the advantages and disadvantages of the rights vocabulary for the human rights movement. Questions about the content of human rights pertain to the scope and weight of particular rights and to whether contemporary lists of human rights are plausible and realistic. Questions of justification ask whether there are any grounds for believing in universal human rights, whether these grounds are transcultural, and what steps are involved in justifying a right. Questions about the universality, inalienability, and weight of human rights arise here as well.

This book addresses these questions, moving from analytical questions to issues of justification and from these to questions of content and affordability. Overall, the book sketches a defense of the contemporary idea of human rights against a variety of philosophical and practical objections. As part of this, considerable attention is given to economic rights and issues involving resources and affordability.

At the conceptual level, my intention is to explain the concept of rights and to demonstrate the numerous ways in which specific human rights can be qualified so as to avoid many familiar objections. This endeavor goes against the tendency of writers in the last decade to emphasize the power and uniqueness of the rights vocabulary. I oppose this tendency because I fear that it makes human rights too difficult to justify.

The account given here of the nature and justification of the rights in the Universal Declaration does not take such specific rights to be ultimate moral standards that are underived and unchanging. Instead, it sees these particular rights as attempts to identify the implications for the political morality of a particular era of deeper and more abstract considerations pertaining to life, freedom, and fairness.

(1966), and the International Covenant on Social, Economic and Cultural Rights are appended. These documents can also be found in Ian Brownlie, ed., *Basic Documents on Human Rights* (Oxford: Clarendon Press, 1971).

As this approach suggests, the justification of human rights has several stages. The most basic stage involves trying to justify one's claims about the abstract considerations that underlie human rights. The second stage involves trying to show that some specific human rights follow from these abstract considerations—that they express the implications of these considerations for the problems and institutions of a certain period of time. Using an analogy to chess, I will often refer to this stage as the "middle game." A third stage of justification involves defending the choices that have to be made when rights are implemented and applied. To extend the analogy, this might be thought of as the "end game."

This book gives considerable attention to the middle game. Philosophers generally focus on ultimate justification, and political scientists and lawyers usually focus on the end game, with the result that the middle level is largely ignored. I try to remedy this lack of attention by developing an account of the kind of case that needs to be made for a specific right at the middle level of justification. The result may seem insufficiently theoretical to philosophers and insufficiently practical to political scientists and lawyers, but that is a risk I willingly take. I hope to make it obvious that the middle level of justification is a significant area in which the concerns of abstract theorists and human rights practitioners must be brought together. One of my key contentions is that considerations of cost or affordability cannot be confined to the end game, or application stage.

Despite this concern with affordability, this book does not advance or explore political strategies for increasing respect for human rights around the world. A philosophical account of the nature and justification of human rights is not a recipe for progress. It is rather an attempt to define in international terms what it would mean for such progress to occur.

I am indebted to many individuals and institutions for their support and help. People who have provided much-appreciated suggestions and encouragement include Joseph Beatty, Nancy Davis, Allan Fuchs, David Falk, Kent Greenawalt, Louis Henkin, Dale Jamieson, Ellen Lutz, Rex Martin, Philipe Nonet, Philip Selznick, and M. B. E. Smith. Special thanks go to Fred Berger, Regina Celi, Virginia Held, Steve Munzer, and Carl Wellman for writing comments on earlier drafts of this book. This is a much better book than it could have been without their help. I would also like to express my appreciation for grants in support of this work from the American Council of Learned Societies, the National Humanities Center, and the Rockefeller Foundation.

Some of the material in chapters 2 and 3 first appeared in "Are Human Rights Utopian?" *Philosophy and Public Affairs* 11 (1982): 246–264. An earlier version of the section on the right to employment in chapter 8 was published in "Is There a Human Right to Employment?" *Philosophical Forum* 11 (1980): 149–170. And the test for the priority of rights propounded in chapters 6 and 8 was first elaborated in "On the Feasibility of Welfare Rights in Less Developed Countries," in Kenneth Kipnis and Diana Meyers, eds., *Economic Justice: Private Rights and Public Responsibility* (Totowa, N.J.: Rowman & Allanheld, 1985), 217–225. Permission to use this material is gratefully acknowledged.

1. The Contemporary Idea of Human Rights

The United Nations and Human Rights

Today's idea of human rights is a compound that was brewed in the cauldron of World War II. During that war it took no stretch of the imagination to see that one dangerous aspect of Hitler's rule was its lack of concern for people's lives and liberties. Because of this, the war against the Axis powers was easily defended in terms of preserving human rights and fundamental freedoms. The Allied governments asserted in the "Declaration by United Nations" of January 1, 1942, that victory was "essential to defend life, liberty, independence and religious freedom, and to preserve human rights and justice."[1] In his subsequent message to Congress, President Franklin D. Roosevelt identified four freedoms that the war effort was to secure: freedom of speech and expression, freedom of religion, freedom from want, and freedom from fear of war.[2]

The incredible carnage and destruction of World War II led to a determination to do something to prevent war, to build an international organization that could defuse international crises and provide a forum for discussion and mediation. This organization was the United Nations, which has played a key role in the development of the contemporary view of human rights.

The creators of the United Nations believed that reducing the likelihood of war required preventing large-scale violations of people's rights. Because of this belief, even the earliest conceptions

1. For the text of the "Declaration by United Nations" of January 1, 1942, see H. F. van Panhuys et al., eds., *International Organization and Integration* (The Hague: Martinus Nijhoff, 1981), vol. 1A.

2. See Douglas Lurton, *Roosevelt's Foreign Policy, 1933–1941: Franklin D. Roosevelt's Unedited Speeches* (Toronto: Longmans, Green, 1942), 324.

of the United Nations included a role in promoting rights and liberties. Early drafts of the UN Charter (1942 and 1943) contained a bill of rights to which any nation joining the organization would have to subscribe, but difficulties arose concerning enforcement of such a bill of rights. Reflecting concern for their sovereignty, states were willing to agree to "promote" human rights but not to "protect" them.[3]

It was ultimately decided to include only a few references to human rights in the UN Charter and to charge the Commission on Human Rights, a committee of the United Nations created by a provision of the charter, with the job of writing an international bill of rights. The charter itself reaffirmed "faith in fundamental human rights, in the dignity and worth of the human person, in the equal rights of men and women and of nations large and small." Its signatories pledged themselves to "take joint and separate action in cooperation with the Organization" to promote "universal respect for, and observance of, human rights and fundamental freedoms for all without distinction as to race, sex, language or religion."[4]

The Human Rights Commission prepared an international bill of rights that was approved by the General Assembly on December 10, 1948. This bill, the Universal Declaration of Human Rights, was proclaimed "a common standard of achievement for all peoples and all nations." The rights it declared were to be promoted by "teaching and education" and by "progressive measures, national and international, to secure their universal and effective recognition and observance."[5]

The first twenty-one articles of the Declaration present rights similar to those found in the Bill of Rights in the U.S. Constitution as amended to date. These civil and political rights include rights to equal protection and nondiscrimination, due process in legal proceedings, privacy and personal integrity, and political participation.

3. For an overview of the history of the Universal Declaration of Human Rights and an outline of the key issues that were debated prior to its adoption, see Louis B. Sohn, "A Short History of the United Nations Documents on Human Rights," in Commission to Study the Organization of Peace, *The United Nations and Human Rights: Eighteenth Report of the Commission* (Dobbs Ferry, N.Y.: Transnational Publishers, 1968), 43–56; reprinted in Louis B. Sohn and Thomas Buergenthal, eds., *International Protection of Human Rights* (Indianapolis: Bobbs-Merrill, 1973), 505. See also John P. Humphrey, *Human Rights and the United Nations: A Great Adventure* (Dobbs Ferry, N.Y.: Transnational Publishers, 1984).

4. Ian Brownlie, ed., *Basic Documents on Human Rights* (Oxford: Clarendon Press, 1971), 93–105.

5. Ibid., 107. The text of the Universal Declaration is appended.

But articles 22 through 27 make a new departure. They declare rights to economic and social benefits such as social security, an adequate standard of living, and education. These rights assert, in effect, that all people have rights to the services of a welfare state.

Human rights, as conceived in twentieth-century human rights documents such as the Universal Declaration, have a number of salient characteristics. First, lest we miss the obvious, these are *rights*. The exact import of this status is unclear—and will be one of my subjects of inquiry—but the word at least suggests that these are definite and high-priority norms whose pursuit is mandatory.

Second, these rights are alleged to be *universal*, to be held by people simply as people. This view implies that characteristics such as race, sex, religion, social position, and nationality are irrelevant to whether one has human rights. It also implies that these rights are applicable all around the world. One of the distinctive features of human rights today is that they are international rights. Compliance with such rights has come to be seen as a legitimate object of international concern and action.

Third, human rights are held to *exist independently* of recognition or implementation in the customs or legal systems of particular countries. These rights may not be *effective* rights until legally implemented, but they exist as standards of argument and criticism independently of legal implementation.

Fourth, human rights are held to be *important norms*. Although they are not all absolute and exceptionless, they are strong enough as normative considerations to prevail in conflicts with contrary national norms and to justify international action on their behalf. The rights described in the Declaration are not ranked in terms of priority; their relative weights are left unstated. It is not claimed that some of them are absolute. Thus the rights of the Declaration are what philosophers call prima facie rights.

Fifth, these rights *imply duties* for both individuals and governments. These duties, like the rights with which they are linked, are alleged to exist independently of acceptance, recognition, or implementation. Governments and people everywhere are obligated not to violate a person's rights, although a person's own government may have the main responsibility to take positive measures to protect and uphold that person's rights.[6]

---

6. On whether governments other than one's own must uphold one's human rights, see James W. Nickel, "Human Rights and the Rights of Aliens," in Peter G.

Finally, these rights *establish minimal standards* of decent social and governmental practice. Not all problems deriving from inhumanity or selfishness and stupidity are human rights problems. For example, a government that failed to provide national parks for its citizens might be criticized for being cheap or insufficiently concerned with recreational opportunities, but that would not be a matter of human rights.

Although human rights are viewed as setting minimal standards, contemporary rights declarations tend to posit rights that are numerous and specific rather than few and general. The Universal Declaration replaces Locke's three generic rights—to life, liberty, and property—with nearly two dozen specific rights. Among the civil and political rights asserted are rights to freedom from discrimination; to life, liberty, and security of the person; to freedom of religion; to freedom of thought and expression; to freedom of assembly and association; to freedom from torture and cruel punishments; to equality before the law; to freedom from arbitrary arrest; to a fair trial; to protections of privacy; and to freedom of movement. The Declaration's social and economic rights include rights to marry and found a family, to freedom from forced marriage, to education, to the availability of a job, to an adequate standard of living, to rest and leisure, and to security during illness, disability, and old age.

The Universal Declaration states that these rights are rooted in the dignity and worth of human beings and in the requirements of domestic and international peace and security. In promulgating the Universal Declaration as a "common standard of achievement," the United Nations did not purport to describe rights already recognized everywhere or to enact these rights within international law. Instead, it attempted to set forth the norms that exist within enlightened moralities. Although the goal of many of the participants was to enact these rights in both domestic and international legal systems, they were held to exist not as legal rights but as universal moral rights.

Descendents of the Universal Declaration include not only bills of rights in many national constitutions but also a number of international human rights treaties. The first and perhaps most signifi-

Brown and Henry Shue, eds., *The Border That Joins* (Totowa, N.J.: Rowman & Littlefield, 1983), 31–45.

cant of these is the European Convention on Human Rights. This convention, created within the Council of Europe in 1950, has been the most successful system yet developed for the international enforcement of human rights.[7] It declares roughly the same rights found in the first twenty-one articles of the Universal Declaration. It contains no economic and social rights; these were relegated to the European Social Covenant, a document committing its signatories to promote as important government goals the availability of various economic and social benefits.

Some advocates of an international bill of rights in the United Nations wanted not a mere declaration but norms backed by an enforcement procedure capable of applying international pressure to countries violating human rights on a large scale. The plan within the United Nations was to follow the Universal Declaration with analogous treaties. Drafts of the International Covenants were submitted to the General Assembly for approval in 1953. To accommodate those who believed that economic and social rights were not genuine human rights or that they were not enforceable in the same way as civil and political rights, two treaties were prepared, the Covenant on Civil and Political Rights and the Covenant on Economic, Social, and Cultural Rights.

Because of the Cold War hostilities of the time and the termination of support for human rights treaty making by the United States, action on the Covenants was long delayed. They were not approved by the General Assembly until 1966. During the years when it appeared that the Covenants were doomed, the United Nations produced a number of much narrower human rights treaties dealing with relatively uncontroversial topics such as genocide, slavery, refugees, stateless persons, and discrimination.[8] These treaties were

7. On the European system, see Frede Castberg, *The European Convention on Human Rights* (Dobbs Ferry, N.Y.: Oceana Publications, 1974); James E. S. Fawcett, *The Application of the European Convention on Human Rights* (Oxford: Clarendon Press, 1969); and the Secretary to the European Commission of Human Rights, *Stock-Taking on the European Convention on Human Rights: A Periodic Note on the Concrete Results Achieved Under the Convention* (Strasbourg: Council of Europe, 1979).

8. Many of these documents can be found in Brownlie, ed., *Basic Documents on Human Rights*. Relevant documents therein include the Convention on the Prevention and Punishment of the Crimes of Genocide (1948), 116–120; the Slavery Convention (1926, amended by Protocol, 1953), 121–127; the Supplementary Convention on the Abolition of Slavery, the Slave Trade and Institutions and Practices Similar to Slavery (1956), 128–134; the Convention Relating to the Status of Refu-

generally signed by a large number of nations—although not by the United States—and through them the United Nations began to acquire some experience in administering human rights treaties.

Between the Universal Declaration of 1948 and the General Assembly's final approval of the International Covenants in 1966, many African and Asian nations, recently freed from colonial rule, entered the United Nations. These nations were generally willing to go along with the human rights enterprise, but they did modify it to reflect their own interests and concerns: finishing off colonialism, condemning Western exploitation of developing countries, and destroying apartheid and racial discrimination in Southern Africa. The Covenants that emerged in 1966 reveal these concerns; both contain identical paragraphs asserting rights of nations to self-determination and to control their own natural resources. The Universal Declaration's right to property and to remuneration for property taken by the state were deleted from the Covenants.

After General Assembly approval in 1966, the Covenants required the signatures of thirty-five countries in order to be binding on the signatories. The thirty-fifth nation signed in 1976, and the Covenants are now in force as international law.

Distinctive Features of the Contemporary Conception of Human Rights

Although the contemporary idea of human rights was created during World War II, that new construction used a number of familiar ideas about freedom, justice, and individual rights. It would not be a great distortion to view the recent rise to prominence of the vocabulary of human rights as simply the popularization of an old idea. The notion of a natural or divine law binding on all people and requiring decent treatment of all is an ancient one, and this notion was wedded to the idea of natural rights in the writings of theorists such as Locke and Jefferson as well as in declarations of rights such as the French Declaration of the Rights of Man and the Citizen and

---

gees (1951), 135–152; the Convention Relating to the Status of Stateless Persons (1954), 153–169; the International Convention of the Elimination of All Forms of Racial Discrimination (1966), 237–252; and the Declaration on Elimination of Discrimination Against Women (1967), 183–187.

the U.S. Bill of Rights. The idea of individual rights vis-à-vis, or against, government is not a new one, and one could argue that today's idea of human rights is merely a development of this concept. But if we take the Universal Declaration and the Covenants as representing, broadly, the contemporary view of human rights, we can say that today's view of human rights differs from earlier, particularly eighteenth-century, conceptions in three ways. Human rights today are more egalitarian, less individualistic, and have an international focus.

Egalitarianism

The egalitarianism of recent human rights documents is evident, first, in the great emphasis they place on protections against discrimination and on equality before the law. Although eighteenth-century rights manifestos sometimes declared equality before the law, protections against discrimination are nineteenth- and twentieth-century developments. Victory over slavery came in the nineteenth century, but the struggle against racist attitudes and practices is a central struggle of our time. The demand for equality for women in all areas of life has also been placed on the human rights agenda.[9]

Second, the egalitarianism of contemporary human rights documents can be seen in the inclusion of welfare rights. Earlier conceptions of political rights generally viewed their role as keeping government off the backs of the people. Abuse of political power was seen as a problem of governments doing things they should not, rather than failing to do things they should. The duties generated by these rights were mainly negative ones—duties of restraint. Positive duties were mainly found in the duty of governments to protect people's rights against internal and external invasions.

Due process rights (rights to a fair trial, freedom from arbitrary arrest, freedom from torture and cruel punishments) were seen as remedies for abuses of the legal system. These abuses included manipulating the legal system to favor the friends and disadvantage the

9. On women's rights in the international context, see Margaret K. Bruce, "Work of the United Nations Relating to the Status of Women," *Human Rights Journal* 4 (1971): 365–412; Margaret E. Galey, "International Enforcement of Women's Rights," *Human Rights Quarterly* 6 (1984): 463–490; Terry Ellen Polson, "The Rights of Working Women: An International Perspective," *Virginia Journal of International Law* 14 (1974): 729–746; and Jane P. Sweeney, "Promoting Human Rights Through Regional Organizations: Women's Rights in Western Europe," *Human Rights Quarterly* 6 (1984): 491–506.

enemies of those in power, jailing political opponents, and ruling through terror.

Rights of privacy and autonomy (rights to freedom from invasion of the home and correspondence, freedom of movement, free choice of residence and occupation, and freedom of association) were seen as remedies for invasions of the private sphere, which included governmental prying into the most intimate areas of life and attempts to control people by limiting where they are able to live, work, and travel.

Rights of political participation (rights to freedom of expression, to petition government, to vote, and to run for public office) were seen as remedies for such abuses as refusing to consider complaints, suppressing dissent and opposition, crippling the development of an informed electorate, and manipulating the electoral system to stay in power. Avoiding these various abuses mainly required governments to leave people alone. Satisfying these rights, however, requires provision of positive benefits such as fair trials, free elections, and protections against abuses by police and other government officials.

But as Marx and other socialists often pointed out, even if government were restrained from the abuses just listed, such social and economic problems as slavery, poverty, ignorance, disease, discrimination, and economic exploitation would be undisturbed. Since Marx, movements for social change have been as much concerned with these social and economic problems as with violations of traditional kinds of political rights. One result has been to broaden the scope of the rights vocabulary to include these problems within the human rights agenda.

The vehicle for delivering the services these rights demand is the modern welfare state, a political system that uses its taxation powers or control of the economy to collect the resources required to supply essential welfare services to all of the country's residents who need them. Marxists and socialists were not alone in promoting welfare rights; Roosevelt's "four freedoms," for example, included freedom from want.

Three beliefs seem to be involved in the process by which these social and economic problems come to be seen as problems to be solved by government and hence, if left unsolved, as violations of political rights. One of these beliefs is that poverty, exploitation, and discrimination are threats to human welfare and dignity as serious as deliberate violations of traditional political rights.

A second belief is that human misery and severe inequality are not inevitable but result from changeable social, political, and economic conditions that can be subjected to moral or political control. One basis for this optimistic view is the high levels of wealth attained in Europe, North America, Japan, and Australia and the emergence in these countries of effective systems of politically implemented welfare rights.

Last is the belief that political, economic, and social systems cannot really be separated—that government power is often used to create and maintain economic and social institutions that favor certain groups. If government helps to support an economic system that gives vast wealth to a few while leaving many in misery, and if such a system is not inevitable and could be replaced by one far more supportive of everyone's welfare and dignity, government may reasonably be charged with complicity in the evils resulting from the existing system.

As these beliefs have become common, governments have been charged with the task of providing remedies through the use of their resources and redistributive powers.

Reduced Individualism

Recent rights manifestos have tempered the individualism of classical theories of natural rights. Current documents conceive of people as members of families and communities, not as isolated individuals who must be given reasons for entering civil society. The Universal Declaration, for example, declares that "the family is the natural and fundamental group unit of society and is entitled to protection by society and the State." In the Covenants, rights of groups have been brought within the human rights framework by giving a prominent place to the rights of nations to self-determination and to control of their natural resources. Further, human rights are no longer closely associated with social contract theory—although John Rawls has tried to rebuild the linkage.[10] There are few references to the philosophical foundations of human rights in contemporary documents. Postwar efforts to formulate international human rights norms have gone forward in the face of undeniable and unchangeable philosophical and ideological divisions. To gather as much support for the movement as possible, the philosophical underpinnings for human rights were left unspecified.

10. John Rawls, *A Theory of Justice* (Cambridge, Mass.: Harvard University Press, 1971).

International Rights

The third difference between today's human rights and eighteenth-century natural rights is that human rights have been internationalized.[11] Not only are they prescribed internationally—which is nothing new—but now they are also seen as appropriate objects of international action and concern. Although eighteenth-century natural rights were viewed as rights of all people, they served more often as criteria for justifying rebellion against existing governments than as standards whose violation by governments could justify investigations and the application of diplomatic and economic pressure by international organizations. Although states remain jealous of their sovereignty and anxious to prevent outsiders from interfering in their affairs, the principle that international inquiries and nonmilitary sanctions are justifiable in cases of large-scale violations of human rights is now well established.[12]

At present the most effective system for the international enforcement of human rights is found in Western Europe under the European Convention on Human Rights. This convention provides a bill of rights, a Human Rights Commission to investigate complaints, and a Human Rights Court to deal with issues of interpretation. Any state ratifying the European Convention must accept the authority of the Human Rights Commission to receive, investigate, and mediate complaints from other member states about human rights violations. Liability to complaints by individuals is optional, as is the procedure of referring to the Human Rights Court all issues not resolvable by the commission.

The Human Rights Commission, which receives hundreds of complaints each year, examines them for admissibility and investigates and mediates the admissible ones. Friendly negotiation with the parties involved is a standard procedure, but when this fails an issue can be referred to the court or to the Committee of Ministers of the Council of Europe. The commission and court have by now

11. See Louis Henkin, *The Rights of Man Today* (Boulder, Colo.: Westview Press, 1978), xi–xiii.

12. On intervention, see Richard B. Lillich and Frank C. Newman, "How Effective in Causing Compliance with Human Rights Law Are Coercive Measures That Do Not Involve the Use of Armed Force?" in Lillich and Newman, eds., *International Human Rights: Problems of Law and Policy* (Boston: Little, Brown, 1979), 388–482; or Richard B. Lillich, "Intervention to Protect Human Rights," *McGill Law Journal* 15 (1969): 205–219.

dealt with many cases and have built up a sizable body of procedure and law. In general they have proceeded quite cautiously, but this caution has been rewarded by the member states' confidence in the integrity of the system and by their continued willingness to accept the limitations on their sovereignty that the system requires.

The International Covenant on Civil and Political Rights, created within the United Nations, also provides a procedure—albeit a weaker one than its European analogue—for the international protection of human rights. This covenant established a Human Rights Committee to supervise compliance, a committee with three main functions. The first is to examine the reports that states adhering to the covenant are required to submit "on the measures they have adopted which give effect to the rights recognized herein and on the progress made in the enjoyment of these rights." The second activity is to receive, consider, and mediate complaints by one member that another is violating the terms of the covenant. A state is vulnerable to such complaints only if it accepts the competence of the committee to receive complaints. Only sixteen of the eighty-one states that have ratified the covenant have agreed to be liable to complaints made to the committee. The third activity of the committee is to receive, consider, and mediate complaints by individuals that states are violating their obligations. The optional protocol that indicates willingness to have the Human Rights Committee receive such individual complaints has received enough signatures to come into force. How effective the committee will be in enforcing the covenant's norms remains to be seen, but it is clear that few if any sanctions of weight are at its disposal.

A similar system for the protection of human rights exists within the Organization of American States (OAS). The Inter-American Commission on Human Rights was established in 1959 and was made an official organ of the OAS in 1970. This commission played an important role in investigating and exposing rights abuses in Latin America during the seventies.[13] In 1969 the American Convention on Human Rights was approved by a special conference sponsored by the OAS.

13. For a discussion of the Inter-American Commission see, among others, "Regional Approaches to Human Rights: The Inter-American Experience: A Panel (Burgenthal, Vargas Carreno, Schneider, Armstrong, Oliver)," *American Society of International Law Proceedings* 72 (1978): 197–223; C. S. White IV, "Practice and Pleadings Before the Inter-American Commission on Human Rights," *Human*

The American convention received enough ratifications to enter into force in 1978. It establishes two institutions, the Inter-American Commission on Human Rights and the Inter-American Court of Human Rights. The commission is a successor to the one established in 1959 and is rooted both in the OAS charter and in the convention. It combines the role of its predecessor with the functions conferred by the convention. The court held its first meeting in 1979 and has since produced a number of advisory opinions. In March 1986 it received its first litigious case.[14] The court consists of seven judges, elected by the states that have ratified the convention. Although the inter-American system is similar to the European system in many respects, the social and political context for its operation is radically different. Further, the human rights problems it faces are much more severe. For these reasons, its evolution will be interesting to watch.

In Africa, the Organization of African Unity recently adopted an African Charter on Human and Peoples' Rights.[15] In the Middle East and Asia, however, regional institutions for the purpose of promoting human rights have not emerged.

Rights 4 (Summer 1975): 413–431; Robert E. Norris, "Observation *in Loco:* Practice and Procedure of the Inter-American Commission on Human Rights," *Texas International Law Journal* 15 (1980): 46–95; and Anna P. Schreiber, *The Inter-American Commission on Human Rights* (Leiden: Sigthoff, 1970).

14. The text of the American Convention is available in Brownlie, ed., *Basic Documents on Human Rights,* 399–427. Concerning the work of the court, see articles by Thomas Buergenthal: "The Inter-American Court of Human Rights," *American Journal of International Law* 76 (1982): 235–245; and "The Advisory Practice of the Inter-American Human Rights Court," *American Journal of International Law* 79 (1985): 1–27. See also Manuel D. Vargas, "Individual Access to the Inter-American Court of Human Rights," *International Law and Politics* 16 (1984): 601–617.

15. See B. Obinna Okere, "The Protection of Human Rights in Africa and the African Charter on Human and Peoples' Rights: A Comparative Analysis with the European and American Systems," *Human Rights Quarterly* 6 (1984): 141–159; and Rhoda Howard, "Evaluating Human Rights in Africa: Some Problems of Implicit Comparisons," *Human Rights Quarterly* 6 (1984): 160–179.

2. The Nature of Rights

Many disputes about human rights have a conceptual dimension: they are partly about how the language of rights should be used. I address these conceptual issues here by presenting an account of the meaning and role of rights that is intended to apply to all kinds of rights. There are many varieties of rights, and it is not wise to generalize from just one or two. In particular, one should not focus exclusively on legal rights.

Human rights are a subset of rights generally. How human rights should be understood will be addressed in chapter 3; the general analysis of rights that is developed here will be used to guide that inquiry.

Elements of Rights

Because rights often involve complex relationships concerning who has the right and when it can be applied, it is helpful to have a detailed analysis of the parts of a fully specified right.

First, each right identifies some party as its possessor or holder. A right's *conditions of possession* may be narrow enough to apply to only one person (e.g., a person named in a will) or broad enough to include the whole human race. Procedures for permanently alienating a right, such as selling, repudiating, or forfeiting it, can also be specified in its conditions of possession.

Second, rights are *to* some freedom or benefit. We can say that the *scope* of a right specifies what it is to. For example, the scope of a right to payment under a commercial contract may specify that the rightholder has a right to be paid $5,000 by the addressee within sixty days after specified goods are delivered. The scope of a right often contains exceptions excluding items that might otherwise be expected to be included. If, for example, the constitutional right to freedom of speech does not include protection for speeches made from the visitors' gallery during sessions of Congress, this exception could be specified in, or be a consequence of, a full statement of the right's scope.

The scope of a right also includes *conditions of operability,* which specify when a right applies and what, if anything, must be done to bring it into play. A right becomes operable when its holder is in a situation in which the right can be put into use, perhaps by being claimed or invoked. It can then be said to be *engaged.* To waive or refuse to exercise one's right when it is operable often prevents the right from being engaged. Some rights, however, seem to be continuously engaged. A person's right not to be tortured would be engaged—and would generate the duty not to torture—even if the person being tortured were too weak to invoke the right.

Rights are commonly classified as negative or positive according to whether the right requires the addressees merely to refrain from doing something or requires them to take some positive action they might not otherwise take. Because most rights impose on their addressees both negative and positive duties, the distinction is misleading when applied to rights and should be restricted to duties. Consider, for example, the right of freedom of assembly, which may seem to be a negative right in view of the fact that its main focus is on getting governments and individuals to refrain from interfering with religious and political meetings. But this right also implies a positive duty of governments to provide protections against government agents or private parties who disrupt meetings.[1]

Third, a fully specified right identifies a party or parties who must act to make available the freedom or benefit identified by the right's scope. These parties are the *addressees* of the right. Here one can distinguish between rights that entail claims against the world at large and rights that entail claims against specific parties.[2]

Finally, the *weight* of a right specifies its rank or importance in relation to other norms. Weight pertains to whether a right can sometimes be overridden by other considerations in cases of conflict. A prima facie right is a nonabsolute right whose weight in competition with other considerations is not fully specified. De-

---

1. For a fuller discussion of this point, see Henry Shue, *Basic Rights* (Princeton, N.J.: Princeton University Press, 1980), 35–64.
2. This distinction between these two dimensions of rights is drawn by Joel Feinberg in *Social Philosophy* (Englewood Cliffs, N.J.: Prentice-Hall, 1973), 59.

scribing a right as prima facie does not imply that it is only an apparent right but rather asserts that it is a genuine right that can sometimes be outweighed by other considerations.[3]

Rights range from abstract to specific (or from general to precise) according to how fully their parts are specified. But indeterminacy can occur not only in regard to scope and weight but also in regard to conditions of possession and operability and in regard to the addressees and their burdens. One of the confusing things about rights is that they are used with differing degrees of abstractness; even very abstract or general rights play important roles in stating grand political principles. The right conferred by the U.S. Constitution to equal protection of the law is vague and abstract, but the principle it states is extremely important. The moral and legal roles of abstract rights are often just as significant as the roles of very specific rights, so we simply have to come to terms with abstractness in rights rather than proposing to get rid of it to achieve some philosophical ideal of precision.

Distinctive Functions of Rights

A tradition of formulating bills of rights was established by the Magna Carta, the French Declaration of the Rights of Man and the Citizen, and the U.S. Bill of Rights. It is therefore not surprising that the authors of the Universal Declaration chose the vehicle of rights to express universal standards of government conduct. But other conceptual vehicles could have done roughly the same job. It is interesting to ask whether the language of rights has unique advantages for formulating standards of behavior for governments and societies.

In explaining a problematic concept it is often helpful to try to identify the distinctive functions of that concept. The focus on what one can *do* with a concept usefully supplements attempts to analyze rights by focusing on their constituent parts. This approach is

3. The vocabulary of prima facie rights was adapted from Ross's concept of prima facie duties; see David Ross, *The Right and the Good* (Oxford: Clarendon Press, 1930). See also the section on defeasibility in Rex Martin and James W. Nickel, "Recent Work on the Concept of Rights," *American Philosophical Quarterly* 17 (1980): 165–180. This essay is reprinted in Kenneth G. Lucey and Tibor R. Machan, eds., *Recent Work in Philosophy* (Totowa, N.J.: Rowman & Allanheld, 1983), 205–225.

closely related to ones that focus on the practices in which a concept plays a role or on the motivations that people typically have when they accept a system of beliefs using a concept.[4]

Goals and Rights

We can begin by comparing rights to high-priority goals. Suppose that instead of formulating a bill of rights, the human rights movement had formulated high-priority goals in areas such as civil liberties, security of the person, due process, and social justice and had asserted that these goals should be pursued by all nations. This vocabulary would have lent itself to the formulation of a long list of things important for governments to do and not do. The resulting "Universal Declaration of High-Priority Goals" could have been even more expansive than the Universal Declaration, but it would have been more aspirational than mandatory.

Some of the distinctive features of the rights vocabulary would be lost if we were to speak exclusively of goals or ideals or if we were to define rights entirely in terms of these goals or ideals. A declaration of high-priority goals might have had much the same effect, and many of the same problems, that the Universal Declaration has had. These high-priority goals might have served as international standards for governments and led to familiar sorts of disputes about the phrasing, relative priorities, and ambitiousness of the goals. Defenders of these high-priority goals might have justified them by appeal to considerations of human welfare, dignity, and equality, and critics might have charged that high-priority goals for such things as civil liberties and due process are Western ideas with few roots elsewhere.

This comparison of goals and rights should help us to recognize some of the distinctive features of rights. Note that I have spoken of high-priority goals—not just goals—to match an apparent feature of rights, namely, that they are important or high-priority considerations. In Ronald Dworkin's phrase, rights are "trumps." What Dworkin means to suggest with this slightly misleading metaphor is not that rights *always* prevail over all other considerations but rather that rights are strong considerations that *generally* prevail in

---

4. See Richard Flathman, *The Practice of Rights* (Cambridge: Cambridge University Press, 1976); Richard B. Brandt, *A Theory of the Good and the Right* (New York: Oxford University Press, 1979), chap. 10; and Richard B. Brandt, "The Concept of a Moral Right," *Journal of Philosophy* 80 (1983): 29–45.

competition with other concerns such as national prosperity or administrative convenience. Dworkin simply makes this stipulation part of what he means by a right; he proposes "not to call any political aim a right unless it has a certain threshold weight against collective goals in general; unless, for example, it cannot be defeated by appeal to any of the routine goals of political administration." [5]

What Dworkin stipulates here seems also to be descriptively true of most uses of the concept of rights. Part of the rhetorical appeal of this concept is that having a right to something means having a strong enough claim to outweigh other claims to that thing. Consider, for example, the right a cellist has under a valid three-year contract to play in an orchestra during a given year. While in possession of this right, the cellist does not need to show that he or she is the best cellist available or that the orchestra's or the public's welfare would be maximized by allowing him or her to play. Apart from competing considerations of exceptional weight, the cellist's right to the position provides a conclusive justification for making it available to him or her.

The assertion that rights are powerful normative considerations does not imply that their weight is absolute or that exceptions cannot be built into their scope. And the weight of a particular right is relative to other considerations at work in a given context. Some rights involve matters that are not of earthshaking importance (e.g., the repayment of a small loan). Such rights are powerful in comparison with other considerations normally at work (e.g., in the context of a small loan, the debtor's convenience). [6]

The vocabulary of goals, if it had been chosen for the Universal Declaration, would have yielded more flexible standards of government behavior. Even high-priority goals can be pursued in various ways and can be deferred when prospects for progress seem dim or when other opportunities are present. Rights, however, are more definite than goals; they specify who is entitled to receive a certain mode of treatment (the rightholders) and who must act on specific occasions to make that treatment available (the addressees).

Consider, for example, a constitutional right to counsel in criminal cases, which requires government to provide competent counsel

---

5. Ronald Dworkin, *Taking Rights Seriously* (Cambridge, Mass.: Harvard University Press, 1977), 92.

6. Despite Joseph Raz, "Professor Dworkin's Theory of Rights," *Political Studies* 26 (1978): 123–137.

to those charged with crimes who are unable to hire their own law-yers. Enacting such a right does more than say that it is desirable to maximize the percentage of those charged with crimes who have ac-cess to competent counsel; rather, it requires that counsel be guar-anteed to every person charged. Because every rightholder must be treated in a specified manner, rights are different from "collective goals," which merely assert the desirability of maximizing some ag-gregate quantity and which can easily be ignored when other goals seem more pressing.

The definiteness and the binding character of rights separate them from most goals, and these features make rights more suitable for enforcement than goals. But one who wished to equate rights with some subset of goals might respond that rights are just those goals that are both high-priority and definite in the sense of having specific beneficiaries and addressees.[7]

It is not clear, however, that having these two characteristics will make a goal into a right. Suppose that a family explicitly commits itself to the goal of providing the resources for its only child to at-tend college. It is clear that such a high-priority goal is a lesser com-mitment than giving the child a right to the resources needed to at-tend college. The mandatory character of a right is still missing. As long as providing the resources is merely a high-priority goal, the parents would do no wrong if they decided to use their resources to pursue some other high-priority goal, for example, providing for their retirement by taking advantage of a very attractive investment opportunity. But if they had given the child a moral right to a col-lege education through an explicit promise, such a decision would be morally wrong. The mandatory character of a right provides a basis for complaint that a high-priority goal does not.

Rights are distinctive not only in their high priority and defi-niteness but also in their mandatory character. It is these three fea-tures—high priority, definiteness, and bindingness—that make the rights vocabulary attractive in formulating minimal standards of de-cent governmental conduct. This character would be lost if we were to deconstruct rights into mere goals or ideals.

To avoid exaggeration here, however, two qualifications need to be stated. First, a right is not a perfect guarantee. To return to our example, a child who has been given a right to college expenses may

7. This view is suggested by Dworkin, *Taking Rights Seriously*, 81–130.

face not only deliberate noncompliance with that right but also the parents' inability to pay when the time arrives or even a conflicting, higher-priority claim on those resources.

The second qualification concerns the fact that rights vary greatly in degree of specificity, ranging from very specific, such as a right to reside in a certain place under a rental contract, to grand constitutional rights such as due process of law. Abstract rights are much less definite in their requirements than specific rights; indeed, very abstract rights may function in a way not too different from high-priority goals. By this I mean that they do not always imply clearly what must be done by whom, and hence actions to comply with and implement them are subject to considerable discretion. But when abstract rights can be made concrete in particular cases, they differ from high-priority goals by conferring on the guidance they provide a binding character that high-priority goals lack and cannot confer (see the figure on p. 20).

Conferring Authority and Benefits

Two of the most familiar accounts of the functions of rights are the *interest* and *will* theories.[8] Interest theories, which are associated with the utilitarian tradition, assert that the function of rights is to promote people's interests by conferring and protecting benefits. Will theories, which are associated with the Kantian tradition, assert that the function of rights is to promote autonomy by conferring and protecting authority, discretion, or control in some area of life. In this kind of theory, the alleged role of rights is to guarantee a specified scope for people's wills, their decision-making capacities.

A representative statement of the will theory of the function of rights is provided by Carl Wellman:

> The function of a legal right is to resolve . . . conflicts by giving legal priority to the desires and decisions of one party over those of the other. A legal right is the allocation of a sphere of freedom and control to the possessor of the right in order that it may be up to him which decisions are effective within that defined sphere.[9]

---

8. See Neil MacCormick, "Children's Rights: A Test-Case for Theories of Rights," *Archiv für Rechts und Sozialphilosophie* 62 (1976): 305–317; H. L. A. Hart, "Bentham on Legal Rights," in A. W. B. Simpson, ed., *Oxford Essays in Jurisprudence,* 2d ser. (Oxford: Clarendon Press, 1973), 171–201; and David Lyons, "The Correlativity of Rights and Duties," *Nous* 4 (1970): 45–55.

9. Carl Wellman, "Upholding Legal Rights," *Ethics* 86 (1975): 52.

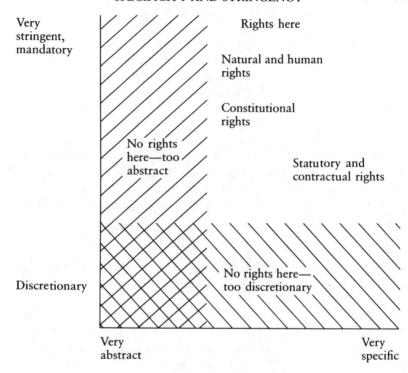

TWO DIMENSIONS OF NORMS:
SPECIFICITY AND STRINGENCY

Very
stringent,
mandatory

Rights here

Natural and human
rights

Constitutional
rights

No rights
here—too
abstract

Statutory and
contractual rights

Discretionary

No rights here—
too discretionary

Very
abstract

Very
specific

The insight that rights often prevent disputes and promote autonomy by conferring and protecting decision-making authority is important. It is illuminating to see property rights, for example, as giving their holders authority over the use of resources—and thus as denying that authority to others and to government. Rights to benefits, such as a cotton grower's right to a minimum price under price-support legislation or an elderly person's right to social security benefits, fit this model less well. The main function of these rights is to confer benefits such as money or services on parties with certain characteristics. The powers these rights confer will merely be powers to decline to apply for or receive benefits or to demand and receive a hearing if benefits are denied or terminated.

We must not exaggerate the extent to which even property rights actually confer control. Consider, for example, a right to repayment resulting from a loan or investment. In a context where there is general compliance with and enforcement of legal norms, a right to repayment may be such a reliable guarantee of getting one's money back that the right itself can be sold for about the same amount as was borrowed. This is roughly what takes place when there are markets in bonds. But a person who has a right to repayment has, after all, only a normative position or status; he or she does not necessarily have complete and effective control.

For a rightholder to have full and effective control over, say, the repayment of a loan, three conditions must be satisfied. One, obviously, is that there must be compliance with the right—and this often requires some means of coercing those who do not comply voluntarily. Note, however, that enforcement is a condition for the effectiveness of the right, not for its existence or possession. A second condition is that the persons who are required by the right to repay be able to do so, and the third condition requires that an engaged right not be overridden in a particular case by stronger normative considerations.

Will theories need also to be qualified to accommodate cases where a right to A is accompanied by a duty to do A. For example, in many countries citizens have both a right and a duty to vote. The right confers no control over whether a citizen will vote, except when officials exclude some people from voting or fail to hold elections. The right protects against these abuses; the accompanying duty requires that people make use of opportunities to vote. Here the most we can say is that the right to vote gives citizens valid claims against government officials to be given regular opportunities to vote; it does not, however, give citizens control over the decision whether or not to vote when elections are being held. Interest theories assert that the function of rights is to promote interests by conferring and protecting benefits. Jeremy Bentham, for example, held that to have a right is to be in a position to benefit from another's duty.[10] John Stuart Mill held that universal moral rights are justified as protections of people's most basic and shared interests.[11] An interest theory would emphasize that although a minority stockholder's property rights provide very little control over the corporation's use of the individual's assets, these rights do place the stockholder in a position to benefit from the earnings of the corporation.

It has often been argued that being in a position to benefit from an obligation does not itself amount to having a right. Repayment of an overdue loan may benefit people other than the lender (e.g., aged parents, whom the lender will now have the means to support), without those beneficiaries having a right to repayment of the loan. Further, one can have rights that are not in fact beneficial. Officials may not benefit by or have interests in all of the powers conferred by their positions. Some of these powers may be merely burdensome and offer no real advantage to their holder. If we nevertheless speak of rights as conferring benefits or goods, we are making a broad generalization with many exceptions.

I submit that we do not need to choose between the will and interest accounts of rights, because rights can have more than one distinctive function. If the will and interest accounts are formulated as theses about one important function of rights, then these accounts are mutually compatible and even correct each other's exaggerations. There is no contradiction between the statements (*a*) "conferring a sphere of authority on rightholders is a distinctive function of rights," and (*b*) "conferring benefits on rightholders is a distinctive function of rights." A contradiction arises only if we assert that each is the only distinctive function of rights. Nothing requires us

10. Jeremy Bentham, *Works,* ed. John Bowring (New York: Russell & Russell, 1962), 3 : 159, 181, 220–224. See also David Lyons, "Rights, Claimants and Beneficiaries," *American Philosophical Quarterly* 6 (1969): 173–185; and Hart, "Bentham on Legal Rights," 171–201.

11. John Stuart Mill, *Utilitarianism* (1863), chap. 4. See also David Lyons, "Human Rights and the General Welfare," in David Lyons, ed., *Rights* (Belmont, Calif.: Wadsworth, 1979), 175–186.

to make this stronger claim. Considerable tension exists between the associated Kantian and utilitarian traditions in moral and legal philosophy, but it is perfectly consistent to take both conferring and protecting authority and conferring and protecting benefits to be important functions of rights. To combine the two theories it is necessary to say only that rights serve to direct behavior in ways that make available to rightholders freedoms, protections, opportunities, immunities, powers, and benefits.

This broad description of rights has the advantage of emphasizing the wide variety of things that rights can be *to*. Within a particular legal system one might have rights to act in certain ways (e.g., to leave the country), to be treated in certain ways (not to be subjected to cruel punishments), to have certain protections (those provided by police and fire departments), to have certain opportunities (to vote or to attend free public schools), and to receive certain goods (free school lunches or social security payments). It is implausible to select any part of the range of things that rights are *to*—whether liberties, authority, or benefits—as canonical. In what follows I will sometimes speak, for reasons of linguistic convenience, of all the various things to which there can be rights as "goods," but this term should be understood as a loosely used shorthand device.

The variety of normative positions that rights confer and protect can be seen from the widely accepted Hohfeldian classification of rights into liberty rights, claim rights, power rights, and immunity rights (although Hohfeld himself advocated reserving talk of rights for claim rights alone).[12] A liberty right to do A, which consists in the absence of any duty on the rightholder's part to refrain from A, is matched with other people's lack of a claim against the rightholder that he or she not do A. A claim right to A is matched by duties of the addressees to act in ways that will make A available to the rightholder. A power right to do A confers competence to perform an act that will create, or at least bring to bear, moral or legal consequences for the addressee, and it is matched by the addressee's liability to that particular power. Finally, a right to immunity from A is correlated with a lack of authority by the addressees to do A; hence the correlative of an immunity is a disability.

---

12. Wesley N. Hohfeld, *Fundamental Legal Conceptions* (New Haven, Conn.: Yale University Press, 1964) (the two papers printed under this title first appeared as articles in the *Yale Law Journal*, one in volume 23 [1913]: 16–59, and the other in volume 26 [1917]: 710–770).

Claiming Things as One's Due

A third thesis emphasizes the role of the rights vocabulary in the practice of claiming things as one's due. This thesis is sometimes accompanied by the assertion that because rights allow one to claim one's due, they provide especially firm support for one's dignity or self-respect. Joel Feinberg states this as follows:

> Even if there are conceivable circumstances in which one would admit rights diffidently, there is no doubt that their characteristic use and that for which they are distinctively well suited, is to be claimed, demanded, affirmed, insisted upon. . . . Having rights, of course, makes claiming possible, but it is claiming that gives rights their special moral significance. . . . Having rights enables us to "stand up like men," to look others in the eye, and to feel in some fundamental way the equal of anyone.[13]

It is not very controversial to suggest that the presence of moral and legal guarantees of important freedoms, benefits, and powers supports people's self-respect. And we can readily concede that the existence of assignable rightholders to whom the addressees have duties (or other normative burdens) is a key feature in giving rights a more definite meaning than mere goals. It is much more problematic, however, to assert that the activity of *claiming* the things that are or should be guaranteed is somehow central to the meaning of the rights vocabulary or the existence of self-respect.

One problem with this assertion is that the notion of claiming a right is very ambiguous: it can involve either (1) seeking recognition that one has a right to something or (2) invoking a right that one has already been recognized to have. The latter divides into several different possibilities. These include (*a*) seeking to invoke or trigger a right so that it will be engaged (e.g., requesting unemployment benefits when one is out of work); (*b*) demanding compliance with a recognized right in the face of a threatened violation of it (e.g., a black person insisting on nondiscrimination from a realtor who is giving him or her the runaround); and (*c*) taking steps to bring

13. Joel Feinberg, "The Nature and Value of Rights," in Feinberg, ed., *Rights, Justice and the Bounds of Liberty: Essays in Social Philosophy* (Princeton, N.J.: Princeton University Press, 1980), 151 (originally published in *Journal of Value Inquiry* 4 [1970]: 243–257). An even stronger version of this view is put forward in Lyons, "Human Rights and the General Welfare."

about enforcement, compensation, or punishment when one's right has been violated (e.g., taking legal action to stop the FBI's continual invasions of one's right to privacy). Another problem concerns who must do the claiming. Must it be the rightholder? If so, only rightholder claiming can serve as the distinctive function of the rights vocabulary. Or can interested-party claiming, where one person claims something for someone else, serve as well? This difference is important: a self-effacing society might rely almost entirely on interested-party claiming.

These questions illustrate the imprecision of the assertion that the distinctive feature of rights is found in the activity of claiming one's due. A further problem with this thesis is that we can easily imagine the concept of a right functioning in cultures where actions such as demanding, claiming, and protesting are frowned on as unmannerly. If we generalize from the close connection between rights and claiming in many Western societies, we risk giving an ethnocentric account of the functions of rights—one that overemphasizes social and legal procedures for bringing about the recognition of rights—and suggesting that other cultures cannot have or import the concept of rights unless they are or become pushy and litigious.

Finally, it is not necessary to identify some particular speech act—claiming or anything else—as the single act which it is the special role of the rights vocabulary to perform. Most words can be utilized in a great many speech acts. Just as the word "good" can be used to perform many speech acts besides commending, the phrase "P has a right to A" can be used to perform many speech acts besides claiming a right to A.[14] Besides claiming rights, we can recognize them, question them, take them into account, disregard them, respect them, and use them as a basis for decision. With these other activities to give the rights vocabulary a functional role, it is not clear that we should say anything stronger about the connection between rights and claiming than that claiming things as someone's due is one of the characteristic things that people use rights talk to do.

Correcting the overemphasis on first-person claiming should not lead us to ignore the importance of activities such as claiming and

14. See John Searle on the "speech act fallacy," *Speech Acts* (Cambridge: Cambridge University Press: 1969), 147.

protesting in gaining recognition for rights and making them effective as protections. Liberties and powers to claim one's rights and protest their violations are often associated with rights, particularly institutional rights; the justification of rights often requires the justification of such powers and liberties.

The Focusing Function

By identifying in its scope a freedom or benefit to be made available, a right identifies the rationale of the various powers, immunities, duties, and liabilities that are part of the right. This is one way in which rights are different from duties. Richard Brandt makes this point as follows:

> A manifesto of the Women's Movement might list innumerable duties of men, corporations, or government, in respect of women. But such a list would lack focus. After all there is a target here: that women have an equal opportunity for a good life. That is what all these duties are aimed at; the duties are what other people must do if women are to have an equally good life. In talking of a right to equal opportunity, we focus attention on the intended good.[15]

Multiple Functions

If my arguments in this section are sound, there is no single function of the concept of rights. Among other things, rights characteristically (1) provide a normative category that is binding, high-priority, and definite; (2) confer and protect a sphere of authority; (3) confer and protect benefits or goods; (4) provide a normative vocabulary that allows for "claiming" in a variety of senses, by either rightholders or interested parties; and (5) provide a focus for a number of connected Hohfeldian elements.

Moral and legal discourse would not be devastated if it were deprived of the concept of rights. With the vocabularies of duties and justice one can formulate nearly all the assertions commonly stated in the vocabulary of rights. The vocabulary of high-priority goals could do much of this work as well. But moral and legal discourse would be handicapped by the loss of this useful concept. It does not follow from the fact that something is not utterly irreplaceable that it is not extremely useful.

15. Brandt, "Concept of a Moral Right," 44.

Rights and Duties in Morality and Law

Rights are found in various normative systems, such as moralities, the regulations of organizations, and local, state, national, and international legal systems. It is common to classify rights in terms of the kind of normative system in which they are rooted. A *positive legal right* is one that is recognized and implemented within some group's legal system. It may be included among constitutional norms, but recognition of this sort is compatible with the right's being merely a nominal or "paper" right.

Moral rights can be divided into those that exist in actual moralities and those that exist as theoretical constructs in critical or justified moralities—even if they are not part of any actual moralities. An *accepted moral right* is one that exists within the actual morality of some group or groups. For example, a group's moral code may give people a right not to have their clothes forcibly removed by other persons. Such a right may exist prior to the group's having a formal legal system, and it may be recognized and enforced by the formal legal system once such a system comes into being. Rights often exist both as accepted moral rights and as positive legal rights.

When a right is part of a group's actual morality, it is likely to be used as a standard of argument and as a guide to the evaluation of conduct and social policy. Those who refuse to comply may be scolded, shamed, ostracized, exiled, beaten, or killed. For some rights such recognition and implementation at the moral and social level may be all that is possible or desirable. Legal or governmental implementation may be impossible (as with, say, a right to revolt against repressive governments), or it may be inappropriate because it would be too costly or because its enforcement would require unacceptable violations of other norms.

Many people believe that their moral rights include not only those accepted within their society but also some unaccepted rights they believe to be justifiable. This belief suggests that there is an additional category of *justified moral rights*.

Positivists and skeptics hold that we should take legal rights as our exclusive paradigms of rights and thus treat moral rights as degenerate or phony.[16] Closely connected issues here are whether it

16. Classic representatives of the positivist tradition include Thomas Hobbes, Jeremy Bentham, and John Austin. See H. L. A. Hart, *The Concept of Law* (Oxford:

should be made a matter of definition that rights are partially constituted by the duties or other normative burdens of the addressees,
and whether legal and moral rights are rights in the same sense of
the word.

Three broad positions can be taken in response to these questions. These positions can be seen as corresponding to three stages
in the evolution of a legal right. The first stage is the recognition
that it is very important for people to have some good available to
them—that people are somehow entitled to that good. The second
stage involves identifying moral duties, disabilities, and liabilities of
some parties that, if they are complied with, will result in the availability of that good. The third stage involves constructing parallel
legal duties, disabilities, and liabilities and providing measures for
their enforcement; at this stage a legal right emerges.

There are three corresponding positions on when it is appropriate to speak of a right. One, which I call the *entitlements theory,*
endorses a very liberal use of the language of rights and holds that it
is proper to speak of rights whenever one can justify on moral or
legal grounds the proposition that people are entitled to enjoy specific goods—even if we cannot say who should bear the burden of
making these goods available or how these entitlements should be
implemented and enforced. A somewhat more restrictive view,
which I call the *entitlements-plus theory,* holds that entitlements
alone cannot constitute full-fledged rights but must be supplemented by the identification of addressees who have appropriate
moral duties, disabilities, or liabilities. These burdens on the addressees are the "plus" added to the entitlement to yield a full-
fledged right. The third and narrowest position, which I call the *legally implemented entitlements theory,* agrees with the previous
theory in holding that genuine rights are more than mere entitlements, but it holds that this "something more" must include legal
implementation. In this view, it is not proper to speak of rights at
the earlier stages; the real thing does not emerge until one has legal
implementation.

All three theories have been forcefully advocated in various forms,
and I want to explore the advantages and disadvantages of each. In
doing so I propose to appeal to the following desiderata for analyses
of rights.

Oxford University Press, 1961); see also Rex Martin, "Human Rights and Civil
Rights," *Philosophical Studies* 37 (1980): 391–403.

1. *Accuracy:* The analysis captures all of the important features of rights.

2. *Inclusiveness:* The analysis covers the entire range of intelligible uses of the rights vocabulary.

3. *Penetration:* The analysis allows us to identify important differences among rights and between rights and other concepts.

4. *Economy:* The analysis does not multiply rights unnecessarily; it does not inflate the rights vocabulary by confusing rights and goals.

5. *Exportability:* The analysis allows rights to be used in a variety of cultures and legal traditions; it does not tie the idea of rights to a particular legal or cultural tradition.

Because these criteria are unranked, difficult to interpret, and possibly incomplete, no claim can be made that they will conclusively settle the issues. But they at least provide explicit standards in an area in which standards of analysis are often left unspecified.

The Entitlement Theory

Broadly, this theory holds that a right is a very strong moral reason why people should have a certain freedom, power, protection, or benefit. H. J. McCloskey expounds a theory of this kind; he believes that rights are best "explained positively as entitlements to do, have, enjoy, or have done, and not negatively as something against others, or as something one ought to have." [17] McCloskey's view implies that a full-fledged right need not specify who bears the burden of making available what the right is *to;* a right is not to be equated with claims against other parties. Of course, rights do often give rise to duties, but McCloskey wishes to emphasize the logical priority of entitlements to the duties they generate. An entitlement seems to be a strong set of reasons, rooted in the nature of human beings, for ensuring that a certain good is available to people. Since McCloskey believes that entitlements—and thus rights—can exist even when it is not feasible to implement them, he finds no difficulty in saying that a right to medical care, for example, is a universal human right.

The entitlement theory has the advantage of accounting for the

17. See H. J. McCloskey, "Rights—Some Conceptual Issues," *Australasian Journal of Philosophy* 54 (1976): 99–115, at 99.

wide range of actual uses of the rights vocabulary. McCloskey emphasizes that people often speak of rights when it is unclear who must bear the burdens of these alleged rights.[18] Thus McCloskey would have no objection on linguistic grounds to reformers who declared a new right even though they were unable to specify who would bear the burdens of this right, what exactly these burdens would be, or whether resources were available to meet such burdens. Such rhetorical uses of the rights vocabulary are very common, but a key issue here is whether we should endorse them.

A second advantage of the entitlements theory is that its notion of rights is readily exportable. Talk of entitlements is tied neither to possibly parochial activities such as claiming things as one's due or seeking remedies for wrongs nor to legal implementation. Thus the vocabulary of rights can easily be put to use in diverse cultures.

Viewing rights as mere entitlements, however, is likely to have inflationary results. A moral right will exist whenever there are conclusive moral reasons for ensuring the availability of a certain good. Hence there is danger that the list of entitlements will be nearly as long as the list of highly desirable goods. To extend the economic metaphor, this conception has no built-in assurance that the demand side of rights will not outrun the supply side—the side involving addressees who bear normative burdens.

Another way to say roughly the same thing is to suggest that the entitlements theory is insufficiently penetrating because it is unable to distinguish between rights and high-priority goals. In making this distinction, I appeal to the definiteness of rights (the fact that they have assignable holders and addressees) and to their mandatory character. The entitlement theory comes close to collapsing rights into high-priority goals by diluting the mandatory character of rights and by cutting out essential reference to their addressees.

The Entitlements-Plus Theory

These problems can be remedied, it seems, by adding essential reference to specific addressees and burdens to our conception of a full-fledged right. This is what the entitlements-plus theory does. It holds that a right cannot be constituted by an entitlement alone—

---

18. Ibid. See also the discussion of "rights against" in H. J. McCloskey, "Rights," *Philosophical Quarterly* 15 (1967): 118–119.

that moral or legal norms directing the behavior of the addressees are essential to the existence of moral or legal rights and must be added to an entitlement to constitute a right. A version of the entitlements-plus theory of rights is put forward by Joel Feinberg, who makes a useful distinction between claims to benefits and claims against parties to supply those benefits. A claim to is what I call an entitlement, and a claim against is the "plus" that can be added to an entitlement. Feinberg's position is that a full-fledged claim right is a union of a valid claim to and a valid claim against. He allows, however, that rights in a weaker, "manifesto," sense can be constituted by a claim to or entitlement alone.[19] Feinberg's approach makes clear that justifying a right requires one to justify not only an entitlement, or claim to but also a claim against, that is, the burdens that the right will impose on at least one other party.

The entitlements-plus theory fits well with the traditional view that rights are simply duties seen from the perspective of one who stands to benefit from their performance.[20] In this view the difference between Jones's right against Smith and Smith's duty to Jones is mainly the difference between the active and the passive voice. From Smith's perspective the normative relation is a duty and from Jones's perspective it is a right, but the relation is really the same. This traditional view seems to assume (1) that all rights are claim rights and (2) that rights can be constituted by a single norm, such as a duty to a particular person.

Both assumptions are dubious. Rights are typically constituted by liberties, immunities, and powers, as well as by claims to what one is due.[21] For example, the right to rebel against oppressive governments, much emphasized by Locke and Jefferson, seems primarily to be a liberty right, meaning that a person does no wrong in revolting against oppressive governments. As David Lyons points out, the right to freedom of speech in U.S. constitutional law is mainly an immunity right; it deprives Congress of the power to pass laws abridging freedom of speech and thus makes people immune

19. See Feinberg, "Nature and Value of Rights"; and *Social Philosophy*, chap. 4.
20. See Ross, *The Right and the Good*, 48–56; Richard B. Brandt, *Ethical Theory* (Englewood Cliffs, N.J.: Prentice-Hall, 1959); and S. I. Benn and R. S. Peters, *The Principles of Political Thought* (New York: Free Press, 1965).
21. See Wellman, "Upholding Legal Rights." See also Martin and Nickel, "Recent Work on the Concept of Rights."

to such laws.[22] The truth here, which is skewed by equating rights and duties, is that a meaningful right must imply some normative direction of the conduct of its addressees. This direction can be achieved not only by imposing duties but also by giving right-holders liberties, powers, and immunities and giving addressees corresponding "disadvantages."

The second assumption, that a right can be constituted by a single duty to some person, fares no better. Consider an example that clearly has a duty at its center. Smith borrows money from Jones by signing an agreement to repay at a certain time, and thus Smith has a duty to repay and Jones has a right to repayment. Jones's right consists not only of Smith's duty but also of Jones's immunity against Smith's unilateral cancellation of the duty to repay. Jones's right probably also includes liberties and powers to extend the due date, forgive the loan, demand payment on the due date, and sue if Smith fails to repay. This example illustrates that rights are often families of Hohfeldian relations, not single relations—as the equation of rights with duties suggests.

Clearly, formulations of the entitlements-plus theory should avoid suggesting that what needs to be added to an entitlement to turn it into a moral right is always and only a duty. We should rather say that what needs to be added are norms that will direct the conduct of the addressees in ways not fully subject to the addressees' discretion. I will often refer to the Hohfeldian disadvantages that do this as "normative burdens."

The entitlements-plus theory need not require all full-fledged rights to have precisely specified scopes, weights, and addressees. The vocabulary of rights is used in abstract as well as in specific normative discourse, and one cannot expect abstract rights to be fully specified. The description of an abstract right often identifies only key ideas and leaves specific elements to be worked out at the implementation stage. But even when rights are stated abstractly—as they typically are in the Universal Declaration—there must at least be some general idea of what normative burdens are imposed by the right and who will be required to bear them.

The entitlements-plus theory seems to have some important advantages over the entitlements theory. First, it offers a more accurate and penetrating analysis because it recognizes an essential feature of

22. Lyons, "Correlativity of Rights and Duties."

rights, the burdens they impose on their addressees, which the entitlements theory leaves out. Its penetration comes from its ability to distinguish rights from high-priority goals and to explain how both moral and legal rights are rights. Because entitlements-plus holds that even justified moral rights must generate norms that place burdens on addressees, it sees similar normative structures in all kinds of rights, which makes it easier to see that they are all rights in the same sense. Second, the entitlements-plus theory is noninflationary in that it denies that mere entitlements are full-fledged rights, whereas it leaves room for bona fide moral rights.

It is alleged that the entitlements-plus theory is insufficiently accurate and penetrating because it ignores practices of legal recognition and enforcement and thus fails both to emphasize what is most practically important about rights and to mark the very significant difference between legal rights and moral demands. It is to this charge, which is central to the third theory of rights, that I now turn.

The Legally Implemented
Entitlements Theory

It has often been claimed that a "right" is mainly a legal notion, that practices of legal enforcement are central to the existence of rights, and that nonlegal rights are phony rights. To Jeremy Bentham, for example, the idea of rights not created by positive law was nonsense.[23] Bentham might have been willing to allow that entitlements, in the sense defined above, can exist as conclusions to utilitarian arguments and can serve as grounds for wanting corresponding legal rights. But he held that such entitlements are not rights—just as "hunger is not bread."

Bentham held that talk of moral and natural rights is politically dangerous and ultimately unintelligible. An advocate of Bentham's view might point out that when, for example, the right to leave one's country is not legally recognized, respected, or enforced in a particular nation, we sometimes say that people in that country do not have the right to leave or that this right does not exist there. But this mode of speaking proves nothing. One may mean by these statements that the right to leave is not a legal or effectively implemented right in that country without at all wanting to deny that it

---

23. See Jeremy Bentham, "Anarchical Fallacies," in A. I. Melden, ed., *Human Rights* (Belmont, Calif.: Wadsworth, 1970), 30–31.

exists as an accepted or justified moral right. Indeed, it is precisely to demand reform in cases like these that we may wish to appeal to independently existing moral or human rights. To be as unambiguous and as penetrating as possible here, we have made distinctions among accepted moral, justified moral, and legal rights and among the existence, recognition, and effective implementation of rights.

Bentham regarded appeals to nonlegal rights as a mere rhetorical ploy: without a court of law to determine who has the right and what it means, talk of rights is merely "a sound to dispute about," allowing argument from undefended premises. But an appeal to rights need not substitute for further argument, particularly if the status of the right one is appealing to is challenged. Bentham was eager to settle political questions by appeal to what would maximize utility, but there is no system of courts and judges to answer the question of whether a particular policy maximizes utility. Thus, if we accept Bentham's premise that a normative concept without an adjudication procedure merely gives us a sound to dispute about, we must conclude that such a sound is all we are given by the principle of utility. Subtract Bentham's exaggerated claims about the determinacy of his preferred standard, and it becomes clear that Bentham's attack on the vocabulary of his opponents would, if it succeeded, undermine his own appeals to utility.

As Mill and other utilitarians have allowed, norms justifiable by considerations of utility may constitute moral obligations and rights to which one can appeal whether or not they are already recognized in the legal system. There is likely to be controversy about which rights are justifiable and about the scope and limits of the rights and obligations in question; but that key concepts are open to controversy does not show them to be unintelligible.

A third argument against the existence of nonlegal rights is that recognition and enforcement are such important features of our paradigm that unenforced rights cannot be said to have the same sense as enforced rights. According to this view, only by saying that nonlegal rights are rights in a different or phony sense can we adequately reflect the importance of recognition and enforcement to what rights are all about. But important differences often exist within a single generic category. There are huge differences between small economy cars and giant long-distance trucks, but this does not require us to say that they are vehicles in a different sense of "vehicle." They are different kinds of vehicles, but not vehicles in a different sense.

One might respond along these lines to the claim that conceiving all rights as legally implemented entitlements is more accurate and penetrating than less restrictive views. Although noninflationary, the equation of all rights with enforced legal rights excludes talk of many important moral rights and severely limits the exportability of the concept of rights. Another disadvantage is that restricting full-fledged rights to legal ones gives important argumentative advantages to defenders of existing social, political, and legal arrangements.

Overview

What has been suggested here is that rights are complex high-priority norms, typically involving several Hohfeldian elements, with scopes, weight, addressees, and conditions of possession. These components enable rights to provide very definite guidance to behavior, although many rights—particularly those found in constitutions and bills of rights—are too vague or abstract to make full use of this potential.

By prescribing the availability of a good to rightholders and imposing on the addressees normative burdens that direct their conduct toward making this good available, rights serve to confer and protect important freedoms, powers, immunities, protections, opportunities, and benefits. Such normative structures can exist in actual and justified moralities and in local, state, national, and international legal systems. Legal enforcement is often important to making rights effective, but such enforcement is not essential to the existence of rights.

3. Making Sense of Human Rights

The Universal Declaration makes claims that appeal strongly to one's idealism and hope for humankind and offers a long and attractive list of specific rights. But the exact meanings of its claims are often unclear, and its long list of rights is of problematic consistency and affordability. In this light, making sense of the Universal Declaration is no easy task. There is little reason to regard the Declaration as sacrosanct, and I am willing to revise or jettison parts that seem indefensible. Nevertheless, to save the rest will require plausible answers to most of the following questions:

1. In what sense are the rights of the Declaration real rights?

2. How can such rights exist independently of enactment as law in particular countries?

3. Who are the addressees of the Declaration; that is, for whom does it generate duties or other burdens?

4. How should we interpret the Declaration's claim that human rights are "universal" and "inalienable"?

5. Since the Declaration does not resolve most issues of priority, scope, and trade-offs, what does it imply for practice?

6. Does the Declaration's long list of rights make any sense? Are the rights on the list consistent and defensible? In particular, is the idea of economic rights intelligible?

These are hard questions, which set the agenda for the rest of this book. This chapter sketches general answers to them; subsequent chapters explore them in greater depth. My goal is to show that these questions can be answered well enough to justify continued use of something like the Universal Declaration's conception of human rights. In interpreting claims about human rights my tendency will be to give weak rather than strong accounts, the effect of which will be to make those claims less distinctive but easier to defend.

If we can make sense of human rights, and bring our conceptions of them down to earth a little, the intelligibility and usefulness of appeals to human rights in social and political discourse will be strengthened.

Human Rights and Their Existence

A good understanding of the general nature of rights does not by itself enable one to make sense of human rights. At most, the analysis offered in chapter 2 identifies some of the questions that need to be asked and provides a framework within which answers can be constructed.

Human rights are often held to exist independently of acceptance or enactment as law. The attraction of this position is that it permits critics of repressive regimes to appeal to human rights whether or not those regimes accept human rights or recognize them in their legal systems. But the contention that human rights exist independently of acceptance or enactment has always occasioned skepticism. If human rights were mere wishes or aspirations, we could say they merely exist in people's minds. In order to be norms that are binding on all people, human rights must be far more than wishes or aspirations.

One might try to sidestep skeptical doubts about the independent existence of human rights by pointing to their place in international law. For example, the right to leave a country is found in article 12 of the International Covenant on Civil and Political Rights, a treaty that is now part of international law. Under this agreement, a Russian, say, who asks to be allowed to emigrate to Israel (and who is not fleeing debts or criminal prosecution) has in this right a strong justification, and the government of the Soviet Union has a corresponding obligation to allow him to go. The Soviet Union has signed this covenant, thereby undertaking this obligation in international law.

As this example suggests, human rights can exist as legal rights within international law. Some may doubt whether the institutional grounding and support for compliance under the International Covenant on Civil and Political Rights are sufficient to make the rights recognized there into full-fledged legal rights. But the grounding and support provided under the European Convention on Human Rights permits us to say without exaggeration that the

European system establishes human rights as international legal rights. The institutions established by this convention include a Human Rights Commission to investigate and arbitrate complaints and a Human Rights Court to deal with matters the Commission cannot resolve.[1]

When human rights are implemented in international law, we continue to speak of them as human rights; but when they are implemented in domestic law we tend to describe them as civil or constitutional rights. It is possible for a right to exist within more than one normative system at the same time. For example, a right to freedom from torture could be a right within a justified morality, a right within the domestic legal system, and a right within international law. This kind of congruence is an ideal of the human rights movement, which seeks conformity between various levels of law, existing moral codes, and the standards of enlightened moralities.

Because human rights are now enacted within many national and international legal systems, positivist worries about unenforced moral rights are no longer fatal to taking human rights seriously. As Louis Henkin observes, "Political forces have mooted the principal philosophical objections, bridging the chasm between natural and positive law by converting natural human rights into positive legal rights."[2]

But such positive norms of national and international law can confer rights only on people in countries that have appropriate domestic laws or that have ratified international human rights treaties. Many countries in the world neither have domestic laws that recognize and implement human rights nor adhere to any human rights treaties. For human rights to be universally available, they must be moral norms that are independent of recognition in positive law.

Many have followed this line of thought, and thus human rights are commonly characterized as moral rights. In such characterizations the word "moral" seems to be doing much of the work that the word "natural" did when it was fashionable to speak of natural rights. Describing rights as natural implied that they did not depend

1. See Frede Castberg, *The European Convention on Human Rights* (Dobbs Ferry, N.Y.: Oceana Publications, 1974); and Hans Danelius, "A Survey of the Jurisprudence Concerning the Rights Protected by the European Convention on Human Rights," *Revue de droits de l'homme* 8 (1975): 431–473.

2. Louis Henkin, *The Rights of Man Today* (Boulder, Colo.: Westview Press, 1978), 19.

on convention or enactment as legal rights do. The same independence is implied by describing human rights as moral, although the idea of a moral right does not imply, as the idea of a natural right seems to, that moral norms or laws are somehow part of the natural universe.[3]

Accepted moral rights can exist before a formal legal system is established and later become legal rights. We should recognize, however, that some moral rights are unsuitable for legal enforcement (e.g., a right not to be lied to concerning one's health by one's friends and family). It is not a matter of definition that moral rights call for the creation of legal rights.

Accepted moral rights are found in most human groups, but it is not clear that parochial norms are adequate to support rights of international applicability. If human rights are to be generated by the various accepted moralities that exist around the world, those moralities must share a commitment to principles of the sort found in the Universal Declaration. But it is very doubtful whether there is sufficient agreement worldwide to support anything like the full range of rights declared in contemporary manifestos.[4] All moralities may make some provision for personal security against rape and murder, for example, but they probably do not all condemn racial discrimination or provide for freedom of conscience.

A human rights advocate who asserts that human rights are binding on governments independently of acceptance needs to construe human rights as existing within justified moralities rather than within all accepted moralities. John Stuart Mill, for example, a nineteenth-century advocate of what we now call human rights, would have allowed that there is little agreement worldwide in accepted moralities about basic rights but would have claimed nonetheless that human rights exist within justified moralities—which, in his view, would all give a prominent place to the principle of utility.[5] This view requires some commitment to the "objectivity" of moral norms. At a minimum it requires the consistent human rights advocate to hold that some moral norms are more defensible than others.

The analysis of rights offered in chapter 2 held that full-fledged

---

3. See L. W. Sumner, "Rights Denaturalized," in R. G. Frey, ed., *Utility and Rights* (Minneapolis: University of Minnesota Press, 1984), 20–41.

4. See chap. 4 for a fuller treatment of this issue.

5. John Stuart Mill, *Utilitarianism* (1863), chap. 5; and *On Liberty* (1859).

rights are entitlements-plus, which implies that for a justified moral right to exist, two things must obtain. First, there must be a justifiable entitlement to a freedom or benefit; it must be possible to make a strong moral case for making that freedom or benefit available to all. Second, it must be possible to justify the duties or other burdens involved in making this freedom or benefit available to all. To assert the existence of a justified moral right, in this view, will be to specify an entitlement with holders, scope, weight, and addressees and to assert that it is possible to defend this entitlement and its associated burdens with good moral reasons. At the level of moral theory, the identification of these elements may be fairly abstract, with many details left unspecified. Nonetheless, at least a vague conception of the content of these elements must be present for one to have a full-fledged right.

A justified morality does not need to be accepted or practiced by anyone, nor does it necessarily have a social or institutional dimension. Thus the question arises: even if we are not skeptical about the possibility of identifying a morality that differs from all or most existing moralities in ways that make it more justifiable, are the principles and rights that constitute such a justified morality sufficiently robust to be binding in actual situations here and now? What the knowledge of human rights comes to in this view is—at a minimum—knowledge of good reasons for adopting a certain morality.[6] The Universal Declaration can then be seen as an international attempt to specify the content of such a justified morality.

Legal positivists doubt that the principles of justified moralities are sufficiently knowable to be worth talking about or that in our contemporary Babel, with its many competing voices and views, it is worth talking about principles everyone would be justified in adopting. They prefer the cold steel of legally implemented rights to the hot air of justified human rights.

One who views human rights as justified moral rights may have

6. Jan Narveson puts this nicely: "What there 'is' when there 'are' rights, if indeed there are some, must be certain features or properties of those who 'have' them such that we have *good reason to acknowledge* the obligation to refrain from interfering with, or possibly to sometimes help their bearers to do the things they are said to have the right to do, or have the things they are said to have a right to have. Their rights will be as real as those reasons are strong. Or rather, they will be as real as the features or properties mentioned above, given sufficient reason to accept the obligations in question" ("Contractarian Rights," in Frey, ed., *Utility and Rights,* 164).

the same preference but believe that even without shared norms that can be implemented everywhere through domestic and international law it is worthwhile to continue discussing, and trying to identify, justifiable norms. The hope of human rights advocates is that humans have sufficient capacity for moral understanding and progress to make it worthwhile to talk and argue about how we ought to behave and organize our societies.

The Universal Declaration is usefully seen as an attempt to formulate some fixed points in this discussion, to identify some rights that are widely accepted and strongly supported by good reasons. The belief that it is possible to formulate such a list rests on the belief that human beings have a substantial capacity for moral understanding and progress, but the need for such a list presupposes that the unaided conscience will not generally provide fully adequate beliefs about how people ought to behave and how society ought to be organized.

The Addressees of Human Rights

The analysis of rights offered in chapter 2 holds that rights have assignable addressees, people or agencies who bear normative burdens such as duties, liabilities, and disabilities. This connection between rights and the assignment of burdens is the basis for a frequently voiced question: who bears duties in regard to human rights? On hearing, for example, that people have rights to food and employment, one may wonder whether there is a general duty to try to provide these things out of one's own resources.

International human rights must be formulated broadly enough to cover countries with very different institutions, practices, and levels of resources. We cannot expect a formulation to specify in detail what will be required of whom. Appropriate expectations are (1) that we have a rough conception of how governments and individuals would act if they were guided by the right in question and (2) that this conception be compatible with the abilities and resources of at least most countries today.

The standard answer to the question of who bears the burdens of human rights is that governments do. Historically, the struggle for civil and human rights has been a struggle to restrain abuses of state power. This focus on governments as those who are burdened by human rights norms continues in the human rights movement, particularly because the movement has been intimately connected with the United Nations, an organization of states.

A look at the Universal Declaration suggests, however, that the matter is more complex. When article 4 asserts, "No one shall be held in slavery or servitude, slavery and the slave trade shall be prohibited in all their forms," the wrong addressed is not primarily caused by governments. Slaveholders have generally been individuals, although governments have often supported and institutionalized slavery. The right to freedom from slavery obligates individuals and governments not to hold slaves and further requires governments to implement this right in domestic law by making slavery illegal.

The preamble to the Declaration states that human rights have implications for the conduct of individuals when it says that "every individual and every organ of society, keeping this Declaration constantly in mind, shall strive by teaching and education to promote respect for these rights and freedoms and by progressive measures national and international to secure their universal and effective recognition and observance." Clearly, the authors of the Universal Declaration believed that both states and individuals have obligations in regard to human rights.

States have obligations to respect the human rights of people everywhere and to protect and uphold the human rights of residents of their territories. These obligations are not only negative (not to violate) but are also positive (to uphold or implement). Because of the failures of many states to respect and uphold the rights of residents, it is tempting to assign these tasks to international organizations such as the United Nations or to hope that a world federation or government will soon emerge to assume them.

International organizations, however, do not have the authority or power to enforce rights around the world; national governments are unlikely to give them this authority, and a world federation or government seems at best a distant possibility. There is at present no alternative to assigning sovereign states the main responsibility for upholding the rights of their residents.

Individuals are obligated not only not to violate rights themselves but also to encourage their governments to respect human rights, perhaps by their votes or protests. Although this view requires human rights to be complex enough to have multiple addressees, it is sensible for a number of reasons. One is that many human rights problems have both governmental and private aspects. Implementing the right to freedom from racial discrimination in a country with a history of institutional racism would require both social and political reforms. And torture and kidnapping may be practiced not only by police but also by private groups, such as "death squads." Thus the right not to be tortured must hold against both individuals and governments if it is to be effective.

Another reason to deny that governments are the only addressees of human rights is that genuine human rights rest on extremely powerful normative considerations dictating that humans be treated in certain ways and not in others. It is not surprising that such weighty considerations can generate obligations for a number of parties, even if the main burden often falls on governments. If the moral grounds for human rights are substantial enough to override domestic law and justify risks of international conflict, they are also likely to generate obligations for individuals in matters subject to their control.

A third reason for including individuals among the addressees of human rights is that individuals have some responsibility under democratic principles for the actions of their governments. If government by the people is a reality—and rights to political participation dictate that it ought to be—the obligations of governments will be obligations of their peoples.

Universality and Inalienability

The Universal Declaration's assertion that human rights are both universal and inalienable is attractive in our egalitarian age because it gives all persons claims to essential freedoms, protections, and services. We assert that human rights are universal to avoid leaving the oppressed noncitizen, minority group member, or social outcast without rights to appeal to. We assert that human rights are inalienable so that oppressive governments cannot say their subjects have forfeited or voluntarily given up their rights.

In discussions of universality it is helpful to refer to the levels of moral and political deliberation distinguished by John Rawls in *A Theory of Justice*. The most abstract and philosophical of these is the "original position," at which one attempts to formulate and defend transhistorical principles of morality and justice. Next comes the "constitutional stage," at which one formulates specific rights and duties that apply the abstract principles to particular countries according to their problems, resources, and institutions. This process continues at the "legislative stage," and finally constitutional and legislative norms are applied at the "judicial stage."[7] As we move from grand principles to application-level principles, more information about contemporary (and eventually local) problems is taken into account, and the norms are likely to become less abstract but more relevant to the problems and institutions of a particular time or place.

The rights vocabulary can be used at any of these levels. For example, one might talk at the grand level of the right to equal respect, at the middle levels of the constitutional right to due process, and at the application levels of a statutory right to have thirty days to prepare for a hearing. But the vocabulary of human rights is used most typically at the middle level—it is used by nations or international organizations to outline in broad but still fairly definite terms what grander principles of morality and justice require in one country or era. Even at the middle level it is impossible to anticipate and treat all possible conflicts between rights and other considerations, and therefore human and constitutional rights will typically be prima facie rights.

Claims of universality and inalienability are plausible at least for some specific rights, if not for all of them. The right to freedom from torture, for example, seems to be universal and inalienable. All persons—including those who lived long ago, young children, the retarded, and the senile—can plausibly be said to have this right, and I can see no objection to the idea that it cannot permanently be given up or forfeited. To the objection that this right is alienable, because we can imagine an extreme case in which torture could be justified as the only way of saving the human race, one good reply is that the example confuses inalienability with absoluteness. According to the distinctions drawn in chapter 2, the assertion that a right is inalienable does not imply that it cannot be set aside by the holder in particular cases, that its scope contains no

---

7. John Rawls, *A Theory of Justice* (Cambridge, Mass.: Harvard University Press, 1971), 195–201. See also Ronald Moore, "Rawls on Constitution-Making," in J. Roland Pennock and John W. Chapman, eds., *NOMOS XX: Constitutionalism* (New York: New York University Press, 1979), 238–268.

exceptions, or that it cannot be overridden in exceptional circumstances by other important norms. Strong claims of universality and inalienability are not valid for many specific human rights. Some of the rights declared in the Universal Declaration cannot be universal in the strong sense of applying to all humans at all times, because they assert that people are entitled to services tied to relatively recent social and political institutions. Due process rights, for example, presuppose modern legal systems and the institutional safeguards they can offer. Social and economic rights presuppose modern relations of production and the institutions of the twentieth-century welfare or socialist state. My point here is not merely that people living ten thousand years ago would not have thought to demand these rights (assuming that they had the concept of a right) but rather that the scope of these rights can only be defined by reference to institutions that did not then exist. Transhistorical rights have to be formulated in much broader terms to avoid this objection, but the result would be very abstract rights, subject to a variety of interpretations and hence less useful in political criticism.

Another question about universality concerns people with severely limited mental capacities. Do we include the very young, severely retarded, comatose, or senile when we assert that all human beings have certain rights? Although we may want to grant these persons rights, for example, to life, due process, and freedom from torture, it would be implausible to argue that they have rights to vote, run for political office, or travel freely on their own. These rights presuppose a greater degree of rationality and autonomy than some human beings possess.[8]

Nor are the rights of noncitizens strictly universal. Although aliens in a country are entitled, as persons, to most of the same basic rights that citizens have, it is not wrong, I believe, to deny al-

8. On this distinction and the issue of what kinds of beings can have rights, see Joel Feinberg, "The Rights of Animals and Unborn Generations" in William T. Blackstone, ed., *Philosophy and Environmental Crisis* (Athens: University of Georgia Press, 1974), 43–68; Tom Regan, *A Case for Animal Rights* (Berkeley and Los Angeles: University of California Press, 1983); Christopher D. Stone, "Should Trees Have Standing?—Toward Legal Rights for Natural Objects," *Southern California Law Review* 45 (1972): 450–501; Mary Anne Warren, "On the Moral and Legal Status of Abortion," in Tom L. Beauchamp and LeRoy Walters, eds., *Contemporary Issues in Bioethics,* 2d ed. (Belmont, Calif.: Wadsworth, 1982), 250–260.

iens some political rights, such as the right to vote or hold public office.[9] The Universal Declaration explicitly recognizes the right of political participation as a right of everyone to participate directly or indirectly "in the government of his country." The Covenant on Civil and Political Rights is even more explicit in formulating political rights as rights of citizens rather than of "everyone."

Similar problems arise from the claim that human rights are inalienable, which I interpret to mean that these rights cannot be permanently forfeited or voluntarily given up.[10] The existence of an inalienable right to A implies that attempts to repudiate permanently one's own right to A, or attempts by others to declare someone's right to A null and void, will be without moral effect. If people lack the moral power to eliminate permanently a right of their own or others, that disability makes the right inalienable. And since the right cannot be eliminated, those who act as if it had been eliminated may violate it.

One problem with this claim is that some of the rights in the Universal Declaration are forfeitable in many legal systems upon conviction of serious crimes. In the United States, for example, one's right to vote is forfeited by a felony conviction—and I cannot see that denying felons the vote violates a still-existing right to political participation. If a person's moral right to vote could survive the revocation of his or her legal right to vote—as an inalienable right could—then subsequent failure to honor the legal right would constitute a prima facie wrong as the violation of a moral right. No such prima facie wrong seems to be involved in denying convicted felons the right to vote, and so this right does not seem to be immune to alienation.

In spite of such examples, advocates of human rights often worry that the idea of forfeiture, if admitted, could consume too many rights. It seems to invite oppressors to say that unpopular groups have forfeited their rights to life, liberty, or decent treatment. But many concepts in the rights vocabulary invite rhetorical abuse; this

9. See James W. Nickel, "Human Rights and the Rights of Aliens," in Peter G. Brown and Henry Shue, eds., *The Border That Joins* (Totowa, N.J.: Rowman & Littlefield, 1983), 31–45.

10. On inalienability, see Joel Feinberg, "Voluntary Euthanasia and the Inalienable Right to Life," *Philosophy and Public Affairs* 7 (1978): 93–123; and Marvin Schiller, "Are There Any Inalienable Rights?" *Ethics* 79 (1969): 309–315.

possibility is not sufficient backing for the theoretical claim that all human rights are immune to forfeiture. The claim that human rights cannot voluntarily be repudiated is also problematic in certain cases. Some eighteenth-century rights theorists asserted the inalienability of natural rights because they wanted to counter the Hobbesian claim that people had agreed to give up all their rights when they left the state of nature and entered civil society. Selling oneself into slavery might amount to a permanent alienation of one's liberty, and perhaps we can agree that some minimal right to liberty is inalienable and hence that individuals lack the power to rid themselves of it.

I doubt, however, whether we can plausibly say that all human rights are immune to repudiation. People give up much of their liberty when they enter monasteries or military service, yet we would not propose forbidding these acts universally. Suppose that a public official repudiated his moral and legal rights to privacy, so that his life would be an open book. This might be a foolish step, but it is not clear that individuals cannot take it or that other persons would be wrong to act in accordance with it. A more realistic example is accepting certain permanent limits on what one can say and publish in order to receive a security clearance for government intelligence work. Although one does well to be suspicious of government secrecy regulations, it does not seem to me that agreements of this sort can be precluded wholesale. I suspect that only some—probably only a few—human rights are immune from permanent repudiation.

One could argue that problems about universality and inalienability arise from misguided attribution to the numerous and specific rights of the Universal Declaration of characteristics ascribed by Locke and Jefferson to very general rights. One could hold that these characteristics can properly be assigned only to abstract rights—that only abstract rights, such as Dworkin's right to equal concern and respect or Benn's right to equal consideration of interests, can be truly said to be universal, inalienable, and absolute.[11]

One may indeed make strong claims about very abstract rights, but the plausibility of the claims results at least in part from the

11. Stanley Benn, "Human Rights—For Whom and for What?" in Eugene Kamenka and Alice Erh-Soon Tay, eds., *Human Rights* (New York: St. Martin's Press, 1978), 59–73; Ronald Dworkin, *Taking Rights Seriously* (Cambridge, Mass.: Harvard University Press, 1977), 150–183, 266–278.

vagueness of these rights: we can attribute universality, inalienability, and absoluteness to them without implying that any specific rights deriving from them have these characteristics. Further, one could agree that some very abstract right is universal, inalienable, and absolute while also wanting to assert that some specific rights have one or more of these characteristics. Moving to the level of grand principle may postpone problems about the conditions of possession and the weight of specific rights, but it will not make them go away.

Scope and Trade-Offs

The Universal Declaration declares the existence of a wide variety of human rights, including rights to due process (such as a fair trial and freedom from cruel punishments), rights to personal security and autonomy (such as protection from crime, freedom of movement, privacy, and freedom of thought and religion), rights to political participation (such as voting and speaking), rights to equality (such as freedom from discrimination and equality before the law), and economic and social rights (such as rights to a decent standard of living, education, and medical care). The social and political ideal this list of rights suggests is that of a prosperous, egalitarian, democratic welfare state. Some countries now come close to realizing this ideal, but in much of the world the resources, attitudes, and institutions that would convert this vision into reality are still far from being developed. Many people, including those who are sympathetic to the general idea of human rights, have found the Universal Declaration's list of human rights too expansive and have hoped to shorten or qualify it. My concern here is with the various ways in which human rights can be made less likely to conflict with one another and with other norms.

There are at least two reasons for criticizing the Universal Declaration as utopian: First, its rights are stated in broad terms with few qualifications. Second, no ranking is provided for these rights even though it is obvious that they can conflict. The position I develop here suggests that most human rights must be understood to contain implicit exceptions or qualifications.

Scope concerns what a right is *to*. For present purposes we will not need a sharp distinction between conditions of operability (when a right can be brought into play) and scope. Weight concerns the ranking or priority of a right when it conflicts with other considerations. To be exceptionless is a matter of scope, and to be absolute is a matter of weight. But it is often difficult to know whether the failure of a right to outweigh competing considerations and to dictate the result that should be followed, all things considered, in a particular case is best described as an instance of its containing an implicit qualification (scope) or as an instance of its being overridden (weight).

Suppose that Jones wants to exercise his right of free speech by marching into the courtroom in which Smith is on trial and telling the jury some fact that is barred from them by the standards of evidence (e.g., about Smith's criminal record). Here Jones's right to speak would conflict with Smith's right to a fair trial. Suppose further that we agree that Jones should not be allowed to speak to the jury and that the relevant rights do not, all things considered, require that he be allowed to do this. There are two possible ways of describing the failure of Jones's right to freedom of speech to prevail here. One says that the right to free speech, properly understood, does not include within its boundaries a right to enter a courtroom and tell the jury things about the defendant they are precluded from knowing. Here the matter is treated as one of scope.

The other description says that Jones's right of free speech applied in this situation and would normally have required that he be allowed to speak, but it was overridden in this unusual case by Smith's right to a fair trial, which is of higher priority. Here the matter is treated as one of weight.

In this instance it is probably best to see the matter as one of scope. One might hope that all conflicts between norms could be dealt with as they arose by redrawing boundaries and inserting exceptions—boundaries would eventually be adjusted to minimize or eliminate conflicts, and the relative priority of different norms would be reflected in the expansion or retraction of their boundaries when they covered contiguous areas.

But at least three barriers stand in the way of this program. One is that we cannot anticipate all conflicts between rights and with other norms, and we are often uncertain about what we should do in the cases we can imagine. A second barrier is that a right containing sufficient qualifications and exceptions to avoid all possible conflicts would probably be too complex to be generally understood. Third, relieving a conflict by building in an exception will sometimes incorrectly imply that the overridden right did not really apply and that we need feel no regret about our treatment of the person whose right was overridden. In the most awful moral dilemmas there are conflicts not at the edges of rights or other norms but at their very centers. Adding exceptions to cover such cases may lead us to see what is happening as nontragic, rather than as calling for regret and—if possible—compensation. Retaining the vocabulary of weight and overriding may help us to remember that not all moral dilemmas can be anticipated or resolved in advance and that in hard cases even our best efforts may result in injury.[12]

When we describe human rights as prima facie rights because we cannot provide in advance adequate accounts of how to deal with conflicts between human rights and other important considerations, we render irrelevant the sorts of objections that could be made if we claimed that human rights are absolute or near absolute. Prima facie rights are far easier to defend, but their implications for practice are often unclear. If no substantial competing values are present, a prima facie right will tell us what to do. But in countries where wholesale violations of human rights occur, the violators almost always believe they have good reasons to justify infringing human rights. When claims about substantial competing considerations are genuine, prima facie rights are often silent. Thus the danger is that prima facie rights will provide no guidance in the cases where guidance is needed most.

Two responses can be made to this. First, there is no reason why the scopes of prima facie rights cannot be defined in more detail or principles for ranking them in relation to competing considerations worked out. Classifying a right as prima facie implies not that this sort of work cannot be done, but that we recognize that the work will always remain partially finished, at best.

Second, appeals to human rights should be seen as *part* of moral and political argument, not as the whole of it. The presence of claims about human rights does not mean that less specialized forms of moral argument cannot be invoked. If we have a disagreement about the weight of a recognized right to a fair trial in a conflict with a value such as national security, a clarification of facts and concepts will probably be necessary and deeper normative considerations may have to be appealed to. One advantage of seeing

---

12. Herbert Morris, "Persons and Punishment," *Monist* 52 (1968): 499.

specific human rights as middle-level norms is that the possibility of moving the argument to a deeper level is preserved.

Minimally Good Lives as the Focus of Human Rights

The great range of rights in the Universal Declaration, including privacy, due process, nondiscrimination, and welfare, raises the question of whether any unifying idea ties human rights together. One familiar and helpful view suggests that the idea of a decent or minimally good life for all people is such a unifying concept. Human rights do not promise the good life and the great society; the vision is rather of a decent life for all and of societies that can at least be described as civilized. If life on earth were such that people could easily provide for their needs and develop and protect their capacities, perhaps disputes about how to live and how to organize society could emphasize the heights to be attained and ignore the depths of misery to be avoided. But in our world, minimal standards are indispensable.

Conceiving human rights as minimal international standards has two advantages. First, it helps sidestep many issues of cultural relativity by limiting the role of human rights to providing a common set of minimal requirements. Second, this conception of human rights makes it more likely that they will be affordable in poorer countries.

The distinction between a minimally decent life and a good life is not sharp. It is often difficult to say whether a certain deprivation merely makes people's lives less good or whether it actually deprives them of freedom or frustrates basic needs. For this reason, among others, it is not surprising that the authors of the Universal Declaration were not entirely successful in applying this distinction. Some aspects of the democratic welfare state prescribed by the Declaration are defended more appropriately as instruments of human flourishing than as requirements of a decent life for all. And in a few cases—most notable is the right to holidays with pay—the authors of the Declaration clearly confused these categories. Nevertheless, I suggest that the most plausible conception of human rights sees them as minimal standards and that the content of the Declaration is generally compatible with this conception.

That human rights are minimal standards does not mean that all human rights are negative rights or that welfare rights cannot be included among human rights. A right to police protection against crimes is clearly a positive rather than a negative right, but it belongs in the Declaration as part of a minimal right to security. The right to adequate nutrition is clearly a welfare right, yet it is concerned with ensuring people decent conditions of life, not the conditions that would allow them to develop and use their capacities to the fullest possible extent.

During good times in richer countries, minimal standards may seem trivial and irrelevant, and there may be pressure to incorporate more ambitious political agendas into the human rights framework. But no country, however rich and peaceful, can be confident that periods of political or economic crisis will not occur, and it is during crisis periods that minimal standards are most needed. This is one good reason for resisting the incorporation of much more ambitious standards within the human rights framework. If this sounds unduly conservative, let me add that the government of a prosperous and peaceful country that generally complies with human rights standards does not thereby become immune to moral and political criticism. More ambitious standards can be formulated and defended and governments criticized in terms of them. I contend, however, that there are good reasons for using language other than that of universal human rights to formulate these standards.

How Human Rights Guide Behavior

Some of the ways in which human rights can guide behavior are obvious; in other areas the guidance they provide is complicated or problematic. In the obvious cases, full-fledged rights direct the behavior of their addressees through negative and positive duties. For example, a right to freedom from torture guides behavior by forbidding all agents to engage in torture and by imposing a duty on governments to protect people against torture. But the guidance provided is more problematic when behavior is related to, but not directly involved in, human rights violations. For example, when torture occurs in a country, a formulation of the human right not to be tortured may not provide clear guidance about (*a*) what actual and potential victims of torture may do to defend themselves; (*b*) how private citizens should relate to those they suspect of being engaged in torture (e.g., do they have a duty to try to interrupt torture sessions, or a duty not to sell groceries to torturers?); (*c*) how citizens and officials should respond when the right to be free from torture is not legally recognized; and (*d*) how people and governments from other countries should respond to known cases of torture. I submit that reference to rights violations is essential but insufficient for deciding what is morally required or permitted in such cases. Determinate decisions cannot usually be justified by appeal to human rights alone: other moral and political principles must play an ongoing role. It may be necessary to look back to the abstract moral principles that underlie specific human rights, sideways to moral considerations other than rights, and forward to likely consequences. A list of human rights is only a partial guide to, and not a substitute for, moral and political deliberation about how to respond to the requirements of a minimally decent life for all.

Guidance from Rights That Are Not Accepted or Implemented

Even when a human right is not generally recognized or legally implemented in a country, it can guide the behavior of those who believe it is morally justified. Suppose that Smith is an adherent of the Bahai faith—which is unpopular in some countries—and that she sincerely believes in the right to freedom of religion for herself and others. The validity of this norm is confirmed, she thinks, by its international recognition in the Universal Declaration and other documents. As a holder of this justified moral right, Smith has the moral liberty to hold Bahai beliefs, to engage in Bahai religious practices, and to instruct her children in the Bahai faith. It is clear that Smith's recognition of these liberties, immunities, and duties—whether or not they are socially or legally recognized—can guide her behavior. This right can also guide the behavior of its addressees. As one of these addressees, Smith will have a moral duty not to interfere with the religious beliefs and practices of others. Thus Smith would do wrong to disrupt a religious meeting by Jehovah's Witnesses, and if she were a public official, she would do wrong to sponsor legislation to outlaw the Jehovah's Witnesses from proselytizing or to force the children of its members to undergo instruction in the Bahai faith.

In the same way, international human rights, whether or not they are generally accepted in a particular country, can guide the behavior of rightholders and addressees who accept them. In the case of an abstract human right, however, it may be unclear exactly what the rightholders are permitted and empowered to do and exactly what the addressees are required to do. My present concern, however, is not mainly with the abstractness of the guidance provided but with questions for which even a fairly specific right would be unlikely to provide sufficient guidance.[13]

Rights can provide guidance to behavior not only by directing it with duties and other normative elements (the stronger and more usual case) but also by providing reasons or justification for it (the weaker case). For example, a violation of one's right to freedom of religion, or the likelihood of such a violation, may provide a reason or justification for such actions as refusing to obey a law, engaging in public protest, or seeking to emigrate. The role of a right in justifying actions not identified in the scope of the right illustrates that rights can interact in complicated ways with other norms and values and that not all the guidance obtainable—even from a fairly specific right—is likely to be found in its scope.[14]

What to Do About Systematic Violations

Voluntary compliance with moral rights is often hard to obtain, particularly in areas such as religion, where many people feel that matters of great importance are at stake. Although it is not part of the meaning of assertions about moral rights to call for the creation of corresponding legal rights, there is no doubt that legal implementation is central to making many rights effective.

Governments often have dual and conflicting roles in relation to human rights: on the one hand their sponsorship is needed to make many rights effective, and on the other hand they are often the most significant potential source of violations. The struggle to gain respect for a human right must often attempt both to get the government to restrain itself and to get the government to use its legal powers to restrain others. Where human rights violations are deep

---

13. On whether such questions about specifying abstract rights have unique right answers, see Dworkin, *Taking Rights Seriously*, 81–149.

14. On the justificatory role of rights, see Robert F. Ladenson, "Two Kinds of Rights," *Journal of Value Inquiry* (1979): 161–172. Contrary to Ladenson's view that a justificatory role defines a distinct *kind* of right, I suggest that every human right may play a justificatory role in some contexts.

and systematic, rights advocates must devise strategies for political change that are not in the scopes of human rights. Here respect for and implementation of human rights becomes a goal, and something like consequentialist reasoning must be used to pursue this goal. Suppose that influential citizens of a country are persuaded that within justified moralities there is a right to freedom of religious belief and practice. Because this right is not recognized in the law or accepted morality of their country, these citizens organize themselves into the Alliance for Religious Freedom to promote religious freedom and tolerance. The obstacles they face are formidable: some religions are forbidden by severe penalties; others are permitted but harassed through both private and government actions; and only members of the state religion are given full political rights.

The Alliance can take either of two approaches, broadly speaking, toward bringing about the recognition of a right to freedom of religion in their country. They may focus on changing people's moral attitudes and behavior through persuasion, consciousness-raising, and education, or they may focus on legal implementation of the right—for example, on repeal of legal prohibitions of some religions, on creating a constitutional right to religious freedom, on making possession and exercise of political rights independent of religion, or on outlawing public and private religious discrimination. Both approaches are likely to be difficult and are unlikely to succeed overnight or in the absence of favorable historical conditions. Successful reform movements will probably take both approaches—although differences in emphasis are clearly possible.

The first approach seeks to change people's beliefs and attitudes in the expectation that changes in law and politics will follow. This approach does not need to be exclusively concerned with private behavior. What people believe ought to be done by governments often powerfully influences what governments do and can do. Thus, beliefs about the obligations of governments can be included in the principles that members of the Alliance are attempting to introduce into their country's accepted morality. Suppose that through actions and programs the Alliance persuades most people in the country of the rightness of religious freedom and tolerance. As a result, social and political pressure may be exerted on behalf of religious freedom. Religious discrimination may be criticized and subjected to social pressure. Officials trying to enforce bans on some religions may be given unfavorable media coverage and receive outpourings of critical letters. In these and other ways the acceptance of a right to religious freedom within people's morality can be a powerful force for change in both behavior and institutions.

The second approach might be chosen by members of the Alliance if they have great political influence—if, for example, they had participated in a successful revolutionary movement, justified in part by appeals to human rights, and now have great influence through a ruling group determined to sweep away the old order. In these circumstances, the best strategy might be to let law lead public opinion. The implementation of a right to freedom of religion would probably begin at the legal level, perhaps with the right being declared in the new constitution. Next, laws implementing it would be passed and judges given the power to remedy violations. Contrary laws might be abolished, officials seeking to continue religious discrimination sacked, and religious tolerance made a mandatory part of the school curriculum. This strategy could face resistance from people who are not persuaded, who prefer religious intolerance to compliance with the new laws. In this situation, the government hopes that legal pressure will make persuasion easier.

As this example suggests, social and legal strategies are complementary approaches to the implementation of a human right, and most reform movements attempt to use both. If the second approach is chosen and fails, the rights declared in the new constitution will end by being mere paper rights, representing a standard the government cannot, and perhaps has ceased to want to, enforce.

This extended example shows that we cannot deduce from the content of a human right alone the best strategy to secure respect for that right within a country. The same is true, I believe, at the international level. How large a role countries should play in promoting human rights abroad cannot be settled by appeal to human rights alone. Other relevant considerations include the means chosen (e.g., diplomacy, pressure, intervention), the likelihood of success, the weight assigned to the principle of nonintervention in the domestic affairs of other countries, and competing claims on national energy and resources.[15] As before, these additional considerations do not seem to be part of the rights themselves but must rather

---

15. On human rights and foreign policy, see Peter G. Brown and Douglas Mac-Lean, eds., *Human Rights and U.S. Foreign Policy* (Lexington, Mass.: D. C. Heath, 1979); David P. Forsythe, *Human Rights and World Politics* (Lincoln: University of Nebraska Press, 1983); Stanley Hoffmann, *Duties Beyond Borders* (Syracuse, N.Y.:

come from one's general moral and political principles. Human rights do not provide complete guidance to political action—not even to political action directed at human rights violations.

Legal Guidance

The paradigm of legal implementation at the national level for a human right has two parts: (1) enactment in abstract terms in a constitution or bill of rights, and (2) enactment in more specific terms in statutes that become part of the day-to-day law of the realm. In the implementation of freedom of religion, a constitutional norm might commit a country to religious freedom and tolerance, separation of church and state, and state neutrality between different religious groups. For example, article 4 of the Constitution of the German Federal Republic (West Germany) prescribes religious freedom in the following terms:

1. Freedom of faith and of conscience, and freedom of creed, religious or ideological (*weltanschaulich*), shall be inviolable.

2. The undisturbed practice of religion is guaranteed.

3. No one may be compelled against his conscience to render war service involving the use of arms. Details shall be regulated by a federal law.[16]

As section 3 of this article suggests, legislation will usually be needed to apply these general principles to specific national problems, which might include the institutional status of the dominant religious group, tax exemptions for religious organizations, the policy toward parochial schools and toward religious education in the public schools, and exemptions from military service for conscientious objectors. Legal enforcement of the standard sorts—with powers to complain and sue, court procedures to determine the facts and apply the law, punishments for violators, and remedies for victims—are more likely to be specified in legislation than in constitutional or human rights documents. Only a few countries pro-

---

Syracuse University Press, 1981); Richard B. Lillich and Frank C. Newman, eds., *International Human Rights: Problems of Law and Policy* (Boston: Little, Brown, 1979), 824–871; Louis B. Sohn and Thomas Buergenthal, eds., *International Protection of Human Rights* (Indianapolis: Bobbs-Merrill, 1973).

16. German Federal Republic, Basic Law, 1949, in Ian Brownlie, ed., *Basic Documents on Human Rights* (Oxford: Clarendon Press, 1971), 19.

vide for legal enforcement of constitutional norms through suits and judicial review.[17]

Persuasion and legislation are obviously not mutually exclusive. In fact, education of the population in moral and political principles that are believed to be justified is often one of the main goals of human rights legislation. The capacities of governments to penalize violations are usually very limited; most compliance must be voluntary and based on acceptance as well as on fear of penalties. Constitutional and statutory norms concerning human rights play an ongoing role in education and persuasion; domestically the task is to persuade the new generations, both children and immigrants, to accept and follow these principles. Internationally, a country's constitution proclaims its fundamental values—what it takes to be most basic to a decent human society. Unfortunately, national constitutions frequently serve not to set the real agenda for legislation and practice but as showcase documents, not for domestic consumption.

International human rights neither can nor should deal with specific modes of application in different countries. Human rights can only provide general guidance, prescribe that some reasonable mode of implementation be found, and perhaps suggest some broad outlines for institutions (e.g., that all legal systems give criminal defendants a right to legal counsel as an aspect of due process). This sort of guidance leaves much to be decided at the legislative and application stages. Human and constitutional rights guide but seldom fully determine these decisions. No constitutional or statutory norm can cover all questions to be decided; even after legal implementation it will still be necessary to appeal to international human rights and background moral and political principles to decide how to apply legal norms.

Overview

The existence of human rights cannot be adequately explained in terms of legal enactment (either domestic or international) or acceptance in existing moralities. Unfortunately, not all countries have accepted human rights treaties or enacted these rights in domestic law,

---

17. On judicial review, see Henkin, *Rights of Man Today,* 40. On constitutionalism, see J. Roland Pennock and John W. Chapman, eds., *NOMOS XX: Constitutionalism* (New York: New York University Press, 1979).

and it is doubtful whether moralities worldwide share enough content to allow one to find in that content such definite and high-priority norms as human rights. A third alternative, which preserves the universality and independence of human rights, holds that human rights exist—at the most basic level—as norms within justified moralities. This alternative is attractive, but it requires its advocates to argue that at least some moral norms can be known to be rationally justified. Further, because agreement on which human rights are rationally justifiable is unlikely—even if possible in principle—universality and independence may be purchased at the price of some uncertainty about what these norms require.

Human rights are best conceived as implying duties for both governments and individuals. According to the Universal Declaration, these duties support human rights in a wide variety of areas, including due process, personal security and autonomy, political participation, equality, and welfare. The Universal Declaration's long list of human rights probably needs to be pruned to fit better with the attractive idea that human rights are minimal standards. But the view that all genuine human rights are negative should be rejected because the drastic surgery it proposes would exclude many important rights.

To serve as international standards that are not subordinate to domestic laws and practices, human rights must be of high priority in competition with other considerations. Guaranteeing this high priority by saying that human rights are absolute should be avoided, however, as this guarantee exposes one to many objections and accomplishes little.

Although claims that human rights are universal and inalienable are attractive ways to specify very strong conditions of possession of these rights, not all human rights seem to have these characteristics. In some cases, at least, claims about the universality of human rights need to be qualified to restrict these claims to the modern era, to people with some minimal level of rationality and autonomy, or to citizens of each state. Inalienability has two aspects: immunity to repudiation and immunity to forfeiture. Some human rights may have neither of these characteristics, or they may have one without the other. When claims about the absoluteness, universality, and inalienability of human rights are qualified, these norms are made somewhat easier to defend and less vulnerable to the charge that they are too rigid for our messy and difficult world.

Full-fledged human rights provide direct guidance to their holders and addressees, although this guidance may be stated abstractly. Such rights do not, however, provide complete guidance as to details of implementation, appropriate responses to noncompliance, and strategies for promoting compliance. Thus a list of rights cannot serve as an alternative to political thought and deliberation.

4. Universal Rights in a Diverse World

The people who created the international human rights movement after World War II were under no illusion that universal assent to human rights already existed. The horrors of the holocaust, with its genocidal attempt to destroy European Jewry, were too much in view to permit any such illusion. The Soviets clearly had reservations about traditional civil and political rights. The proletarian revolutions they desired would require rough treatment or worse for members of the overthrown classes.

But with the optimism that often accompanies idealism, the advocates of international human rights hoped that substantial agreement on standards of government behavior could be found or created among the members of the United Nations. They expected these standards to express the hopes of millions of people around the world who yearned for freedom and a better life. The achievements of the human rights movement in the decades that have followed have shown both that these optimistic beliefs were not entirely without foundation and how difficult it is to create genuine international agreement about how governments should behave.

Although this movement has made significant progress in formulating and gaining acceptance for human rights, it has also been faced with massive violations of these rights in many parts of the world and with the hypocrisy of governments that use the rhetoric of human rights while ignoring them in practice. So much diversity and disagreement may lead to doubt about the reasonableness of believing in human rights and raise two questions that I want to pursue here. First, does this disagreement mean that there is no rational basis for universal human rights? Second, would not an enlightened moral position prescribe different standards for different groups and tolerance between groups?

Divergent Perspectives

That the peoples of earth display enormous diversity in customs, languages, religions, moral norms, and political practices is both inescapable and difficult to accommodate philosophically. Extended first-hand exposure to cultural differences often has a powerful impact. People who become intimately acquainted with other ways of life often respond by advocating tolerance and moral flexibility. This response is not limited to anthropologists; it can be found among travelers and missionaries as well. But these people disagree about how much to tolerate abhorrent practices and about the feasibility of introducing new standards.

Although I cannot offer anything like a comprehensive survey of worldwide attitudes toward human rights, it may be helpful to sketch in broad strokes some of the most familiar and representative positions. One could divide the world by regions, levels of economic development, ideologies, or religions, but I will use the familiar division of countries into first, second, and third "worlds," thus combining several of these categories into one. This crude trichotomy designates the developed Western countries of Europe and North America, plus Japan and Australia, as the First World; the non-Asian communist countries as the Second World; and the remaining, generally less developed, countries as the Third World.

The First World

Many of the institutions we now associate with the implementation of human rights first emerged in Europe and North America, so it is not surprising that one finds the most favorable public attitudes toward human rights in the developed, noncommunist West.[1] Since World War II, these countries have generally been constitutional democracies that tolerate a variety of political parties and points of view, protect some degree of public political discussion, and select their leaders through regular elections. I hasten to add that this does not mean that these governments have never tried to manipulate public opinion or suppress dissent. And while showing some respect for the rights of their citizens, they have often sup-

---

1. See Richard P. Claude, "Western European Public Opinion on American Human Rights Advocacy," in Jack L. Nelson and Vera M. Green, eds., *International Human Rights* (Stanfordville, N.Y.: Earl M. Coleman, 1980), 97–117.

ported extremely repressive regimes abroad when that was thought to be in their interests.

The welfare state has now emerged in all of the countries of the First World. Socialism and the labor movements have been influential in bringing to all these countries some degree of central economic direction and the provision of educational, medical, and economic benefits through public institutions. The idea of the welfare state has been generally accepted, although many would deny that people have rights to the benefits the welfare state provides. But very large economic and social inequalities remain, and these comprise, or are connected with, the most severe human rights problems in these countries. Poverty, unemployment, racism, and sexism are far from being eliminated, and it is in these areas that the struggle for human rights is most intense and political disagreements most heated.

It is only a slight exaggeration to say that the international human rights movement was started after World War II by people from the First World, acting in the hope that an international system to promote and protect human rights would help to avoid repetition of the tragedies of World War II. Although the United States took a leading role in this endeavor in the late forties, the onset of the Cold War terminated U.S. leadership, and since then the United States has been unwilling to ratify human rights agreements such as the International Covenants. The countries of Western Europe have carried on this task and have been the most consistent supporters of the international human rights movement both in the United Nations, where they were among the early signers of the International Covenants, and in the Council of Europe, where through the European Convention they developed the most effective international system for protecting human rights that has emerged to date.

The Second World

Even if one confines one's attention to Eastern Europe and the USSR and ignores Asian communist states, the communist world is no longer monolithic. Substantial differences exist between communist countries in their attitudes and practices in regard to human rights. Yugoslavia and Hungary have moved some distance toward political liberalization, and the people of Czechoslovakia and Poland would clearly like to do the same. For our purposes here, however, a focus on the Soviet Union will provide the dominant perspective.

As their Marxist heritage leads one to expect, contemporary communists have had negative or mixed attitudes toward the human rights movement. On the one hand they have endorsed the contemporary movement's commitment to economic and social rights and deemphasis of the right to property, and they have recognized the rhetorical advantages in international arenas of being in favor of human rights. But on the other hand they remain opposed to many of the elements of liberal democracy that contemporary human rights prescribe. Soviet leaders have been loath to permit opposition to the Communist party and its policies to emerge publicly.

When the Universal Declaration was accepted by the General Assembly in 1948, the USSR and its allies abstained. Since the 1960s, however, the Soviet Union has participated in the human rights endeavors of the United Nations. It has ratified the International Covenants and thus enjoys the advantages of going on record in support of human rights, while generally opposing strong international machinery to apply pressure against countries that flagrantly violate human rights.[2] The Soviet Union has often alleged that any criticism of its own human rights conduct amounts to illicit interference in its domestic affairs.

It is probably fair to say that the disagreement between the First World and Second World concerns how to achieve societies in which all people can enjoy a high degree of welfare and freedom, rather than the desirability of this goal. Thus the Soviets can agree to most of the norms of the Universal Declaration as prescriptions for the societies they hope will emerge from the revolutionary process, but they are little inclined to tolerate pressure to implement these standards in the present—particularly when that pressure seems to threaten central control of the direction of the revolution. Human rights seem to be viewed by the Soviets merely as goals and not necessarily even as high-priority goals. Further, the Soviets tend to emphasize the duties of individuals as much as their rights, and in conflicts between the interests of individuals and the goals of the

2. See Peter B. Reddaway, "Theory and Practice of Human Rights in the Soviet Union," in Donald P. Kommers and Gilbert D. Loescher, eds., *Human Rights and American Foreign Policy* (Notre Dame, Ind.: Notre Dame University Press, 1979); Eugene Kamenka and Alice Erh-Soon Tay, "Human Rights in the Soviet Union," *World Review* 19 (1980): 47–60; A. Glenn Mower, Jr., "Human Rights in the Soviet Union," in Nelson and Green, eds., *International Human Rights,* 199–228. See also Inga Markovitz, "Socialist vs. Bourgeois Rights—An East-West German Comparison," *University of Chicago Law Review* 45 (1978): 612–636.

country, the Soviets seldom favor the individuals. It should be emphasized, however, that the countries of the Second World have generally made good progress in providing for the material well-being of their citizens and thus in implementing economic and social rights.

The Third World

This is a very diverse group of countries, about which broad generalizations are risky. The salient characteristic of these countries is a lower level of economic development than is generally found in the first two worlds. Latin America, Africa, the Islamic countries, and the countries of Asia and the Pacific constitute the Third World. Most of the world's population lives here, about half in Asia alone.

The Third World shares little in the way of values or ideology, except for a desire for economic improvement and a better life for the masses. In many Third World countries pressing problems include feeding and educating a growing population and putting it to work, establishing the authority of the central government over diverse peoples, and ending a history of colonial domination and foreign economic exploitation.

Many Third World religious and cultural traditions emphasize human brotherhood, human dignity, and the duties of justice and generosity. But, as elsewhere, these values are often contradicted by a reality of oppression, cruelty, corruption, and gross inequality.

Latin America, with its European and Christian heritage, has a tradition of support for human rights measures in international bodies, and the Organization of American States has developed its own system for the protection of human rights that parallels the European system.[3] But the political and economic background for these measures has often been one of rising but unmet expectations, massive unemployment, runaway inflation, leftist agitation and guerrilla activity, rightist retaliations, political and labor unrest, and military coups.[4] Military governments, in order to establish their authority and to obtain international assistance, often im-

3. See Thomas Buergenthal and Robert E. Norris, *Human Rights: The Inter-American System* (Dobbs Ferry, N.Y.: Oceana Publications, 1982); Carlos Alberto Dunshee de Abranches, "The Inter-American Court of Human Rights," *American University Law Review* 30 (1980): 79–125. Also see pp. 11–12, note 13, above.
4. See Richard R. Fagen, "Equity in the South in the Context of North-South Relations," in Albert Fishlow et al., eds., *Rich and Poor Nations in the World Econ-*

pose economic austerity on the populace, emphasize industrial development over agriculture or social services, and repress those with liberal and leftist views through imprisonment, kidnapping, torture, and murder—the last often involving mysterious disappearances.[5] Repression has often been assisted or tolerated by First World governments.

The Islamic world generally finds the idea of human rights compatible with its religious traditions, particularly because the Koran emphasizes duties of respect, justice, and mercy.[6] Further, Muslims have long traditions of religious and social tolerance—at least for other monotheists. Conflict between human rights norms and Islamic beliefs and practice are found chiefly in the authoritarian and undemocratic character of many Islamic states and in such matters as full equality for women, full religious freedom and political equality for unbelievers, and, in the most conservative states, the use of cruel punishments, such as the amputation of a hand for theft.

In Third World countries under leftist control, political repression has often occurred as the left tried to consolidate its power. In a few cases this revolutionary process has been relatively bloodless; in others, such as Cambodia and Vietnam, it has led to brutal repression and massive movements of refugees. Here the attitude of government leaders is likely to resemble that of the Soviet communists: human rights are nice things that will, with luck, emerge after the revolution succeeds.

---

omy (New York: McGraw-Hill, 1978), 165–214. See also Noam Chomsky and Edward S. Herman, *The Political Economy of Human Rights* (Boston: South End Press, 1979).

5. Amnesty International, *Torture in the Eighties* (London: Amnesty International Publications, 1984); *Amnesty International Report 1983* (London: Amnesty International Publications, 1983); Amnesty International USA, *Disappearances: A Workbook* (New York: Amnesty International USA Publications, 1981), 1–30; Amnesty International, *Testimony on Secret Detention Camps in Argentina* (London: Amnesty International Publications, 1980); Inter-American Commission on Human Rights, "Report on the Status of Human Rights in Chile," prepared by Thomas Buergenthal, *International Legal Materials* 14 (1975): 115–134. See also Margaret E. Crahan, "National Security Ideology and Human Rights," in Margaret E. Crahan, ed., *Human Rights and Basic Needs in the Americas* (Washington, D.C.: Georgetown University Press, 1982), 100–127.

6. See David Hollenbach, "Human Rights and Religious Faith in the Middle East: Reflections of a Christian Theologian," *Human Rights Quarterly* 4 (1982): 94–109; Seyyed Hossein Nasr, "The Concept and Reality of Freedom in Islam and Islamic Civilization," in Alan S. Rosenbaum, ed., *The Philosophy of Human Rights: International Perspectives* (Westport, Conn.: Greenwood Press, 1980), 103–112.

In spite of their diverse attitudes about human rights, Third World countries have been generally willing to participate in human rights activities in the United Nations. When the Universal Declaration was formulated after World War II, few African and Asian countries were members of the United Nations. Although the Declaration differed from earlier bills of rights in being international and in containing social and economic rights, in other respects it was clearly a descendent of the French Declaration and the U.S. Bill of Rights. African and Asian countries entering the United Nations during the fifties accepted the Charter's commitment to human rights and the Universal Declaration. But when the International Covenants were finally approved by the General Assembly in 1966, they clearly reflected the concerns of Third World members in a way that the Universal Declaration did not. The rights of nations to self-determination and to control of their own national resources, along with a right to freedom from racial discrimination, had, at the insistence of the new members, been placed prominently at the beginning of both covenants. And the Declaration's right to property, with its requirement of compensation for appropriated property, had been entirely omitted.

Third World leaders and intellectuals often have reservations about the human rights movement, and their reasons are easy to understand. People who seek radical change in their societies—whether revolutionary transformation or the imposition of "discipline" by a rightist military regime—may worry that appeals to human rights will block the changes they believe are needed and exclude harsh tactics to promote those changes. Third World nationalists, jealous of their national sovereignty after long periods of foreign domination or colonial rule, may worry that alleged violations of human rights in their territory will give other nations a pretext for infringing their sovereignty. Third World intellectuals may worry that the human rights movement is still another attempt by ethnocentric Europeans and Americans to impose their values and institutions on the rest of the world. Although the human rights movement is far from being the only, or even the main, cause of Westernization, it clearly encourages countries to develop Western-style political institutions. These worries are likely to result in support for self-determination and nonintervention, but they have not kept Third World countries from participating in the human rights movement in the United Nations, for several reasons.

One is undoubtedly that the idea of freedom and human rights

appeals to many peoples, not just to rich Westerners. Many groups
have tried to devise means to protect people against the tyranny and
corruption of officials, unfairness in the application of criminal penalties, and gross economic inequalities. Second, the human rights
movement has provided Third World countries with some useful
tools for condemning colonialists and racists and for justifying a
new international economic order. Finally, it is possible to obtain
the rhetorical advantages of supporting and appealing to human
rights without coming under much pressure to comply.

Moral Relativism
and Human Rights

When the Universal Declaration was being formulated in 1947,
the executive board of the American Anthropological Association
warned of the danger that the Declaration would be "a statement of
rights conceived only in terms of the values prevalent in Western Europe and America" and condemned an ethnocentrism that trans-
lates "the recognition of cultural differences into a summons to action." To a large extent the concern of the executive board was
merely to condemn intolerant colonialist attitudes and to advocate
cultural and political self-determination. The board allowed that
"freedom is understood and sought after by peoples having the
most diverse cultures" and suggested that in attempting to influence
repressive regimes "underlying cultural values may be called on to
bring the peoples of such states to a realization of the consequences
of the acts of their governments, and thus enforce a brake upon discrimination and conquest." In addition to these sensible suggestions the board also made some stronger assertions—that "standards and values are relative to the culture from which they derive"
and thus "what is held to be a human right in one society may be
regarded as anti-social by another people." The board also asserted
that "respect for differences between cultures is validated by the scientific fact that no technique of qualitatively evaluating cultures has
been discovered."[7]

These assertions express the position known as "moral rela-

7. "Statement on Human Rights," *American Anthropologist* 49 (1947): 539–
543. See also Peter L. Berger, "Are Human Rights Universal?" *Commentary* 64 (September 1977): 60–63; and Jack Donnelly, "Cultural Relativism and Universal Human Rights," *Human Rights Quarterly* 6 (1984): 400–419.

tivism," which is often embraced by those who recognize cultural differences and which many believe to be incompatible with a commitment to human rights. Moral relativism consists of a number of distinguishable claims that do not necessarily stand or fall together; it will be useful to distinguish these and consider them separately.[8]

Let us begin with the factual claim that there are fundamental differences among groups in their moral norms and values and accompanying world views. We might call this the *diversity thesis*.

This claim is often accompanied by an explanatory hypothesis, namely, that a group's moral norms and values derive their content and character from—and thus are relative to—the culture and survival needs of the group. We might call this the *relativity hypothesis*. It not only denies that humans have a universal moral sense or conscience but also asserts that moral beliefs must be explained entirely in terms of the culture and survival needs of the group.

One who believed the diversity thesis and the relativity hypothesis might count them as evidence for the view that there is no rational method of choosing or justifying moral norms and values and hence that moral norms cannot be known to be true or false. This view, which we might call *skeptical relativism*, rejects the idea of a justified morality.[9]

One could hold that substantial differences among moral attitudes and practices are a good thing and ought to be respected. This view, which we might call *prescriptive relativism*, is itself a moral position, namely, that it is desirable and proper for different groups to have different moral standards if their cultures or circumstances are different. Prescriptive relativism implies, or at least is usually accompanied by, a prescription of tolerance for the practices of other groups.

It is sometimes alleged that skeptical relativism implies prescriptive relativism. The board of the American Anthropological Association argued, for example, that "respect for differences in cultures" is supported by the "scientific fact" that there is no way of evaluating cultures—which is, in effect, to justify a norm by assert-

---

8. On moral relativism, see the essays in John Ladd, ed., *Ethical Relativism* (Belmont, Calif.: Wadsworth, 1973). See also N. L. Gifford, *When in Rome: An Introduction to Relativism and Knowledge* (Albany: State University of New York Press, 1983).

9. See Kai Nielsen, "Scepticism and Human Rights," *Monist* 52 (1968): 573–594.

ing that there is no way of justifying moral norms. Skeptical relativism is not merely the useful warning that because our moral knowledge is tenuous we ought to be very careful about imposing our moral beliefs on others. It also asserts the impossibility of moral knowledge or justification. If norms are impossible to justify, so are norms that prescribe diversity and tolerance. Prescriptive relativism is not supported by skeptical relativism.

In the rest of this section I will discuss the diversity and relativity theses and skeptical relativism. Prescriptive relativism is a very different kind of thesis, which I discuss in the concluding section.

The Diversity Thesis

There are obvious differences among the moralities of different groups around the world but it is not obvious how deep these differences are. It is known, for example, that some positive moralities allow the killing of the aged, but the interesting question is whether this killing involves the absence of respect for human life (or of a general prohibition against harming the innocent) or is merely an exception based on economic necessity or cosmological beliefs.

Kai Nielsen argues that when background beliefs are taken into account, such extreme practices appear not to involve completely different moral frameworks:

> The Norse believed that to have an honoured place in Valhalla a warrior must die a violent death in battle or in circumstances that would give an old warrior such an honoured place. For a person who sincerely believes such cosmological accounts . . . it is at least understandable, quite within our "moral geometry" . . . that a morally concerned individual would so club—and indeed regard it as a duty to do so—his aged but loved father to death. . . . It is not that the Norseman has no appreciation of the fact that such an act is an act of violence, that acts of violence cause harm and that to harm a person is *prima facie* wrong. . . . Rather with his cosmological beliefs about how the gods behave and about a man's prospects for an after-life, his act is not a cruel act showing no concern with the avoidance of harm or the infliction of suffering.[10]

It is clearly possible to find deeper agreement beneath surface differences in moral norms and values, but it is far from certain that we can explain away all disagreements in this way. Many anthropol

---

10. Kai Nielsen, "On the Diversity of Moral Beliefs," *Cultural Hermeneutics* 2 (1974): 289–290.

ogists have concluded that we cannot. Further, even if it could be shown that all peoples accept some prohibition against killing human beings, the exceptions (e.g., that the prohibition protects only male heads of households) may be substantial enough to count as a deep disagreement. Finally, such agreement as exists may pertain to basic values rather than to rights or duties. Thus it is reasonable to accept the diversity thesis, especially if it can be construed in a way that makes it compatible with the existence of significant areas of agreement.

The Relativity Hypothesis

This view holds that existing ethical standards are inevitably relative to culture or circumstance. It denies the possibility of transcultural moral criticism that appeals to international human rights to create a shared standard of argument. If the moral norms and values of a group are uniquely determined by cultural or environmental factors, then it is impossible for them to be changed by, say, human rights campaigns that encourage peoples and governments to adopt a different and allegedly more justifiable political morality.

Anthropologists have often tried to identify functional connections between the moral beliefs of groups and aspects of their cultures, circumstances, or survival needs. One who holds, as I do, that a morality should promote people's survival will be able to accept many of these claims and may even be committed to some of them. But as a strong claim about causal relationships, the relativity hypothesis is open to many objections.

This thesis may be seen as simply a consequence of universal determinism—if everything has a cause, then moral beliefs must have causes. But two possibilities are left open in this case. One is that a wide range of factors can influence moral beliefs, including knowledge of the moral beliefs of people in other societies, which might be provided by a document such as the Universal Declaration. Another is that beliefs about the outcomes of moral decision making are among the causes of moral beliefs. In some cultures, at least, people may be more committed to certain methods of decision making than to particular norms, so that norms and customs can change when these methods are believed to yield results incompatible with existing moral beliefs.

As an imperfect analogy, consider beliefs about the natural world. If everything has a cause, then these beliefs have causes. But once experimental methods have been learned and internalized the methods themselves begin to influence beliefs about nature. One kind of cause thus displaces another. We do not find it surprising when groups change their beliefs about nature in response to new results of scientific investigations.

Another reason to reject the view that moral beliefs are uniquely determined by cultural or environmental factors is that the efforts of missionaries, colonialists, and revolutionaries have led people to adopt new moral beliefs. One of the clearest examples of this is the adoption of Marxist egalitarianism by millions of Chinese in the last thirty years. Through a revolutionary struggle, Marxist ideas were transplanted to an Asian country whose indigenous norms were quite different. Although many factors make it difficult to change a group's norms and practices, such change is not impossible, as, indeed, the considerable influence of the human rights movement around the world illustrates.

A final objection is that the diversity thesis suggests more uniformity of moral beliefs within societies than one is likely to find today. At least on issues involved in human rights violations, opinion within a group or country is likely to be divided even in advance of outside criticism. This point is well stated by Thomas Scanlon:

> Like many forms of relativism, this argument [that human rights have a special place in our tradition but not in others] rests on the attribution to "them" of a unanimity that does not in fact exist. "They" are said to be different from us and to live by different rules. Such stereotypes are seldom accurate, and the attribution of unanimity is particularly implausible in the case of human rights violations. These actions have victims who generally resent what is done to them and who would rarely concede that, because such behavior is common in their country, their tormentors are acting quite properly.[11]

Skeptical Relativism

Given the deficiencies of most attempts to justify human rights and the widespread disagreement about such rights, one might be inclined to think that skeptical relativism is the most appropriate response. Skeptical relativism incorporates the diversity thesis; it acknowledges that there are great cultural differences worldwide

11. Thomas M. Scanlon, "Human Rights as a Neutral Concern," in Peter G. Brown and Douglas MacLean, eds., *Human Rights and U.S. Foreign Policy* (Lexington, Mass.: D. C. Heath, 1979), 88.

and that few moral norms are universally accepted. Skeptical relativism infers from the diversity thesis that there is no rational method of justifying norms and values and hence that there are no grounds for preferring the standards of the human rights movement to any others. In this view, the norms of groups neither derive from nor are justifiable in terms of rational considerations; consequently, the human rights movement has no rational basis and must be viewed as a raw, if constantly rationalized, attempt by some people to impose their values on others. The skeptical relativist need not be a prescriptive relativist; he or she might agree with those who view the human rights movement as a form of cultural imperialism but then disappoint the advocates of that view by denying that any condemnation of cultural imperialism can be justified.

A milder form of skeptical relativism might allow that some of the broad outlines of morality are justifiable by rational considerations but maintain that many important details can only be filled in by convention. In its weaker versions this view may be held by people who do not consider themselves moral skeptics.

Neither the weak nor the strong forms of skeptical relativism are proven true by the diversity thesis, that is, by the existence of deep moral disagreements. The nonskeptic can respond that disagreement only shows that some people hold justified moral beliefs and others unjustified ones or, more plausibly, a mixture of the two. Disagreement only shows that not everyone successfully uses a rational method of settling moral questions, not that such a method is unavailable or impossible. Some people may not know the method, or they may be incapable of using it well because of bias, irrationality, or lack of knowledge about relevant facts.

Interestingly, the negation of the diversity thesis also implies nothing about the truth of skeptical relativism. Even if there were complete agreement on moral issues worldwide, skeptical relativism could still be correct if this agreement derived from irrational grounds and was impossible to justify by appeal to rational ones. Skeptics appeal to disagreement and nonskeptics to agreement as evidence for their views, but neither appeal is conclusive. The issue must be argued on other grounds.

One may hope to settle the matter in favor of skeptical relativism by arguing that if there were a rational method for settling moral disagreements everyone would know it or, at least, that moral philosophers would be able to specify its steps adequately. This argument does not work. It took millennia for human beings to develop rational methods for deciding disputes in scientific matters, and even now there are very significant disputes about the methods of physical sciences. Further, philosophers have offered numerous accounts of rational argument about moral questions, one of which may be correct.

It seems safest to conclude that we do not know whether skeptical relativism is true—although we are not precluded from making guesses. A thorough inquiry into this matter would require us to examine the methods philosophers have proposed for deciding moral questions and to judge whether these methods are partially or fully adequate.

Deep moral disagreement may place a question mark before the international human rights movement and certainly makes the work more difficult, but it does not undermine the human rights movement or show its endeavors to be irrational.

Prescriptive Relativism

Prescriptive relativism is a moral position that endorses normative diversity and tolerance among groups. The prescriptive relativist denies that there are any (or at least that there are many) universal and exceptionless norms, except for a norm requiring tolerance of other people's mores and practices. This position is the antithesis of the view that there are numerous universal and absolute moral standards that admit of no exceptions. The strongest form of prescriptive relativism holds that the only valid universal norm is one requiring tolerance. The prescriptive relativist need not be a moral skeptic: he or she may hold that it is possible for the standards of a particular group to be objectively justified, but to bind only the members of that group.

In its more modest forms, prescriptive relativism holds that universal norms should be few and broad so that most local standards and practices will be compatible with them. This modest version seems to have much to recommend it from a moral point of view. The enormous differences among groups in traditions, social arrangements, world views, levels of economic and political development, and problems faced make it unlikely that we can defend the existence and universal applicability of numerous detailed and exceptionless norms. A norm setting out a father's obligations in European societies may be inappropriate in a society where many responsibilities for children are assigned to their maternal uncles. Standards of blasphemy appropriate to a highly religious society might be inappropriate in a secular one. The relaxed legal standards appropriate to a homogeneous, stable, and peaceful society may be insufficient to provide order in a troubled, ethnically divided new state.

Prescriptive Relativism and Human Rights

Prescriptive relativists often dislike the idea of human rights, particularly in cross-cultural contexts. We saw that high priority and definiteness were distinctive features of rights, allowing them to express moral and legal requirements that leave relatively little room for discretion and interpretation. Prescriptive relativists are likely to be suspicious of such inflexible norms. Even modest prescriptive relativists who endorse minimal standards of international political morality may not wish to see these standards stated in the language of rights; they may prefer the more flexible language of high-priority goals.

But rights can be modified by abstract language and exceptions to make them more flexible. The human rights movement has often modified its norms in this way, and I suspect that these norms are sufficiently limited in scope, broad in terms, and liberal in exceptions to permit a reasonable amount of diversity among social systems, legal practices, and forms of government. In what follows I will illustrate some ways in which the norms of the human rights movement permit diversity and will then consider, and attempt to rebut, some arguments in favor of even stronger forms of prescriptive relativism.

Human rights standards have a number of characteristics that allow diversity. Perhaps the most obvious and important is that they provide only minimal standards in a limited number of areas. For example, the rights one has as a parent, home owner, teacher, or union member depend not on human rights but on the morality, laws, and customs of one's country. It is possible, of course, that some of the rights found in the Universal Declaration and other human rights documents are insufficiently basic and that one who wanted to preserve local flexibility against international human rights would set the criterion for a "minimal standard" or "basic right" rather high.

Second, the terms used in formulating human rights are often broad or abstract enough to allow some latitude to local interpretation. For example, article 9 of the International Covenant on Civil and Political Rights includes the provision: "No one shall be subjected to arbitrary arrest or detention. No one shall be deprived of his liberty except on such grounds and in accordance with such procedures as are established by law." Here the vague word "arbitrary" allows considerable room for interpretation in judging arrests, and the reference to "procedures as established by law" requires only formal legality. Another example, article 10 of the same covenant, requires that people in prison be "treated with humanity and with respect for the inherent dignity of the human person." This permits the operation of varying conceptions of human dignity. What counts as an indignity usually depends on how most people live and are treated and on what the local culture finds repulsive. If many people work in the fields pulling plows because there are no tractors or beasts of burden, then a punishment involving such work would be no indignity. But if such work is normally done by tractors, and only prisoners are required to pull plows, this may amount to a substantial indignity.

Those who formulate human rights may be pulled both ways in regard to precision and detail. Standards that are definite in requiring, for example, particular kinds of institutions, are easier to interpret and make it more difficult for repressive regimes to pretend that they are complying when they are not. But institution-specific requirements may condemn perfectly adequate alternatives; for this reason and others the modest prescriptive relativist is likely to be uncomfortable with them. Except in the area of fair criminal procedures, the human rights movement has leaned toward broad and flexible standards that allow for a variety of implementations.

Third, the possibility of overriding some human rights in emergency situations is explicitly allowed. The European Convention allows countries to derogate from their duties during "time of war or other public emergency threatening the life of the nation." Similar provisions, found in the International Covenant on Civil and Political Rights, are discussed and evaluated in chapter 8.

Fourth, the duty to comply with human rights standards is conditional on the ability to do so. Part 2, article 2, of the International Covenant on Economic, Social, and Cultural Rights explicitly requires a state to "take steps . . . to the maximum of its available resources, with a view to achieving progressively the full realization of the rights recognized in the present Covenant." Even without such a statement, the principle that "ought" implies "can" implicitly holds that rights are inoperable when it is genuinely impossible to implement them. Thus a country so poor that it could only afford a rudimentary system of due process in criminal cases would not be in violation of the requirement of due process of law.

Finally, the human rights movement has supported diversity within a structure of basic principles by endorsing the principle of self-determination and, in the UN Charter, the principle of nonintervention in matters "essentially within the domestic jurisdiction" of a state. It should be understood, however, that these principles are subject to some important qualifications. The domestic jurisdiction clause does not relieve a country of obligations undertaken in international law even if they pertain to domestic matters. The principle of self-determination was asserted in the International Covenants: "All people have a right of self-determination. By virtue of that right they freely determine their political status and freely pursue their economic, social and cultural development." The clearest implication of this broad principle is to forbid colonial rule. Perhaps armed intervention in the affairs of another country is also prohibited; if so, the right to self-determination would preclude "humanitarian intervention" to eliminate large-scale violations of human rights. But the principle of self-determination as internationally understood does not forbid attempts to influence governments through public forums, appeals to public opinion, and denial of economic advantages such as loans, trade, and aid. Thus the principle of self-determination seems compatible with most forms of international pressure for compliance with human rights.

Strong Prescriptive Relativism:
Pros and Cons

The standards of the international human rights movement are for the most part compatible with a modest prescriptive relativism, but some people desire even greater diversity in norms and practices than is permitted by these standards. I now turn to some arguments for and against greater relativism.

The appeal of indigenous standards. One might try to defend strong prescriptive relativism by arguing that indigenous moral and political norms and practices, flowing from long experience, are likely to be well suited to a group's needs and thus advantageous to its welfare. Imported standards, it might be argued, are likely for the same reasons to function poorly or not at all. One might try, for example, to defend the practice in some Arab states of cutting off the hands of thieves on the grounds that it is deep-rooted, indigenous, and has survived because it is well suited to local needs.

But the superiority of indigenous standards, on which this kind of argument rests, is often exaggerated. We know from our own culture that indigenous institutions often work badly and become outdated. Social and technological changes often make older norms and practices ill suited to a group's needs. For example, when education and wide availability of radio and television make people more knowledgeable about politics and less willing to have no influence on important political decisions, the absence of even rudimentary democratic institutions becomes a problem. Further, one cannot assume that the existing norms and practices that violate human rights are in fact indigenous. Techniques of repression are often imported (sometimes with the help of the great powers) and thus a cessation of torture or the release of political prisoners may be more in accord with traditional norms and values than continued torture and imprisonment.

The second part of this claim, namely, that imported standards generally function poorly or not at all, is also an exaggeration. Many transplanted institutions are successful, especially if a transition period is planned. The parliamentary institutions created in Japan after World War II are one striking example of successful transplantation. Borrowing between countries occurs constantly and ranges from political institutions (civil service systems, judicial review, ombudsmen, income tax) to technology and economics (assembly line production, worker self-management).

It should also be noted that compliance with human rights norms may require not a change of practices but merely an expansion of existing practices. Some Soviet citizens are already permitted to travel abroad; compliance with the human right to travel would simply require making this liberty available to all. Similarly, some of those accused of crimes in repressive countries already receive a fair trial. Thus compliance with the human right to a fair trial would not require new norms or institutions, merely the extension of present ones.

The value of cultural diversity. This argument asserts the great value of preserving the diverse cultures and ways of life that now exist. Because distinctive values and practices are essential parts of culture, the argument concludes that we must refrain from encouraging countries to adopt the Western norms and practices that are commended by the documents of the human rights movement.

Cultural diversity is an important value, I think, but it is not absolute nor does it rule out many of the changes involved in complying with human rights. One may see the value of preserving, say, the cultural and religious traditions of India without concluding that the Indian caste system should be preserved. Cultures and value systems typically have many parts, and it is sometimes possible to preserve the best and most distinctive features while jettisoning the most repugnant—particularly when making the changes required for compliance with human rights. These rights have the behavior of governments as their central focus, and government practices are seldom central to the identity and persistence of a culture. A group's culture is not likely to be destroyed if torture and cruel punishments are eliminated, political prisoners are released, political dissent is permitted, and programs to combat hunger and illiteracy instituted. Although the human rights movement is part of the general trend toward Westernization in cultures around the world, it is a relatively small part, and terminating it would do little or nothing to terminate Westernization. The question for our era is not whether rapid cultural change should occur—it is occurring—but rather what direction such change should take.

Human rights as barriers to development. This argument contends that economic and political development will be slower in a country that respects human rights, particularly rights to political participation and dissent. A developing country may be troubled by ethnic conflict, a weak central government, an ailing economy, an uneducated population, or a lack of experience with democratic processes. Progress toward economic and political development requires people to be mobilized and unified. Public opposition to government programs and policies may, if permitted, make this mobilization more difficult. Thus, the argument concludes, harsh measures to silence political opposition are sometimes justifiable. A weak form of this argument might try to justify the absence of freedom of expression or the failure to hold regular elections. A stronger form might use the same premises to justify even harsher measures, such as torture, political murder, and holding large numbers of political prisoners.

This kind of argument may seem to be mere common sense. A country with limited resources cannot do everything at once, and establishing government authority must be one of the first priorities. Further, the issue cannot be posed as a simple conflict between economic and welfare concerns on one side and human dignity and rights on the other. Providing the food requisite to the enjoyment of the right to life is an important goal of development in many countries, as security against criminals is necessary for the protection and enjoyment of many other rights. Thus people's rights are present on both sides of the balance. The trade-off, if one is required, will sacrifice some rights and aspects of welfare to other rights and aspects of welfare.

The strong form of this argument—which tries to justify such harsh tactics as murder, torture, and holding political prisoners—is much more vulnerable than the weaker form. An atmosphere of terror is not conducive to innovations, solidarity, or confidence in government, and the record of the most repressive countries is generally one of chaos and stagnation, not of great development and progress. Torture does not do much to raise a country's agricultural production or gross national product. If great emphasis is to be placed on the development of effective political institutions, it is important to ask whether a very repressive government is worth having or if it can endure for long.

The weaker form of this argument might be invoked by a relatively benign government that was greatly respected internationally. Torture, murder, and mass arrests would be repudiated by such a government, but it might nevertheless be a one-party state in which no elections were held, one person or group remained in power for an extended period, and laws against criticizing the government and against political assemblies made political opposition very difficult. Here the claim would be that these practices give the country a better chance for stability and development.

Philosophical theorists of human rights have sometimes been willing to endorse this position. John Stuart Mill allowed that his arguments for freedom of expression would not apply when a society had not yet advanced to the point where it was capable of being improved by public discussion of important issues.[12] John Rawls, who criticized utilitarianism for being excessively flexible, has argued that political rights may be temporarily subordinated to economic and social development in situations where the levels of such development are so low that these rights cannot meaningfully be implemented.[13]

An advocate of the weak position might argue not only that restrictions on rights of political participation will often increase a country's chances for economic development but also that the putative human rights these restrictions violate are not directly linked to human well-being and dignity in the way that, say, the rights against being murdered or tortured are. Torture destroys a person's rational autonomy and subjects him or her to severe pain, but being denied an opportunity to vote or express one's political opinions does neither. Thus, one might argue, if rights of political participation are human rights at all, they are of lower priority than other human rights.

Although I agree that rights of political participation are of lower priority than, say, rights not to be murdered, tortured, or arbitrarily imprisoned and am willing to allow that they may be restricted at the lowest extremes of economic and political development, I doubt whether conditions in most countries today are this extreme. Further, a country that restricts these rights renders itself more vulnerable to tyranny, corruption, and bad political choices. As I will argue in chapter 5, rights of political participation play an important role as indirect protections of the integrity of a political system. If it eliminates regular elections, a country loses the possibility of throwing corrupt or inept leaders out of office by peaceful means. When people are prevented from expressing their grievances, petitioning government, or organizing to work peacefully for political change, the advantages of competition among political ideas, so eloquently described by Mill's *On Liberty*, are lost. The connection between rights to political participation and fundamental interests of people is often indirect, but it is substantial and regular nonetheless.

12. John Stuart Mill, *On Liberty* (1859).
13. John Rawls, *A Theory of Justice* (Cambridge, Mass.: Harvard University Press, 1971), 542.

5. Starting Points for Justifying Rights

In a world of diverse cultures and ideologies, claims about human rights are often controversial. Those who promote and defend human rights are often challenged—even by people who are generally sympathetic—to justify the strong claims they make about international rights. These challenges are not merely topics for rainy day reflections and coffee house discussions; they arise too frequently and have too much practical import to be relegated to that status.

One job a justification of human rights could do is to make plausible my earlier claims about justified rights as norms that are independent of recognition or enactment. A plausible account of the justification of rights might also suggest the degree to which we can discount disagreement about human rights. If rational, knowledgeable, and unbiased people from various regions and cultures would be persuaded by the case that can be made for human rights, cultural and ideological differences in this area would be less theoretically troubling.

A justification needs to originate somewhere; a chain of reasons eventually has to go back to something that is accepted without argument. A justification for a human right (R) must show the reader or listener that some acceptable proposition, or group of propositions, provides substantial or conclusive support for R. I will call the premise or premises that are most central to a justification its *basic premise(s)*.

One difficult question about philosophical justifications, including justifications of human rights, is how deep they should go in locating their basic premises. The answer may seem obvious, as no one wants a superficial starting point if a deep one is available. But to avoid the negative and misleading connotations of "superficial," we can talk about basic premises being distant or close instead of deep or superficial. A proposition is distant from another if it involves substantially different categories or subject matters. A justification for human rights that started from a theory of human evolution would have a distant proposition as its basic premise. A justification for human rights that started from an ideal of democracy would have a close proposition as its basic premise. Like the notion of human rights, an ideal of democracy is clearly normative. The best sort of basic premise would have two features. First, it would clearly support R. We might call this *unproblematic derivation*. Second, the premise would be either widely accepted or such that people could be easily persuaded to accept it; this is *unproblematic acceptance*.

When we ask whether a premise is unproblematic, we find that different people have very different beliefs and that we must ask, "Unproblematic to whom?" One way to deal with variations between the premises people will accept is to custom tailor premises, to plan one's justification so that its premise is likely to be accepted by particular listeners. But one who is writing for a general audience rather than speaking to particular people will find it difficult to custom tailor premises in this way. Unless one uses a shotgun approach that offers many justifications in the hope that every reader will find at least one of them plausible, it will be necessary to find a premise that everyone, or nearly everyone, will accept. This is what many philosophical justifications try to do. They try to avoid premises that work only for known individuals and to find premises that any genuinely rational person would accept. But such widely accepted starting points are often rather distant from controversial claims about human rights.

The criteria of unproblematic acceptance and unproblematic derivation often work against each other. What is accepted easily is likely to be conceptually distant from R and difficult to derive. Getting R out of a distant premise may seem like pulling a rabbit out of a hat. But if the derivation is easy, the premise is likely to be conceptually close to R and hence infected by whatever controversy afflicts R. When this happens, we may say that appealing to that premise for justification begs the question.

In order to find basic premises that do not beg the question and that will appeal to everyone (and thus avoid custom tailoring), philosophers seeking justifications for rights tend to choose premises that are distant and abstract. This approach often leads to difficult derivations and accompanying controversies about whether the premise really supports R.

As these considerations suggest, justifications of human rights are usually complicated philosophical arguments involving many premises and inferences. Further, many philosophical arguments are not fully specified; they are argument sketches. Hence most justifications of human rights will be vulnerable to objections; philosophical arguments about matters of substance are seldom bulletproof. One looks for overall plausibility and promise rather than invulnerability and hopes that the deficiencies can be overcome.

Prudential Reasons

A general justification for human rights avoids custom tailoring by trying to identify reasons that all, or nearly all, people have—in spite of the great diversity that we find among humans. There are different kinds of reasons (e.g., technical, prudential, moral), and attempted justifications can differ with the kinds of reasons they invoke. In this section I present and discuss a prudential justification for human rights, which views good reasons for accepting and complying with rights as prudential reasons—reasons relating to a person's own interests. Here, the basic premises pertain to what prudent persons, fully aware of their own status as persons and of the circumstances in which they live, would find it reasonable to accept.

Let us say that something is a fundamental interest of a person if it is necessary to that person's ongoing existence or ability to develop and express central features of human personality. Fundamental interests will be general in the sense that all people will have them, and they will be strong in the sense that they will generally outweigh other interests. Their strength comes from their foundational character. As conditions of having a life as a person, they will generally prevail over interests within a person's life. Examples of fundamental interests include, for example, security against deadly violence, some degree of freedom of action, and the material necessities of life (food, shelter, and so forth).

A prudential argument from fundamental interests attempts to show that it would be reasonable to accept and comply with human rights, in circumstances where most others are likely to do so, because these norms are part of the best means for protecting one's fundamental interests against actions and omissions that endanger them. We can begin by discussing the right against physical violence. Here, a prudential argument might take the following form:

1. I have fundamental interests in life and health that can be undermined by physical violence directed against me by others.

2. The best way to protect these interests essentially includes—whatever else it may involve—getting other people to accept and comply with a system of moral norms that protects these interests, that is, getting other people to accept and comply with moral restrictions on physical violence.

3. If something is an essential means to protecting my fundamental interests, then I have a fundamental interest in the availability of that means.

4. Hence, I have a fundamental interest in getting other people to accept and comply with a system of moral norms that protects my life and health against physical violence.

5. Other people's interests in having such a norm accepted are the same as mine and of roughly the same strength.

6. Both I and others will find the burdens involved in complying with and maintaining this system of moral norms to be tolerable, and hence these burdens are insufficient to outweigh my fundamental interest in the availability of this system.

7. Thus, in a context where most others will accept and generally comply with moral norms protecting our fundamental interests in life and health against physical violence, all of us have good prudential reasons for agreeing to accept and comply with these norms.

This form of argument works equally well for other fundamental interests, but I have initially stated it in terms of protections against physical violence because this is its classical form, as we find it in Hobbes.[1] The first premise is intended to help one recognize one's own strong interests in security against physical violence. In a famous passage from *Utilitarianism,* John Stuart Mill made the case for a fundamental interest in security as follows:

> All other earthly benefits are needed by one person, not needed by another; and many of them can, if necessary, be cheerfully foregone or replaced by something else; but security no human being can possibly do without; on it we depend for all our immunity from evil and for the whole value of all and every good, beyond the passing moment, since

---

1. Thomas Hobbes, *Leviathan* (1651), chap. 13.

nothing but the gratification of the instant could be of any worth to us if we could be deprived of everything the next instant by whoever was momentarily stronger than ourselves.[2]

The second and third premises assert that the best methods of protecting one's life and health against physical violence involve formulating moral norms restricting violence and making them part of other people's most basic beliefs. The strong assertion that moral restrictions on physical violence are, or are part of, the *best* way of protecting one's security serves to ensure that a system of moral restrictions on violence can be said to be the *most* reasonable means of protecting one's fundamental interests. Morality, as a social institution, is likely to involve firm teaching of standards and ideals of behavior, using social pressure against violators of these standards, and developing the capacity to feel guilt about one's own violations of the standards. If these measures are effective, the problem of free riders should be reduced to tolerable size. Firm teaching of standards, inculcating the capacity for guilt feelings, and the threat of social sanctions will prevent most people from gaining protection from moral standards without paying the price in terms of consistent compliance.

Premise 6 deals with costs. One issue here concerns how much the prohibition of violence should be qualified to make its costs bearable to oneself and others. A system of unqualified restrictions on violence could harm my interests more than it helped them if it prevented me from defending myself, or someone I care for, against physical violence. The solution, obviously, is to build in a qualification permitting the use of violence in self-defense. This solution illustrates a general possibility, namely, making the cost of a principle more bearable by building in exceptions for circumstances where it would be exceptionally costly to comply with it in its unqualified form.

Another issue related to costs concerns the time frame. There is no doubt that in particular instances one's important interests may conflict with the prohibition against the use of physical violence. For example, one may be able to achieve the goal of marrying a particular person if one can get rid of another lover, and a little physical violence may be an effective way to frighten the lover off. Genu-

2. Samuel Gorovitz, ed., *Mill: Utilitarianism* (Indianapolis: Bobbs-Merrill, 1971), 50.

ine conflicts of this kind occur frequently and cannot be wished away. It may be possible to navigate around most of them, however, by taking a longer-term view. If one surveys social institutions from the perspective of a person who expects to live a long life, with the consequent uncertainties about what may happen over the next sixty or seventy years, the benefits and costs to oneself of restrictions on physical violence will probably even out. This does not mean that there will not be substantial costs along the way, merely that the overall balance is likely to be favorable. With this move to a longer-term perspective, we must modify our description of the basic premises. We should say that they construe good reasons as those that appeal to the prudence of a rational agent over the long term.

A prudential justification for human rights of this sort is often described as "contractarian," suggesting that most people can recognize their fundamental interests and respond by engaging in a cooperative endeavor to create and maintain a morality. One question here concerns the effects of imbalances of knowledge and power on the outcome. Will the weak and unproductive be included, and have full status, in the moral community? This question will be addressed at the end of this section.

Security is not the only fundamental interest that people have; there are a number of others for which individuals need strong and stable protections. More broadly, the strongest interests of persons are focused on being able to have and lead a life that is not so miserable and disgusting as to be inappropriate to a human being. This proposition suggests two basic interests: (1) *having* a life, which includes avoiding premature death or incapacitation caused by the invasions of others, as well as the availability of assistance from others, when needed, in obtaining the necessities of life and in protecting one's fundamental interests; and (2) *leading* a life, which means being able to make and carry out the key decisions about the kind of life one will live and avoiding having one's life, body, and time treated as resources that others may use without consent.

Life

A central interest is security against actions of others that lead to death, destruction of health, or incapacitation. Having and leading a life, however, requires more than merely being free from harm and interference. One's body must be capable of most normal functions, and to maintain bodily capacities one must satisfy physical needs for food, water, sleep, shelter, and so forth. People can usually supply these things for themselves through work. But everyone goes through periods when self-supply is impossible—typically, childhood, illness, unemployment, disability, and advanced old age. During these periods, one may need protections not only against harmful actions but also against failure to aid. From the perspective of a whole lifetime, anyone can anticipate periods when aid will be needed and see the importance of the interest in obtaining that aid; someone's refusal to help at crucial points can do as much to undermine one's life, health, and agency as violent assaults.

Worries about cost may arise when one considers whether to accept an obligation to aid others. The world has many needy people, and it may seem that the costs of aiding these people will outweigh the worth of the aid that one is likely to receive. The costs of aid involve providing services or money, not merely refraining from something one would like to do or tolerating others doing things of which one disapproves. In short, the duties here are mainly positive duties, whereas in regard to security and liberty most of them are negative.

This objection assumes that positive duties are always very burdensome and that negative duties are generally less costly. The actual situation is not so simple. Negative duties are often very burdensome, because substantial costs may be associated with not being able to do things one wants to do, or use methods one wants to use, and with having to tolerate actions that one believes wrong, offensive, or harmful. For example, a government's (negative) duty to refrain from interfering with the freedom to leave a country may result in the loss of many talented people.

Positive duties need not be extremely burdensome, for the costs can be spread over many people through charitable institutions or taxes. Further, we have here the same ability to exclude extremely high costs that we used to make tolerable the costs of the principles pertaining to liberty and harmful invasions. Strategies will include assigning responsibility for aid to families whenever this is workable and efficient, encouraging prevention and self-help through education, and setting upper limits on what individuals can be expected to contribute. How to implement these strategies in modern societies will be discussed in later chapters. In any case, some measures to aid people will be affordable, and the importance of such aid at critical times will at least ensure that these costs are worth bearing.

Liberty

A justification for norms protecting liberty can be constructed along lines similar to those used in the argument for security. The first premise would assert that one has a fundamental interest in being able to *lead* a life, in being able to choose the key features of one's life for oneself. James Griffin states this well:

> Choosing one's own course through life, making something of value out of it by one's own lights, is what makes one's existence human. . . . Even if I constantly made a mess of my life, even if you could convince me that if you managed my utility portfolio . . . you would do a much better job than I am doing, I would not let you do it. . . . [But] the right to liberty is not to do whatever fancy prompts (so that *any* restriction on satisfaction of desires is *some* restriction of liberty) but only, more narrowly, to do what is essential to living a human life.[3]

A prudential argument for liberty will begin by asserting that one's fundamental interest in liberty needs to be protected by getting other people to accept and comply with a moral principle prescribing protections for liberty. It will continue by claiming that other people have the same fundamental interest and that the costs of complying with the liberty principle are tolerable. Where most others will accept and comply with a principle of liberty, every person has good prudential reasons for agreeing to accept and comply with a morality containing that principle.

Interesting questions arise here about costs and scope. A system of unqualified protections for liberty would license other people to act in ways that would be very harmful to oneself; such a morality could harm one's interests more than it helped them. The solution, as before, is to build some restrictions into the principle of liberty. Some of these follow, obviously, from the restrictions on violence already discussed. As we are trying to decide which liberties to include or exclude, we will have to ask whether a particular liberty is essential to our status as persons and agents and whether the costs

---

3. James Griffin, "Towards a Substantive Theory of Rights," in R. G. Frey, ed., *Utility and Rights* (Minneapolis: University of Minnesota Press, 1984), 138–139.

of respecting and protecting it are likely to be so high that it is not worth protecting through moral norms.

In this section I have constructed some prudential arguments for accepting and complying with some basic moral principles in support of specific human rights. One problem with this approach is the possibility that a powerful group will create a system that victimizes a less powerful group—for example, the current system of apartheid in South Africa. Although it may be advantageous for the members of the powerful group to recognize rights among themselves, it may not be advantageous for them to recognize rights, or the full range of rights, held against them by the members of the weaker group. If it is certain that this system of subordination and exploitation will endure for one's lifetime and that the members of the weaker group—or their sympathizers—will be in no position to retaliate through violence or the refusal of cooperation or aid, then it will not be in the interests of the members of the powerful group to accept principles that confer rights on the members of the weaker group.

This kind of objection points out a structural weakness of the prudential approach, namely, that it makes one's claim to rights dependent on one's bargaining power. But this weakness may not make much difference in practical reasoning, since from the perspective of long-term prudence one has good reasons to worry that a system of exploitation will not endure during one's entire lifetime and that the victims or their sympathizers will find ways of retaliating. This is particularly true today, when people are less likely to accept the idea that someone's place at the bottom of the social and economic order is naturally or divinely ordered.

If I am right about this, we can think of prudential reasoning as providing a useful approach to human rights. This approach may not yield universal human rights, but it will get us somewhere in the vicinity. Further, it may help to show how it is psychologically possible for creatures with strong interests of their own to adopt a moral point of view.

Moral Reasons

Discussing moral questions in prudential terms is distasteful to many. The approach of the previous section, where the demand for reasons was taken to be a demand for prudential reasons, may therefore seem to start on the wrong foot. A different, but complementary, approach interprets a demand for reasons as a request for moral reasons, for a case to be made that the fundamental principles of morality require one to accept and comply with human rights. Here one assumes that one's audience has transcended egoism and is prepared to accept arguments that appeal directly to what is reasonable from the moral point of view, whether or not it can be shown that adopting this perspective is likely to promote the long-term interests of the individual.

Transforming Prudential into Moral Reasons

In moving to the moral point of view, one may wish to carry along some of the considerations revealed by a prudential approach—particularly if one thinks that morality has something to do with the protection of strong or fundamental interests of all persons. John Rawls provides a device for doing this in *A Theory of Justice*.[4]

Like someone offering a prudential justification, Rawls asks us to consider what principles of justice a rational person would choose for the society in which he or she was going to live. In order to avoid such possibilities as systems of economic exploitation that are constructed on racial, ethnic, or gender lines, Rawls imposes restrictions on what is known by those choosing principles of justice. Broadly speaking, he asks us to imagine that these people have been deprived of all information about themselves that would allow them to be egoistic, racist, or sexist. They are behind a "veil of ignorance." Further, they do not know what their own life plan or conception of the good life will be; they have to choose principles of justice on the basis of "primary goods," things such as security, liberty, and self-respect that people will want no matter what else they may desire.

The effect of these restrictions is to convert prudential choice into rational choice within the moral point of view. Notice how the underlying conception of good reasons differs from the one presup-

---

4. John Rawls, *A Theory of Justice* (Cambridge, Mass.: Harvard University Press, 1971).

posed by prudential justifications. Here, good reasons are ones relating to the promotion and protection of each person's basic interests. Although prudential considerations are incorporated, they are appealed to within a structure representing the characteristics of the moral point of view. Arguments identifying strong interests that it would be prudent for individuals to protect become moral arguments identifying interests that need moral protections.

Utilitarianism

Rawls assumes—I think rightly—that part of the moral point of view is a concern with protecting the primary goods or basic interests of each person. If the moral point of view imposes impartiality on a prudential concern with important interests, utilitarianism may seem to be the natural result. Utilitarians claim that the fundamental principles of morality are ones that require (1) that no person's interests be ignored or discounted and (2) that the sum of happiness or preference satisfaction be maximized. When one person's interests conflict with those of others, utilitarians will prefer the action or policy that will lead to the highest overall level of satisfaction. For example, if Robinson wants to use loudspeakers to advertise the tomatoes she is selling door-to-door, and if the residents of the neighborhood strongly prefer peace and quiet to the product information Robinson's loudspeakers would provide, then Robinson will have no moral case for being allowed to use her loudspeakers.

In many areas, this balancing of interests—however difficult—is the appropriate method of choosing policies. If we decide on utilitarian grounds that Robinson cannot use her loudspeakers, her loss is not a tragedy. In other areas, however, we may be more reluctant to let the satisfaction of people's interests depend on the compatibility of those interests with the dominant overall direction of preferences and interests. Although utilitarianism assures people that their interests will not be ignored or discounted, it does not assure that their interests, however fundamental, will not be outweighed by the interests of large numbers of other people.

Utilitarianism is like unrestrained free-market capitalism in that it makes success or failure totally dependent on competition within the process. It may usually yield the results we want, but it is far from certain that it will always do so. At the level of moral theory, as well as at the level of national economic policy, one may think that a concern for the interests of all is best served by a system that provides a floor of protection and provision of people's most basic interests—that makes at least minimal satisfaction of these interests independent of their success in competing with other preferences and interests.

One's claim to protections and respect for one's life is among the things at stake here. Normally, there are good utilitarian reasons for not killing people, even if this can be done painlessly. First, killing a person will frustrate his or her own desires to go on living—although the frustration, if we think of it as a psychological state, will last only as long as the dying process. Second, killing someone typically makes the friends, relatives, and dependents of that person very unhappy and induces fear in others. And third, the interests that others have in someone's death are usually not very strong.

It is not hard to imagine variations in these normal conditions that will result in the loss of a person's utilitarian claim to life. If Abel suffers so much pain from physical maladies that his pains outweigh his satisfactions (including his satisfaction in being able to continue to live), and if he has no friends or relatives who care about him, and if his murder would generate little fear, and if there are others who would be made much happier if he were dead (the orphans to whom he has willed his estate), then Abel is likely to have no utilitarian claim to life, even though he passionately desires to go on living. As this illustrates, utilitarianism makes even one's claim to life dependent on one's comparative ability to produce value if one lives, and disvalue if one dies. One's interests will be counted, but in competition with the interests of others they may not count enough to prevail.

Secure Claims

The problems with utilitarianism suggest a need for alternatives. There are a variety of concepts available for formulating these alternatives; one might, for example, start with principles of equality, justice, duty, or rights. Rather than devoting an extended discussion here to the elaboration and evaluation of these alternatives, I will use what I take to be a fairly modest conceptual framework, namely, that of moral claims and duties. I submit that an alternative to utilitarianism should have the following features.

First, it should contain norms that give each person a secure moral claim to life, liberty, and the other minimal conditions of a decent life as a person.[5] A "secure" claim would not depend entirely on one's abilities to generate utility and should be weighty enough to prevail in most circumstances against competing claims based solely on individual or collective welfare.

Second, these claims should generate duties to respond, either directly or through institutions. They should at least assert an abstract obligation of all persons to act in ways, and to support institutions, that promote and protect other people's prospects of being able to have and lead a life.

Third, in dealing with conflicts between the secure claims of different people, substantial inequalities in regard to protection and provision for these claims should be avoided or, if that is genuinely impossible, minimized.

I submit that it is reasonable, when we start within the moral point of view, to choose a moral theory that provides all people with secure claims of this sort to the satisfaction of their most fundamental interests. Some people may not be as well off in a society granting secure claims to all as they would be in a society making all claims subject to a test of utility. But all people will be more secure in regard to the satisfaction of their most fundamental interests, and from the moral point of view, satisfaction of basic interests matters more than small variations in well-being.

A unifying idea for a list of fundamental interests is that of enjoying at least a minimally good or decent life as a person. But because our starting point is the moral point of view, we can also inquire about the basic conditions of life as a moral being, which I take to be life as a member of a human community in which one develops and displays virtues such as responsibility, honesty, and compassion and acts—at least some of the time—in accordance with moral principles. To live as a moral being one needs to be free to participate in social relations, language, thought, teaching, and discussion and to exercise one's responsibilities.

The fundamental interests discussed in the section on prudential justifications can serve here to identify areas in which secure moral claims are appropriate. As a partial list, I suggest the following:

---

5. There are obvious problems concerning when one becomes a person and thus about when these secure moral claims take effect. But any moral theory needs to define the boundaries of the moral community, and hence these problems are not unique to this approach.

1. A secure claim to life, which is a claim to live a life and to enjoy a life span that is not shortened by the harmful or negligent actions of others or by lack of assistance in obtaining the necessities of life and protecting oneself against invasions. The claim to life includes a claim to security; thus it generates negative duties not to murder, use violence except in self-defense, or harm unnecessarily. It also includes a claim to assistance, which implies positive duties to assist people when they need help in obtaining the necessities of life and in protecting themselves against harm.

2. A secure claim to liberty, which is a claim to lead a life and to exercise the capacity for choice in regard to the most important decisions that life presents. This is a claim to freedom from slavery, servitude, and the use of one's life, time, or body without one's consent, as well as a claim to the liberties of a moral being—liberties to learn, discuss, decide, respond, and act. Associated with the secure claim to liberty are duties to refrain from enslaving persons, treating them as if they were mere means to the realization of one's own goals, or preventing them from making and living in accordance with the key decisions about their own lives. The claim to assistance from others, when needed to provision and protect oneself, carves a small exception into the claim to liberty. Within limits that prevent excessive burdens, people can be called on to expend their time assisting others.

Measures to respond to these moral claims are likely to conflict and to scatter their benefits and burdens in ways that are not entirely equal. We cannot escape these conflicts, but we can expect—within the moral point of view—that fair procedures be used in dealing with conflicts and the distribution of burdens. Hence we should add to the list:

3. A secure claim to fairness in trade-offs of rights and in distributions of the costs, burdens, and penalties involved in respecting and upholding them. The primary requirement of fairness is that large and unequal burdens not be imposed on people without good reason. There must be a rational relation between the goals of a policy and the people chosen to bear its burdens. For example, a reasonable basis for selecting people for military service is physical ability to perform the tasks of a soldier, and it is not unfair to choose people for the draft partly on the basis of physical capacity. But it would be unfair to excuse some people from service on the basis of an irrelevant characteristic such as wealth or

hair color. Some characteristics are almost always irrelevant to the assignment of burdens, and hence there may properly come to be a presumption against the fairness of allocating major burdens on the basis of these characteristics. Race and national origin are examples of such characteristics. A Rawlsian device for excluding irrelevant characteristics asks people to choose policies without knowing what characteristics they themselves will have and hence without knowing where they will stand in relation to the policies they choose.

In calling these three principles "claims," I do not mean to suggest that they are merely entitlements, with no associated duties. At a minimum, they have abstract duties attached to them. They assert a general obligation of all agents to act and to try to arrange social and political institutions so that these actions and institutions do not undermine—and provide at least rudimentary protection and provision for—fundamental interests. In this way, these interests come to have a deontological as well as an axiological status. Some of the duties expressed here are obviously positive; negative duties are not given a privileged position.

These principles express a significant but limited commitment to human equality, in that they prescribe a floor of good treatment for every person. Because of this equality, these principles can ground the universality of specific human rights. No person is to be denied provision and protection for his or her fundamental interests except on grounds of impossibility, unbearably high costs to the fundamental interests of others, or as a reasonable punishment for a serious crime.

In spite of this commitment to a degree of equality, these principles are intended as *minimal* standards; they state—in terms broad enough to apply at all times and places—what people are due simply as people. One advantage of minimal standards is that they have a better chance of cross-cultural justification and acceptance. No claim is made that these are the only principles of justice or that a society that fully respected and implemented people's human rights would be immune to all other forms of moral criticism. A theory of human rights, as I conceive it, is not a complete moral and political theory.

Orienting claims and duties by reference to interests leaves us with the problem of how much is to be done to promote and protect people's interests. The broad answer is that the nature and level of protections and provisions to be supplied in response to these principles are to be chosen rationally in the light of the threats present and the institutions and resources available. Social and political justification will therefore always need to look in two directions: backward to the most fundamental interests of persons as the source of claims to restraint, protection, and assistance; and forward to institutions, costs, and resources as ways of determining to which of these claims, and in what ways, it is reasonable to respond. Extreme limits to resources will not extinguish one's claims in relation to these interests but will badly cramp the responses to these claims. As this suggests, these principles are subject to the "ought"-implies-"can" principle. But there are various ways of complying with and implementing these principles, with different levels of costs, and hence they are not likely to be rendered inoperative by scarcity.

These principles are binding on all agents, including organizations and groups, but the discharge of some of their positive responsibilities—duties to provide and protect—will need to be mediated by available social and political structures. In the contemporary world, this means that the implementation of human rights will be mediated by the international system of separate sovereign states. The governments of these states are the only organizations presently capable of providing protection and other services to people all around the world. Hence, appropriate ways of upholding human rights will reflect the prevailing international system, which divides the earth into distinct territories and assigns primary responsibility for the people in each territory to its government. But the burden of particular positive responsibilities falls partly on whomever is able to effectively bear it, and hence in many areas individuals, families, and communities—and even governments of other countries—will also have duties to respond to people's claims.

A full specification of these principles would include limits on the burdens people must bear to avoid harming others, to assist them, and to support institutions that provide protection or assistance. I suggest that such duties are ordinarily limited, both by what a person can do for others without substantially undermining his or her own fundamental interests and by some degree of fairness in the distribution of the burdens of providing aid. The positive duties of states to respect and uphold the rights of all residents will often strain their resources severely. But these duties are limited by the principle that the costs of respecting and upholding human rights must undermine neither the productivity and institutions that will permit respect for and implementation of rights in the future nor the development and maintenance of a rich social, artistic, intellectual, and religious culture.[6] By working back from this limit we are able to estimate, however roughly, the level of resources that can be devoted to upholding rights.

Specific human rights often involve not only claims and duties but also liberties and powers. Powers that need to be justified may include, for example, powers of governments to tax and direct behavior in order to uphold human rights. As we saw in chapter 3, human rights typically play a role in justifying actions and policies as well as in directly guiding behavior. Liberties and powers can be justified by showing that they are necessary to respecting or effectively implementing these principles or the specific rights that instantiate them.

The Scope of Liberty

One can speak of freedom in any area where one is concerned about the impact on action of barriers that have been raised or have been allowed to remain. There are a multitude of areas and ways in which people can be free or unfree. We may wish to assign some degree of value to freedom in each, but an abstract duty to protect every imaginable freedom would not be plausible. Some specific freedoms must be selected as fundamental—and therefore as coming under the freedom principle—by showing that they have very great personal, social, or political importance.[7] To show this, we will need a conception of human nature, of the kind of autonomy that humans are capable of, and of the areas most central to its exercise. We will also need a social and political theory that identifies

6. The position taken here on permissible burdens is less demanding than the positions taken by Henry Shue, *Basic Rights* (Princeton, N. J.: Princeton University Press, 1980), 114–119; and Peter Singer, *Practical Ethics* (Cambridge: Cambridge University Press, 1979), 158–181. See also John Arthur, "Rights and the Duty to Bring Aid," in William Aiken and Hugh La Follette, eds., *World Hunger and Moral Obligation* (Englewood Cliffs, N.J.: Prentice-Hall, 1977), 37–48. A fuller discussion of resources and costs is found in chap. 7, below.

7. For arguments against the view that there is a prima facie right to be free to perform any action whatever, see Ronald Dworkin, *Taking Rights Seriously* (Cambridge, Mass.: Harvard University Press, 1977), 270–271.

some freedoms (e.g., the freedom to express one's opinions in print) as important for social or political reasons.

People often have very different value systems and life plans, and particular freedoms will therefore sometimes have different values to different people. There are at least two ways to deal with this variability. One is to focus on interests or claims that are already morally endorsed, that is, already recognized in fundamental moral principles. For example, we can ask which liberties are necessary to developing a moral personality, to meeting one's moral obligations, to engaging in work that will provide the means of life, or to choosing a life plan. Another approach is to identify liberties requisite to carrying out all, or at least almost all, plans of life. To return to our earlier example, the ability to move freely will be required by virtually any plan of life and hence has a secure place as an important freedom. The use of incarceration as a punishment presupposes this.

Rawls offers the following list of basic freedoms:

> The basic liberties of citizens are, roughly speaking, political liberty (the right to vote and to be eligible for public office) together with freedom of speech and assembly; liberty of conscience and freedom of thought; freedom of the person along with the right to hold (personal) property; and freedom from arbitrary arrest and seizure as defined by the concept of the rule of law.[8]

This list succeeds in identifying some of the most important political freedoms and a few personal freedoms (conscience, personal property), but it is far from a complete list. Important personal freedoms that are omitted include movement, emigration, and privacy. Omitted social freedoms include freedoms to marry, have children, educate one's children, and practice one's religion. Omitted political freedoms include freedom of publication and freedom to organize unions and parties.

Freedoms often conflict with each other. Jones may exercise his freedom of speech, or even his freedom to walk back and forth, in such a way as to interfere with Smith's freedom of speech. In cases of serious conflict, freedoms must be qualified by other freedoms and rights. To deal with this problem, Rawls formulates his principle of equal liberty with the qualification that basic liberties must be "compatible with a similar liberty for others."[9] This is a suitable

---

8. Rawls, *Theory of Justice*, 61.
9. Ibid., 60.

test, but in carrying it out, one must have some conception of the overall system of liberties and rights. Liberties may need to be qualified, not only when they conflict with other liberties but also when they conflict with other human rights. Conflicts of this sort will be discussed under the heading of "conflict costs" in chapter 7.

Why Not Property?

Because I have endorsed secure moral claims to life and liberty, it may be surprising that I have omitted one member of Locke's historic trio, namely, property. Although I see no grounds for a generic claim to property, some matters traditionally associated with property have already been covered. First, the principle pertaining to life includes claims to opportunities to obtain the necessities of life, against deprivation of these opportunities, and to assistance when one is incapacitated. Second, the liberty principle effectively gives one ownership of one's own body and time, as it forbids enslavement and other forms of use without consent.

Beyond these, I am willing to concede that there may be a case for secure claims to acquire, hold, and transfer personal property—intimate possessions that express one's personality and embody one's culture. Further, fairness may require appropriate rewards for those who put a lot of effort into producing things useful to others.

I deny, however, that there is a good case on moral grounds for a secure claim to property rights in land and other major productive resources. In addition, I deny that the expropriation of such property, when it does not threaten one's ability to obtain the necessities of life, is a violation of human rights. Admittedly, private property in productive resources is often a good thing, and expropriation of such property is sometimes a bad thing. But this admission falls far short of conceding that there should be secure moral claims at the most basic theoretical level to acquire, hold, and transfer productive property. It is impossible, in my opinion, to show a direct link between fundamental interests and the ability to acquire, hold, and transfer productive property. We will return to this topic in chapter 9.

Deriving Rights from Other Rights

Instead of starting from something as abstract as prudence or the moral point of view, one might begin an attempt to justify a human right by appealing to another right that is already accepted. A premise about another right would be a very close starting point for justifying a right. Specific rights are sometimes justifiable not because they directly uphold a fundamental interest but because they are part of, or necessary to the implementation of, some other right that is already accepted. This kind of justification is not as general in appeal as the ones previously considered, because its starting points may be rejected by those who deny most or all rights. But if other justifications give us a list of rights, it may be possible to expand the list by deriving additional rights from the already-justifed rights.

There are at least three ways in which one right, R_1, can imply another, R_2. First, R_1 may be a general or abstract right that implies some more specific right, R_2. For example, the general right to freedom of expression implies the more specific right to distribute pamphlets on public streets. The scope of the former includes the scope of the latter. Second, R_2 may serve to make violations of R_1 less likely, even though the two rights operate in different spheres. For example, if the right to freedom of the press is regularly used to expose official misconduct, it will help to deter officials from violating the right to due process in criminal trials. Third, the effective implementation of R_1 may require the implementation of R_2, even though R_2 is not normally thought to be included in the scope of R_1. For example, the effective implementation of the right to freedom of assembly may require the implementation of a right to security against violence. In this section, I will focus on the second and third kinds of implication.

For R_1 to imply R_2 in either of these ways, R_2 must provide support for the implementation or enjoyment of R_1. The support R_2 provides can, at one end of the spectrum, be essential to the effective implementation of R_1 or, on the other end, be merely helpful to the successful implementation of R_1. The more essential R_2 is to the implementation of R_1, the stronger the support that R_1 can provide for R_2.

We can think of this kind of justification as involving a consistency test—as asking whether the successful implementation of R_1 is inconsistent with the nonimplementation of R_2. However, for this test to be adequate, we must count not only logical inconsistency between the implementation of R_1 and the nonimplementation of R_2 but also practical inconsistency, which holds when it is logically possible but extremely unlikely that one can successfully implement R_1 without implementing R_2.

A system for implementing a right, if it is to be affordable and compatible with other rights, cannot deal with every imaginable threat or offer perfect guarantees of nonviolation. Success in implementing a right—in employing people and institutions to prevent violations—is always a matter of degree. The answers to the question of whether implementation of R1 is consistent in practice with the nonimplementation of R2 will sometimes depend on the degree of implementation we have in mind. Very rudimentary protections for R1 may be consistent with the absence of R2. But full or elaborate implementation of R1 may be inconsistent with the absence of R2. In sum, the degree of support that R1 provides for R2 is likely to depend on (1) how essential R2 is to (2) some particular degree of implementation of R1.

Consistency tests are best suited for use at the implementation stage, when we already know what resources are available and the levels at which rights will be implemented. But these tests can also be used earlier if dependency relations can be detected in more abstract formulations of rights. For example, even without information about specific problems in a country, one can discern that the right to freedom of assembly will require for its effective implementation a right to freedom from violence. Suppose that a country purported to implement a right to freedom of assembly without implementing a right to freedom from violence. When an unpopular group attempted to exercise its right of assembly in that country, it could be prevented from doing so by threats of violence, and it would know that no government help would be available to meet those threats.

In *Basic Rights*, Henry Shue appealed to such connections between rights in order to defend rights to subsistence, security, and liberty.[10] Instead of offering distant-premise justifications for human rights, Shue argued that someone who allows that there is at least one human right will have to admit that there are also human rights to security, subsistence, and liberty. A key premise in this argument is that these rights are *basic,* in the sense that no other rights can be effectively implemented if they are not effectively implemented. Shue's starting point is the proposition that there is at least one universal right that ought to be effectively implemented. He then tries

10. Shue, *Basic Rights,* 5–87. For a critique of Shue's claims about dependency relationships, see James W. Nickel and Lizbeth L. Hasse, "Review of Shue's *Basic Rights,*" *California Law Review* 69 (1981): 1569–1586.

to show that whatever this right is, its effective implementation will require the implementation of universal rights to security, subsistence, and liberty.

In his defense of a right to subsistence, Shue is not merely making the point, sometimes made by Marxists, that guarantees of security or political participation are not very valuable if one must constantly worry about where one's next meal is coming from. Instead, he is making the much stronger claim that a person who does not have an effectively implemented right to subsistence enjoys no rights at all. In Shue's view, a person does not really "enjoy" a right—that is, a right is not effectively implemented—unless there are social guarantees to protect the substance of the right against the most common threats. Basic rights protect against things that are threats to the enjoyment of *any* right; they are defined as rights that are necessary to the enjoyment of any other rights.

Shue insists that there is an all-or-nothing core of rights one must enjoy if one is to enjoy any others: "Every right, including every basic right, can be enjoyed only if all basic rights are enjoyed." [11] It follows that a basic right cannot be sacrificed to promote other rights: to sacrifice a basic right would be to sacrifice all rights. Shue's argument has an important limitation, however. Sacrifice of some people's subsistence or security rights might supply the means to implement rights to paid holidays or to medical care for others. Shue's arguments therefore do not show that a society without subsistence rights for everyone cannot provide effectively implemented rights to some people. At most they show that such a society cannot provide any other effectively implemented rights to everyone.

An important question about Shue's arguments concerns the strength of the supportive relationship between security or subsistence and other rights. I doubt whether these relationships are as strong as Shue suggests. Security against violence is a basic right, he says, "because its absence would leave available extremely effective means for others, including the government, to interfere with or prevent the actual exercise of any other rights that were supposedly protected." [12] Here Shue goes beyond the true and important claim that effective protections of security are strongly supportive of many other rights to make the stronger claim—which I think is an

11. Shue, *Basic Rights*, 178, n. 13.
12. Ibid., 21.

exaggeration—that general protections of security are necessary to the implementation of *every* other right.

Consider, for example, the right to asylum. Suppose that there is severe persecution of Hindus by Muslims in one country and that a number of Hindus manage to flee to a neighboring country where there is less persecution. They present themselves to the border guards, request asylum, and ask for safe passage to a third country. The officials of the second country take seriously their obligations under international law to provide asylum to refugees, and with the assistance of international organizations they provide asylum and safe passage to these refugees. It would be quite possible to do all of this, I contend, even if the *general* right to security against violence was not effectively implemented in the second country. As long as these refugees can be provided security by special arrangements, their right to asylum can be effectively upheld. Because the right to asylum can be upheld in such cases without a general right to security against violence, it follows from Shue's strict definition that the right to security against violence is not a basic right.

Because of examples of this sort, I doubt whether there are implicative relationships among rights as broad as those Shue claims to identify. It is clear, however, that many particular interrelations can be appealed to in justifying rights. A variety of supportive relationships is likely to exist within complex systems of rights, and thus many rights may be wholly or partially justified because of the support they provide for other rights that are already accepted as justified. Shue focuses on cases in which one right is strictly necessary to the implementation of another, but the weaker category of being strongly supportive of the other right seems just as serviceable here.

A number of rights can be supported in whole or part by arguments of this type. If there are other justifications as well, these arguments can provide complementary support and, perhaps, justify additional content or weight. For example, a case for the right to education can be made by appealing to the support that education provides to other rights. Successful implementation of a system of rights requires that people know what rights they have and what they can do if those rights are threatened or violated, and this kind of knowledge will not be sufficiently widespread in a society where a great many people are illiterate and uneducated. It may be possible to imagine a system in which official actions make up for the ignorance of the citizenry, but such a system is not likely to be workable or affordable. Upholding a right to education seems to be strongly supportive of, and even perhaps practically necessary to, the successful implementation of many other rights.

Similarly, many rights associated with democracy (e.g., rights to speak, protest, assemble, and vote) receive at least part of their justification from their importance to institutions that play substantial roles in preventing abuses of human rights. If public officials are regularly held accountable to the electorate in meaningful elections, these officials will find it much riskier to engage in systematic abuses of human rights. For democratic institutions to work, the public needs information about the actions and policies of officials. This argument provides support for freedom of expression, including freedom of the news media, as well as for freedoms to assemble and protest.[13]

Rights that are indirectly justified are not immune to the feasibility test. If a specific right, R2, is justified because it is necessary to the effective implementation of an already-justified right, R1, the costs of effectively implementing R1 include the costs of R2. If this fact was not recognized at the time R1 was justified, then its justification will need to be reassessed.

Overview

My goal in this chapter has been to show that a plausible list of abstract human rights can be reached by reasonable steps from several different starting points. These different approaches are complementary in regard to most issues.

The prudential justification for human rights has a rather distant starting point and involves an extended argument with plenty of potential for controversy. If I am right, however, prudential reasoning will get one to universal rights, or somewhere in their vicinity. This approach is remarkable not only in providing a long-distance justification for human rights but also in suggesting that the pru-

13. See Alexander Meiklejohn, *Free Speech and Its Relation to Self-Government* (New York: Harper, 1948); Thomas I. Emerson, *The System of Freedom of Expression* (New York: Random House, 1970); Thomas Scanlon, "A Theory of Freedom of Expression," *Philosophy and Public Affairs* 1 (1972): 204–226.

dential and moral points of view are not so distant from each other as to make the moral point of view psychologically impossible for prudentially minded people to reach.

A case for human rights within the moral point of view can track, to some degree, the prudential reasons already discussed. Considerations of prudence, used within a framework that demands concern for the fundamental interests of all, lead not to utilitarianism but to the formulation of secure moral claims that all people have. Because these claims are fairly abstract, their role in generating specific rights will need further explanation. Paths from abstract moral claims to specific rights will be explored in chapter 6.

Short-distance justifications of the sort discussed are important because they spotlight linkages between rights that increase the stability and coherence of the system. An exploration of these linkages allows one to justify some additional rights and to add content and weight to others.

6. Justifying Specific Rights

The rights of the Universal Declaration are fairly specific. They speak not of abstract liberty or fairness but of freedom of assembly and of the right to a fair trial. Further, these are mainly moral rights that demand the creation of legal rights—that call for implementation through legal and political institutions. In this chapter I try to show how one can justify rights of this sort once some abstract moral principles have been established. The issue is how to make the transition from abstract claims pertaining to life, liberty, or fairness to specific rights requiring political implementation. I identify some steps needed to justify specific human rights and show how one can complete these steps in the case of three particular examples—rights against torture, to a fair trial, and against discrimination.

Broadly, I suggest that the transition from abstract moral principles to specific human rights can be made by looking to abstract principles that guide and limit what specific rights permit and require and to information about contemporary societies that identifies the threats to be dealt with and the institutions and norms to be used in response. If effective use of these considerations is insufficient to yield a determinate right, the choice can be made on other grounds in accordance with democratic procedures.

Rawls's theory of stages suggests that it is useful to imagine proceeding through several levels of deliberation. After the choice of abstract principles of morality or justice, the next step is to draw up constitutional principles for a particular country, perhaps in a constitutional convention. The constitutional principles in turn limit and guide the choice of principles at the legislative stage.

It is useful to insert an "international human rights stage" between the level of abstract principles and the constitutional stage. We thereby recognize the importance of international politics and organizations and partially correct Rawls's excessively narrow focus on the nation state.[1] At this level one formulates specific rights, appropriate to one's historical era, that can provide standards for the behavior of states and guide the choice of constitutional norms. The international human rights stage and the constitutional stage, along with the broader aspects of the legislative stage, are a middle zone of moral discourse and reasoning, which comes between fundamental moral principles on one side and application-level policies on the other. This middle level of discourse is often ignored both by philosophers, who prefer to talk about starting points, and by politicians, who prefer to talk about concrete policy options.

The selection and formulation of a specific political right is not merely a matter of deduction from an abstract principle. Because the transition from an abstract moral claim to a specific political right requires additional information about contemporary institutions, resources, and problems, the claim alone does not deductively entail the specific right. At best, the abstract claim together with this additional information will deductively entail the specific right.

Going from an abstract claim to a specific human right calling for legal implementation involves at least four steps, each of which requires additional information. First, it must be shown that this specific right will protect something of very great importance. Second, there must be substantial and recurrent threats to this aspect of the abstract claim. Third, evidence must be provided that a specific political right is required for an adequate response to these threats—that no weaker norm will do as well. Finally, it must be shown that the obligations or other burdens the right imposes are affordable in relation to resources, other obligations, and fairness in the distribution of burdens. The first three steps will be discussed in this chapter; the fourth step will be given separate attention in chapter 7.

---

1. Rawls might find this additional stage unacceptable because it presupposes universal applicability. In essays written after *A Theory of Justice* (1971), Rawls has emphasized that his theory of justice applies to democratic societies, not to political cultures with radically different presuppositions; see "Kantian Constructivism in Moral Theory," *Journal of Philosophy* 77 (1980): 515–572, at 518; and "Justice as Fairness: Political not Metaphysical," *Philosophy and Public Affairs* 14 (1985): 223–251.

Importance and Threats

The initial steps in justifying a specific right calling for legal implementation are to show (1) that a very important interest is secured by the specific political right and (2) that it is secured against some substantial and recurrent threat. These two tests can be applied both when a list of specific international rights is being formulated and when bills of rights are being drafted for national constitutions. Meeting these two conditions generates a specific claim to respect, protection, or assistance. But these conditions do not show that respect, protection, or provision at this point must be secured by a specific political right. Additional arguments are required.

Importance

In discussing whether economic and social rights are genuine human rights, Maurice Cranston proposed that the test of a human right be that it protects something of "paramount importance."² I agree with Cranston on this point and will refer to the theory of fundamental interests and secure claims developed in chapter 5 as a test of importance. People who start from other normative perspectives can substitute other tests of importance. The importance test must be passed to get a case for a specific right started, and it is often the focus of arguments about whether something is a right.

A consequentialist theory of moral rights might interpret importance as a purely axiological notion; a claim would be very important if it were closely connected with a very strong interest or value. I propose, however, to interpret importance as having essential deontological elements. Principles of duty as well as considerations of value will be used in judging importance. A claim to A will pass the test of importance if A is necessary to meet the requirements of moral claims such as those to life, liberty, and fairness. Because the content of these claims is partly explained by reference to fundamental interests, these interests will be relevant in applying the importance test.

To decide, for example, whether a right prescribing freedom to leave a country passes the importance test, we can ask whether the

2. Maurice Cranston, *What Are Human Rights?* (New York: Tamlinger, 1973), 67.

abstract claim to freedom includes freedom of movement, particularly freedom to flee or emigrate from a country. To answer this question, further guidance can be obtained by considering the roles freedom of movement and freedom to flee a country play in promoting and protecting people's interest in *leading* a life. In this case the answer is easy: freedom of movement is central to being able to lead a life, and the freedom to flee is essential in many circumstances to escape oppression.

In showing that a specific right protects something of great importance, one may refer to abstract concepts such as "fundamental interest" or "secure claim to life." Ronald Dworkin offers a useful account of how to argue about such abstract concepts.[3] He suggests that one should proceed by elaborating *conceptions* of the abstract concept in question. A conception of a concept proposes some general principles that explain why the concept applies in cases where it clearly does and why it does not apply in cases where it clearly does not. To show, for example, that basic freedom is at stake in a particular case that strikes many people as borderline, one may have to elaborate a conception of what is involved in leading a life or of what aspects of human personality are most central. The next step is to use this conception to generate a result for the issue in question. There will generally be competing conceptions of abstract moral and political principles. To choose between them one can appeal to their consistency or "fit" with other well-established principles.

To explore these matters in a more concrete way, I will try to explain the importance of the interests that are protected by several familiar rights. The same rights will be discussed in illustrating subsequent steps.

Torture. Torture assaults many fundamental interests, often leading to death or to the destruction of health and the shortening of life. Thus torture violates the moral claim to *have* a life. It often deprives its victims of their freedom through kidnapping or arbitrary arrest and through forcing them to reveal information against their wills. Further, the practice of torture often coerces people other than its immediate victims: terror makes people act in ways

---

3. Ronald Dworkin, *Taking Rights Seriously* (Cambridge, Mass.: Harvard University Press, 1977), 81–149. See also James W. Nickel, "Dworkin on the Nature and Consequences of Rights," *Georgia Law Review* 11 (1977): 1115–1142.

they would not otherwise choose. Thus it is clear that the claim to *lead* one's own life can be undermined by torture.[4]

The right to a fair trial. Denial of a fair trial to those charged with serious crimes is a paradigmatic violation of the fairness principle, chiefly because the effects of criminal penalties on life and freedom are very serious. We can allow that if a society uses some method other than a trial to establish criminal guilt, and if this method is fair and reasonably effective, then no violation of the fairness principle would be involved. In this way we can imagine compliance with the fairness principle prior to the emergence of formal legal systems. But in the contemporary world, fairness in criminal procedures will require a fair trial or hearing.

The right against racial discrimination. Perhaps racial discrimination is more survivable than torture or unjustified punishment; many people appear to endure it without much damage to their fundamental interests. Heroic figures who stand tall in the face of racist insults and who are strong enough to be little harmed by racist actions and institutions are familiar in many racist societies. But not all those subject to racial discrimination escape harm; many have their lives shortened and their liberty restricted. Martin Luther King, Jr., explained some of the evil effects of discrimination in his "Letter from Birmingham City Jail":

> I guess it is easy for those who have never felt the stinging darts of segregation to say, "Wait." But when you have seen vicious mobs lynch your mothers and fathers at will and drown your sisters and brothers at whim; when you have seen hate-filled policemen curse, kick, brutalize and even kill your black brothers and sisters with impunity; when you see the vast majority of your twenty million Negro brothers smothering in an airtight cage of poverty in the midst of an affluent society; . . . when you are humiliated day in and day out by nagging signs reading "white" and "colored"; . . . when you are harried by day and haunted at night by the fact that you are a Negro, living constantly at tip-toe stance never quite knowing what to expect next, and plagued with inner fears and outer resentments; when you are forever fighting a degenerating sense of "nobodiness"; then you will understand why we find it difficult to wait.[5]

---

4. See Henry Shue, "Torture," *Philosophy and Public Affairs* 7 (1978): 124–143.

5. Martin Luther King, Jr., "Letter from Birmingham City Jail," in Hugo Adam Bedau, ed., *Civil Disobedience* (Englewood Cliffs, N.J.: Prentice-Hall, 1969), 76–77.

Assigning unequal burdens on the basis of race usually cannot be justified rationally. This unjustifiability, together with the harmfulness of a system of discrimination, provides the grounds for saying that racial discrimination violates the fairness principle. Protections against such discrimination pass the importance test.

Threats

Satisfying the importance test does not provide a complete justification for a specific moral or legal right. That specific right must also be shown to protect the important interest against some significant threat. If we recognized specific rights at every point where a fundamental interest is present, whether or not it is threatened at each of those points, we would have more claims—and potential rights—than we could even talk about. The vast majority would eventually be ruled out on the grounds that they do not satisfy two of the requirements, or tests, in the justification process: that no weaker norm is adequate and that the implementation of the right is feasible. The threat criterion serves as an early feasibility test, restricting claims to those with a prospect of passing the other two tests and thus worth talking about.

Although natural forces such as winds and floods often threaten people's fundamental interests, these threats are not directly germane. The threat criterion weighs dangers to human interests flowing from human actions or omissions. There are obvious difficulties in defining what counts as an omission. A person's nonaction in a particular case will count as an omission if that person had a duty to act in that case. This test is sufficient, but possibly not necessary, for an omission. It follows that if people have a moral claim to the aid of others when such aid is needed to protect and provide for their fundamental interests, then failures to aid victims of natural disasters can count as omissions and hence constitute threats.

Human rights address both individuals and governments because threats to people's fundamental interests come from both individuals and government agencies. Threats from individuals may involve murder, harm, negligence, exploitation, and discrimination. Threats from the state—which receive more attention in historic human rights documents—may involve all of the above and, in addition, threats such as (1) using the criminal law system to suppress opposition to and destroy the enemies of those in power; (2) victimizing unpopular minorities (or even majorities); (3) corruption, favoritism, and ineptitude; (4) using imprisonment, torture, and murder to consolidate political power; and (5) using political power to extend and entrench the favorable position of a dominant group. We can formulate the threat criterion to require that a proposed right protect a fundamental interest against some substantial and recurrent threat. This is intended to be a low standard; its main function is to restrict the discussion of claims and proposed rights to those worth talking about because they have some prospect of full justification. Even if, for example, a society experienced little racial discrimination in a particular era it might still be worthwhile to recognize moral and legal rights against such discrimination to deal with the few cases that did arise and to provide a standard. Publicly recognizing the right and teaching it to children and other new members of society may help preserve the fortunate circumstance of having few violations. Of course, if the moral right to freedom from racial discrimination were implemented in a very expensive way in a country where few threats of discrimination occurred (e.g., by having a large bureaucracy to monitor and promote compliance) it might be appropriate to adopt less expensive means of implementation.

Weaker Alternatives to Rights

The existence of abstract claims in morality does not entail the widespread use of specific rights in the legal system. Conceivably a society could rely on collective aspirations or goals, together with feelings of love and solidarity, to produce actions and conditions that satisfy people's abstract moral claims. This vision, dear to many utopians, suggests that an emphasis on specific legal or constitutional rights is not inescapable.

When a potential right passes the first two tests, or steps, of the justificatory process—protecting something of great value, and countering substantial and recurrent threats—we know that there is a claim to social action in this area. It does not follow, however, that protection must be provided by a specific political right. There is much controversy today over whether extensive use in morality and law of the concept of rights is a good thing, and I do not want to beg the question whether the floor of protection and provision that society should make for people is best made by implementing specific rights. To ensure that this question is faced, I suggest that the third step in the justification of a specific human right be to show that a political right, as opposed to some weaker and less costly norm, provides the best form of protection against the threats identified.

Specific political rights have some important advantages as protections because of their characteristic firmness and definiteness. First, the individuated character of rights ensures that identifiable parties will be charged with providing these protections, rather than leaving them to the whims of volunteers. Second, the obligations or responsibilities that attach to rights are mandatory and definite; they require identifiable parties to respond in specified ways to the rightholders. And third, rights are usually claimable. In addition to the pleas for compliance that can accompany any appeal to a norm, specific rights generally give a special place to steps that rightholders or others can take to bring special procedures or protections into play. For example, a legal right may permit an injured party to sue for cessation or compensation or it may empower an official or citizen to monitor compliance and invoke protections.

These general advantages of rights need to be weighed in relation to the distinctive advantages and disadvantages of other forms of protection and provision. The alternatives I will consider are self-help, voluntary aid, and structural modifications that eliminate the threat or make the basic good available in abundance.

Self-Help

One of the most important ways of providing and protecting fundamental interests is for people to help themselves—to seek, find, and defend their own goods. Whether the goods involve liberties, opportunities, services, or commodities, people will often gain and defend these things through their own efforts, particularly when their rights are not recognized. The "selves" that engage in self-help need not be isolated individuals but may rather be families or communities.

Even when people have legal rights, these rights may merely protect their freedoms to engage in various forms of self-help. For example, protection of personal possessions can be achieved in part by rights that go no further than to guarantee people's freedom to engage in self-defense. We might call these *rights that protect self-help*. Stronger rights would protect personal possessions by requiring police protection and legal remedies. Rights of this sort, which provide goods or services to people unable to supply their own, might be called *rights to a supply.* Thus in discussing self-help the option is not simply self-help or rights; it is rather a choice among (1) unprotected self-help, (2) rights that protect and facilitate self-help, and (3) rights to a supply. In the area of property, few argue that rights protecting self-help are sufficient. Protection services are typically advocated as well. But in the welfare area, many conservatives hold that protections of self-help are sufficient. Most debates about welfare rights are not debates about whether there should be some human rights in the welfare area; they are rather about whether these should be merely rights that protect self-help or also rights to a supply.[6] Rights requiring protections for self-help must be justified by showing that unprotected self-help will leave many people unable to provide for their basic interests or needs. Rights to a supply must be justified by showing that even protected self-help will leave many people in the same position. Of course, even when it has been shown that either of these kinds of rights is necessary, the fourth step—which requires that the right be feasible—still remains to be considered.

Social Aid

The use of voluntary aid to supply protection and other goods to those unable to supply their own provides an option intermediate between relying on protected self-help alone and providing supplies of goods or services. Families, friends, neighbors, and charitable organizations are often willing to help those who are unable to satisfy their own needs. This aid may be forthcoming out of sympathy or as a response to socially recognized duties of charity. Duties of charity, however, are "imperfect duties"; that is, they leave the giver discretion about when, where, and how much to give and do not confer corresponding rights.

This discretion creates a danger that aid through charity will produce only an irregular and spotty supply of aid. Because of this danger, people often organize charitable institutions to enable them to discharge their duties to aid others more effectively. Within these institutions, hired or voluntary workers encourage giving and distribute funds to some target group of needy persons. The gains are that gifts are stimulated by collection campaigns; supply is more

6. See chap. 9 for a fuller discussion of economic rights.

regular because funds can be accumulated, budgeted, and spread; there is scope for large projects; and coverage of people in need is broader. The agency is able to seek out people with certain sorts of need, so that assistance does not entirely depend on a needy person's being in the vicinity of someone willing and able to help.

In some areas, protected self-help together with formal charitable organizations may be an adequate response to a claim that passes the first two tests. But when significant numbers of people are left without protection or aid by these measures, mandatory legal norms are often appropriate. State police and welfare systems require everyone to contribute through taxes and offer services to all who need them. The great advantage of systems involving a right to a supply against the state is a substantial increase in regularity and comprehensiveness over random or organized charity. Their disadvantages include greater bureaucratic rigidity, higher costs, and the possible loss of a sense of community if personalized or community-based forms of mutual aid are abandoned. Whether charitable systems need to be supplemented with rights to a supply in a particular area depends on whether self-help together with charity can respond adequately to the justified claims of all.

Structural Changes

Specific legal rights might be unnecessary if we could change the social and economic systems of countries around the world to create an abundance of goods and eliminate most threats to life, freedom, and fairness. We might call these possibilities, respectively, the abundance strategy and the threat-elimination strategy. These can be combined with self-help and mutual aid; when supplies are abundant and threats few, self-help and mutual aid may be effective enough to make specific political rights unnecessary.

An advocate of the abundance strategy might note that we seldom speak of a right to air because an adequate supply is freely available. We do, of course, recognize a right not to be smothered as an aspect of the right to life, and we do have standards in many countries for clean air, but in general people can get the air they need simply by breathing. One might hope to achieve something similar in other areas by generating a very large productive capacity that would make supplies of needed goods and services so plentiful that no one would find it impossible to get an adequate supply. But this level of abundance has been reached nowhere, and most countries are very far from it.

The threat-elimination strategy has sometimes been advocated by those who see the possibility of a transformation of human motivation and consciousness through religion or other forms of enlightenment. They hope that such a transformation will eliminate selfishness, greed, conflict, and corruption. But it is fair to say, I think, that such transformations tend at best to be limited to small groups and therefore do not provide a practical method of eliminating all crime, greed, and corruption. Marxists sometimes advocate a combination of the two strategies. Their hope is that an abundant economy resulting from successful industrialization can be combined with a social and distributive structure that promotes solidarity and mutual aid, thereby eliminating the need for rights guaranteed by the state. They have also hoped that by getting rid of rights one could also abolish the bureaucratic rigidity of many rights-bound institutions and the egoistic character of a rights mentality that always insists on getting its due.[7] This is an attractive goal, but efforts to achieve it have not been conspicuously successful and its prospects for the foreseeable future are slim.

As a general response to the structural-changes approaches, I suggest that we be open-minded about these possibilities but insist that rights be implemented and retained until these plans have clearly succeeded. It would be foolish to give up rights in anticipation of success—particularly when so many attempts along these lines have failed.

The Three Examples

We can now return to the discussion of our three examples: rights against torture, to a fair trial, and against racial discrimination. I will discuss here both the threats these rights respond to and the reasons rights are needed.

Torture. Torture was once widely used as punishment and is still used in interrogation and as a means of ruling through terror in many parts of the world and in all sorts of political and economic systems.[8] Although the systematic use of torture is now uncommon in liberal democracies, it remains a danger, particularly in emergency situa-

7. On this mentality, see Karl Marx, "On the Jewish Question," in Robert C. Tucker, ed., *The Marx-Engels Reader*, 2d ed. (New York: W. W. Norton, 1978), 43.
8. See Amnesty International, *Torture in the Eighties* (London: Amnesty International Publications, 1984).

tions. There is little likelihood that the threat of torture will soon disappear in any society. As with many other human rights violations, certain groups are especially vulnerable to torture, among them political dissidents and members of unpopular minorities.

Only effectively implemented legal rights can provide adequate protection against torture. Although a variety of structural reforms can and should be taken to reduce the inclination to engage in torture, these are unlikely to eliminate the threat of it completely. Self-help is also unlikely to be an adequate means of protection. Although individuals can sometimes save themselves by fleeing, once a person is arrested or kidnapped he or she is under the physical control of others and the possibility of self-defense is severely limited. Voluntary assistance by friends and relatives may be so dangerous to them that such aid will not be forthcoming or effective in many cases. What is needed is a high-priority, exceptionless legal guarantee supported by prohibitions carrying criminal sanctions and by effective measures to supervise police and military conduct. Also needed are legal measures to stop torture sessions when they are suspected, to investigate disappearances, to exclude confessions induced by torture from evidence, and to provide compensation and rehabilitative services to victims of torture. Because individuals who have been kidnapped and tortured are often not in a position to invoke their own legal rights, provision for second-party claiming will be needed.

The right to a fair trial.   Many of the same points can be made about this right. Violations of due process are even more widespread than torture, and no political or economic system seems immune to them. The unpopular, the troublesome, and the powerless are especially vulnerable to being denied fair trials—and anyone can be a victim of the incompetence or laziness of judges and other officials.

Neither general improvements in legal processes, nor self-help, nor charitable assistance will eliminate the possibility of unfair trials in criminal proceedings. Individuals often lack the competence to gain good treatment for themselves within a complex legal system, and persons imprisoned because of an unfair trial may lack means of invoking their legal rights. High-priority legal guarantees that can be invoked by both the defendant and other parties are needed to protect people against the dangers imposed by the coercive powers of criminal justice systems. Provisions for proof of guilt in public before an impartial tribunal, assistance of effective counsel, habeas corpus, and review of convictions on appeal are important parts of such a right.

The right against racial discrimination. Racial and ethnic discrimination most often occurs in societies that have unpopular and economically exploited minorities (or, as in South Africa, majorities). Almost all countries are now multiracial and multiethnic to some degree, and protections against racial and ethnic discrimination are needed around the world. Many have hoped that education and prosperity will eventually diminish racial and ethnic conflict, but there seems little likelihood that these or other structural improvements will eliminate racial and ethnic discrimination in the present era.

Individuals subject to such discrimination are seldom completely protected against the negative influences of biased attitudes and practices either by self-help or by aid from sympathizers. Once again, only institutional guarantees that provide prohibitions of public and private discrimination, sanctions for the violations of these prohibitions, and remedies for the victims of discrimination will deal effectively with this problem.

7. Resources and Rights

Even though specific rights derive from very important moral considerations, they are not immune to being qualified or even deemed unjustifiable on grounds of costs. In this chapter I develop a taxonomy of these costs and make some suggestions about how one might respond to them.

Costs play a powerful role in relation to specific moral and political rights for several reasons. One is that there are limits to the obligations that can be generated even by fundamental principles, and costs help us decide whether these limits are being exceeded. Another reason is that a right may be in direct conflict with other measures that support fundamental moral principles, and this sort of conflict will be included under "costs." For example, the costs of a specific right may include the destruction of some state of affairs that is part of or important to basic freedoms. In this kind of case, the freedom principle may count as much against the right as for it. A third reason is that when resources are limited, the fact that one right is very costly to implement may make it impossible to implement, or fully implement, other rights.

Kinds of Costs

It is useful to try to identify the main kinds of costs rights can entail. In saying this, I do not mean to imply that all those costs can be adequately represented in monetary terms or that different kinds of costs can always be brought together on the same scale.

Conflict Costs

When a new right is introduced, conflicts with other norms, including other rights, may arise. Losses to other norms from recognizing, complying with, or implementing a right might be called conflict costs. Here the cost is what the right requires us to give up from our normative system that we would otherwise keep. For example, a possible conflict cost of a strong right to privacy is that respecting and implementing this right would require us to carve important exceptions into the right of freedom of the press. An especially severe form of conflict cost is involved when a right cannot be implemented without imposing such severe burdens on some people that the imposition violates other important norms, for example, norms of justice in the distribution of burdens. We would probably reject the idea that people who need kidney transplants have a right to them if we knew that the only way to obtain the kidneys needed for these transplants would be by a national lottery in which the persons selected were forced to donate one kidney to a national kidney bank.

As this example suggests, the problem of unacceptable conflict costs will be most severe when the costs of implementing a right cannot be spread among most members of society through taxation but must rather be met through extremely burdensome contributions by a small number of people. In general, however, the costs of the rights in the Universal Declaration can be met by imposing modest tax burdens on most members of society and thereby generating the resources needed to provide the right to all. The development in the last few centuries of government institutions that can efficiently spread large costs through income and other taxes has made it possible to add costly items such as welfare rights to contemporary lists of human rights without incurring unacceptable conflict costs.

Conflict costs, like some of the other costs of rights, can be direct or indirect. A direct conflict cost exists when there is a contradiction between the descriptions of the scopes of two rights (or norms) or between descriptions of what is involved in normal exercise or enforcement of those rights (or norms). Indirect conflict costs occur when the conflict is mediated by an extended causal linkage. For example, prohibiting a previously permitted act may result—via an extended chain of actions—in forms of evasive behavior that violate or undermine other norms or values.

The Costs of Using Weaker Means

A penetrating discussion of the costs of rights needs to acknowledge a distinction between duties not to infringe people's rights and duties to uphold or protect people's rights. The former duties are negative in that they involve only restraints; the latter are positive in that they require one to act so as to provide or protect a good. The right against torture, for example, implies negative duties for both individuals and governments; they are not permitted to use torture as a means to their ends. But governments also have positive duties to uphold this right and to protect against torture people who are threatened by government or private agents.

The costs of upholding rights are obviously often high, but it is sometimes suggested that the costs of noninfringement—because they merely involve *not* doing something—are always low. The truth is that the costs of not being able to act in a certain way, of not being permitted to take a certain course of action when it is the only or most effective means to a desired goal, are often substantial. We might call these kinds of costs the costs of using weaker means.

To illustrate this kind of cost, consider the case of torture. Forbidding governments to use torture will deny some of them a preferred method of criminal interrogation. Human rights are often controversial precisely because they forbid political tactics that are dirty but effective (at least in the short term). In the case of torture this cost does not—in my opinion—call into question the justifiability of a right against torture, but it does illustrate that the loss of effective means to public goals can become a significant cost when the impermissibility of those means impedes attainment of the goals. Thus it cannot be plausibly maintained that negative rights are always costless or low in cost.

Implementation Costs

Most political rights involve duties to uphold, as well as to not infringe. The costs of meeting duties to uphold might be called implementation costs. Duties to protect are paradigms of duties to uphold; such protection may be provided directly through criminal laws and sanctions and through procedures that permit individuals to sue for cessation of violations of their rights or compensation for them. Protection of rights can also be provided indirectly through such institutional mechanisms as checks and balances, executive control of police and military, civil service systems, and regular elections. Implementing a right often requires providing not just protection but other goods as well. Thus governments may be obligated to provide opportunities (to vote or to attend school), services (medical care or occupational guidance), or payments (a minimum income during unemployment, disability, or old age).

When a good is made available as a matter of legal right, government may become the main supplier of the good (as with education or police protection in most countries today) or it may serve only as a supplier of last resort (as is common today with the right to counsel for indigents in criminal cases). Even when something is available as a matter of right, many people may still prefer to supply the good for themselves, and many will want a higher quantity or quality of the good than is guaranteed by right. The expense of implementing a right will generally depend on how many people will continue to create or pay for their own supply after the right is implemented. Upholding rights, where either protecting or providing is involved, is often enormously expensive, and thus cost estimates, as well as cost reduction proposals, usually focus on implementation.

Like conflict costs, implementation costs can be divided into those that are direct and those that are indirect. Direct implementation costs are the immediate costs of providing the services that uphold a right. Indirect implementation costs are negative consequences that follow by an extended causal chain from the activity of implementing a right. For example, collecting the taxes necessary for implementing a right may decrease the supply of venture capital and retard productivity, and implementing a right may use up resources that could have been used to achieve other desirable goals.

Counting the Costs

Because of the number and variety of costs just surveyed, we seldom have a precise idea how much it costs to respect and implement a right. Cost estimates are often hard to make, particularly because they require comparisons with hypothetical alternatives and count different kinds of costs that are difficult to bring together on a single scale. There is often controversy about how much weight should be attached to particular kinds of costs. Finally, it is hard to determine a country's level of resources or what portion of these resources should be used to comply with and implement the human rights of all residents.

In spite of these problems, people regularly assess the affordability of rights, and it will be useful to suggest in broad terms how this should be done. A budgeting process for rights at the national level might begin with an estimate of the resources available for implementing rights. I suggested earlier that this level of overall expenditure on rights should be a portion of national resources that is small enough to (1) avoid putting unfair and destructive burdens on particular individuals, (2) avoid undermining the institutions and levels of economic productivity needed to provide for the general welfare and implement rights effectively over time, and (3) avoid undermining the development and maintenance of a rich social, artistic, intellectual, and religious culture.

Once we have some idea of the resources available (given these criteria) and a preliminary ranking of the rights candidates, together with their costs, we can cut and prune these candidates so as to make the final list of rights compatible with national resources. We should recognize, however, that an analogy with accounting procedures of subtracting the costs from the resources available breaks down severely at this point. In this context neither resources nor costs can be adequately represented on a single scale, and many of the judgments about the weights of competing values and the likely impacts of expenditures are the sort appropriately thought of as political. The possibility of giving a fully adequate reconstruction of these judgments in terms of moral principles alone seems slight.

Governments do not generally use a budgeting process that considers the costs of a whole system of rights—except, perhaps, in those unusual cases in which a new regime is trying to construct an entirely new political and legal system. Most countries have in operation a system of rights that is known to be affordable, and improvements or additions to this system are evaluated one by one as they are proposed. This incremental procedure requires only that one answer the easier question of whether the country's resources will permit a particular addition or improvement.

Making Rights Cheaper

It is not very controversial to propose that costs and resources must be considered at the implementation stage—when human or constitutional rights are being implemented nationally through legislation. The need to consider costs at the implementation stage can be seen by considering the problem of levels of provision. When a right to A includes claims to services such as provision or protection in regard to A, the level of provision or protection to be made available as a matter of right is usually not deducible from the right itself. For example, knowledge that one has a right to police protection as part of a general right to security against crimes does not settle the issue of how much protection one has a right to—for example, whether one has a right to have a police officer pass one's residence on patrol every hour or every day. A formulation of the right at the middle level may tell us that implementation must be above a certain point (or else the right will not be meaningfully implemented at all), but a more precise determination of "how much" must depend on resources, threats, and available technology and institutions.

When we consider costs and resources at the implementation stage, we often find that the costs of the rights at hand exceed the resources available. In this situation, two main options are available for reducing the costs of the rights in question, neither of which should be used unless strictly necessary. International aid may be justifiable on the grounds that it is needed to enable an impoverished country to respect and implement the rights of its people without resorting to these options.

One way of reducing costs, which I call *axing,* involves eliminating some of the candidates from a list of justified rights. This tactic has often been proposed in regard to the Universal Declaration's long list of rights, particularly in regard to its economic and social rights. Of course, axing a right does not preclude weaker forms of provision for the goods involved. It may be possible to make the provision of these goods a priority goal or a subject of private charity.

Another option for reducing the costs of rights, which I call *pruning,* is to cut back several dimensions of a particular right without cutting so deeply or extensively that the right ceases to exist as a meaningful norm. It is clear, of course, that the result of too-extensive pruning will be to ax the right.

If R is a right we need to prune, there are at least five ways in which this can be done.

1. Change the conditions of possession for R so that fewer people have the right. Human rights are universal in some sense and the extent to which one can deny them to certain human beings while still calling them *human* rights is limited. Further, part of the appeal of human rights is that they protect everyone independently

of nationality, race, or sex. But the international rights documents suggest that some human rights are only held by adults or citizens, and some rights might be restricted to those of normal mental capacity or to people who have not committed serious crimes.

2. Reduce R's addressees. Instead of implying responsibilities for both individuals and governments, R might be construed as addressing only one of these parties. If the human right to freedom of expression, for example, were viewed as forbidding only interference *by government* (as is the case with the First Amendment in the United States), the right would be much less costly to enforce than if it were viewed as forbidding private interference as well.

3. Lower R's weight. This would make R more vulnerable to being overridden by other rights and by other considerations, so that R would be operative less often. For example, if the right to privacy was thought to be too costly in terms of its impact on fair trials, its weight could be lowered until it was subordinate to most other rights. As a result, it would always yield in cases of direct conflict.

4. Limit R's scope. This action is closely related to lowering R's weight: roughly the same effect is achieved by building exceptions into R's scope at all points where it might conflict with rights or other important considerations. For example, a government whose resources were severely strained might restrict the right to assistance by legal counsel to serious criminal cases, or a very poor country might restrict the right to education to cover only the eight grades. One advantage of limiting a right's scope over lowering its weight is selectivity. If we lowered the general weight of the right to privacy, it would be subordinated not only to the right to a fair trial but also, perhaps, to other claims by government agencies for information about people. An exception that applies only in the context of trials provides a way to avoid this general subordination.

5. Reduce the level of protection or provision of R. Reducing implementation costs is the kind of cost reduction people are likely to think of first. In regard to protection, it might involve lowering expenditures on police and courts—perhaps by relying more on individuals to bring suits against violators and less on police and prosecutors to detect and prosecute violations. In regard to provision, levels of food aid or income support that are provided to the most needy residents of the country might be lowered.

If these five ways of pruning a right are used too extensively, the result will be to ax the right—and civil libertarians and advocates of human rights do well to be vigilant against such cuts. But short of making a right insignificant or nonexistent, many questions about how extensive a right and its measures of enforcement should be are legitimate subjects of political debate.

Are the Declaration's Rights Affordable?

A common complaint about the Universal Declaration is that it fails to take into account problems of the affordability of rights in many countries; it formulates a list of rights suitable to the rich countries of the First World without worrying about what is possible elsewhere.

Because rights are not magical sources of supply, the issue of affordability can be postponed but not escaped. Recognizing a right to a good will not by itself make that good available in sufficient quantities to provide it to all the rightholders. If a country lacks courts and lawyers, a right to a fair trial will be moot until legal workers can be educated and courts created. More generally, the obligations flowing from a right will be without effect if their addressees are genuinely unable to comply with them or unable to comply while meeting their higher-ranked responsibilities. Even if costs were not used to draw a boundary between justified specific rights and not-yet-justified rights, they would still have to be used to draw a boundary between operative and nonoperative rights. If we do not face the issue of affordability at the justification stage, we will face it in a more severe form at the application stage. We risk undermining the idea of human rights by formulating rights that are clearly not feasible to implement.

Because they are abstract and limit obligations to what is possible, the three secure claims (to life, liberty, and fairness in decisions between rights) formulated in chapter 5 are immune to being totally set aside on the grounds of expense. But specific international or constitutional rights, which define definite duties and liabilities for particular addressees, are more vulnerable to being set aside or rendered inoperative on the grounds that they are too demanding for present circumstances.

The authors of the Universal Declaration faced great difficulties in this area. On the one hand, they wished to formulate rights that were specific enough to give clear guidance; on the other hand, they wanted their formulations to apply to countries facing severe problems and having very different levels of human, institutional, and financial resources.

The approach they took was to formulate a single high standard for the whole earth. The Declaration's list of human rights presupposes the financial, institutional, and human resources needed to construct democratic political institutions, a humane legal system, and a comprehensive welfare state. This approach results in a list of fairly demanding rights, which is useful as a standard of criticism for First and Second World countries. If a much lower level of resources had been assumed, many of the requirements would have been extremely easy for the richer countries to meet and thus would have had little practical significance for them.

Such demanding standards obviously are problematic in relation to poorer countries, but two considerations make this fact slightly less worrisome than it might have been. One is that the specific rights enumerated can serve as standards of aspiration for less developed countries. In particular, these rights identify the areas in which efforts are called for by extremely important moral claims. Even if these claims cannot be viewed as operative rights in the poorer countries, it is still useful to have them formulated. The other consideration is that rights can be protected and upheld in varying degrees, and thus countries can be expected to implement human rights as far as their resources allow. This approach was made explicit in part 2, article 2, section 1 of the International Covenant on Economic, Social, and Cultural Rights:

> Each State Party to the present Covenant undertakes to take steps . . . to the maximum of its available resources, with a view to achieving progressively the full realization of the rights recognized in the present Covenant.

Although this clause was not inserted into other human rights documents, I think that it represented a common view of the implications of human rights norms for poorer countries.

The problem of this approach is that it forfeits many of the advantages of specific rights. Governments unable to implement these rights are merely told to do the best they can. Except that it enumerates a number of areas in which welfare, freedom, and fairness should be promoted, the Declaration offers little more guidance than the three abstract principles of chapter 5.

This lack of guidance is made worse by the fact that the weights of the rights in the Universal Declaration are not specified. If ten rights were ranked, and if resources in poor countries were only sufficient to respect and implement six of them, it would be clear that the four lowest-priority rights were the ones that should be set aside. But without a ranking, it will be unclear which rights are operable and currently binding on all countries. If we assume that under scarcity a right to a fair trial is operative and a right to education is moot, we are implicitly assuming that the former right is of higher priority than the latter. Assumptions about the relative weights of rights are far from noncontroversial; indeed, people probably disagree more about the weights of rights than about which rights should be on the list.

We are now in a position to see the shortcomings of the Universal Declaration's way of dealing with the problem of resources. First, because it neither addresses the issue of human rights in less developed countries nor provides a ranking of rights, it is simply vague. Thus it fails to provide the definite guidance that rights are well suited to provide. Second, it takes rich countries as its paradigms and provides definite guidance for them, although many of the most severe human rights violations occur in countries that are poor and under great political stress. Thus it often fails to provide guidance where it is most needed.

Some of the authors of the Universal Declaration may have hoped that the implications for poorer countries of the idea of human rights would be spelled out in regional documents to be created by representatives of those countries. New regional bills of rights would need to take into account the traditions, problems, institutions, and resources found in the region. But the idea of regional approaches to human rights has never really matured. Rights documents written by regional bodies have avoided the problem of what to do about rights under extreme scarcity and have been nearly as ambitious in their demands as the Universal Declaration. Perhaps one reason the problem of scarcity has been skirted is that variation in levels of resources and development within these regions is often nearly as large as the variation within the world as a whole. What is possible for Nigeria may not be possible for Mali, and what is possible for Brazil may not be possible for Belize.

Cost as a Factor in Ranking

Can the cost of a right tell us anything about its priority in relation to other rights? Suppose that we have two rights, R_1 and R_2, of equal intrinsic importance but of very different costs, where R_1 is much less costly than R_2. It is clear that if we are considering adding R_1 or R_2 to the set of rights that are respected and effectively implemented in a country, and if we can afford R_1 but not R_2, then R_1 will have priority over R_2. To avoid confusion here, perhaps we should distinguish between intrinsic importance, which is not affected by costs, and priority, which *is* so affected. In the example above, R_1 and R_2 are equal in intrinsic importance, but R_1 has higher priority than R_2. Priority combines intrinsic importance with considerations of efficiency, which is not a general test of rights but operates as such at the margin of affordability.

8. Human Rights During National Emergencies

Governments that respond to domestic opposition or resistance by torturing, imprisoning, or killing people they consider disloyal or dangerous often try to justify their infringements of human rights by saying that their opponents left them no choice—that these harsh measures were necessary to protect national survival and security during a period of extreme stress. Periods of national emergency such as wars, disasters, and insurrections are problematic for human rights theory because they present both reasons for infringing human rights and conditions in which it is easy to exaggerate dangers and make mistaken judgments.

Human rights standards will provide substantial guidance in emergency situations only if they are specific about which rights can be infringed in emergencies and about what kinds of considerations can license infringements. The Universal Declaration is silent on these matters. Fortunately, however, the authors of the European Convention on Human Rights and of the International Covenant on Civil and Political Rights were willing to be specific; they proposed a mixed or compromise account that holds a few of the most basic rights, such as rights against murder, torture, and slavery, to be immune to infringement on national security grounds, while leaving most rights open to such infringement when a necessity test can be satisfied.[1]

In this chapter I examine this mixed approach from a philosophical point of view; my goal is to see how well it stands up to detailed

---

1. See Joan F. Hartman, "Derogation from Human Rights Treaties in Public Emergencies—A Critique of Implementation by the European Commission and Court of Human Rights and the Human Rights Committee of the United Nations," *Harvard International Law Journal* 22 (1981): 1–52. See also "Limitation and Derogation Provisions in the International Covenant on Civil and Political Rights," A Symposium, *Human Rights Quarterly* 7 (1985): 1–131.

examination. I conclude that the mixed approach elaborated in the European Convention and in the Covenant on Civil and Political Rights stands up fairly well if one is willing, as I am, to give a substantial role in determining the weight of a right to considerations about the costs of complying with and implementing that right. One worry that emerges, however, is whether these documents give adequate weight to rights to petition government and to due process.

Rights That Cannot Be Suspended

Exceptions and Weight

The rights of the Universal Declaration were formulated in broad language containing few exceptions, and their weights in competition with each other or with other considerations were not even partially specified. But in formulating the subsequent European Convention and International Covenant on Civil and Political Rights, greater precision was thought appropriate—perhaps because these documents were intended to become, as they eventually did, "binding" standards of international law.

As we saw in chapter 2, an *exception* to the scope or definition of a right limits the freedoms or benefits that the right prescribes. A clear example of an exception clause is found in article 2 of the European Convention, which asserts the right to life. This exception permits killings that are strictly necessary: "(*a*) in defense of any person from unlawful violence; (*b*) in order to effect a lawful arrest or to prevent the escape of a person lawfully detained; [and] (*c*) in action lawfully taken for the purpose of quelling a riot or insurrection."

The weight of a right determines its rank or power in relation to competing considerations; it specifies when the right can be overridden by such considerations. Article 15 of the European Convention specifies the weight of some of its rights by asserting that it is impermissible even in emergencies to suspend the right to life or the rights against torture and degrading punishments, slavery and servitude, and retroactive criminal laws. This specification effectively makes these rights absolute in weight; nothing is permitted to override them. Notice, however, that being absolute in this sense is compatible with having numerous exceptions, as is the case, for example, with the right to life.

It is clear that the categories of scope and weight interact. Perhaps only because of its numerous exceptions can the right to life plausibly be said to be absolute or nonderogable. By building in these exceptions, the right to life becomes, roughly, a right against being murdered. Clearly, in evaluating the claim that some right is absolute, we need to pay close attention to any exceptions that are built into the scope of that right.

Three Tests for the Priority of Rights

In order to evaluate the plausibility of the mixed or compromise approach taken by the European Convention and the Covenant on Civil and Political Rights, it will be helpful to have on hand some machinery for ranking rights. The following are three tests useful in determining the proper weight of rights.

The consistency test. Henry Shue's idea of basic rights can be applied by subjecting proposed cuts in rights to a test of practical consistency.[2] If a right, R_1, depends for its effective implementation on the implementation of another right, R_2, then a proposed cut that axed R_2 but not R_1 would be inconsistent as a practical matter, even if there is no logical contradiction involved in endorsing R_1 and rejecting R_2. This practical inconsistency would come from trying to have one right (R_1) without being willing to accept one of its practically necessary conditions (R_2). This test obviously applies to axing rights but can be easily adapted to pruning.

Shue tries to get a lot of mileage out of the consistency test by trying to identify some rights as *basic,* in the sense of being necessary to the effective implementation of all other rights, including all other basic rights. The effect of recognizing a right as basic is to rule out all proposed cuts that ax or substantially prune it but that seek to preserve some other rights. Because the effect of axing a basic right is to make it impossible to implement any other right effectively, basic rights are immune to cuts except when one is willing to ax all rights—or at least to ax all rights for one region of the country. Even if there are few or no rights that are basic in Shue's sense, more modest uses of the consistency test are not ruled out. Limited dependency relations between rights often have interesting results for what it is possible to cut or prune.

2. Henry Shue, *Basic Rights* (Princeton, N.J.: Princeton University Press, 1980), 5–87.

The importance test. Once we have identified cuts that seem to leave systems of rights consistent in practice, the next test is to rank the cuts in terms of the importance of the rights they retain. Importance can be explained in terms of the weight of the values and norms underlying the specific right. The same considerations that justify the right also provide guidance to when it can be restricted. This test is a continuation of the process whereby specific rights are justified. It reexamines the same supporting considerations and compares them with competing ones.

The test is obviously difficult to apply. A right would not be on a list of international human rights unless many people believed that it was very important, and it is obviously difficult to decide which measures protecting life, freedom, and fairness are most crucial. In spite of the obvious centrality of the importance test, therefore, alleged results are likely to be highly controversial.

It may be helpful when dealing with such controversies to break down arguments about the importance of rights into several parts. This can be done by asking the following questions:

1. How *weighty* are the values and principles served by the right? The right to A would not be a human right unless A were closely connected with a fundamental interest of persons. But we can nevertheless ask how central A is to the fundamental interests protected by a principle. Is A a central or marginal aspect of one of these principles? In the area of due process, for example, this criterion might allow us to distinguish between, say, the right to counsel as central and the right to face one's accusers as less central. Similarly, with freedom of movement we need to distinguish the liberty to flee the country, which is at its core, and the liberty to travel as a tourist, which is less central.

2. How *vulnerable* is this freedom or benefit to the threats to which the right in question responds? Are serious threats common or rare? Whether the damage is reparable or irreparable is also relevant here, at least relevant to the justifiability of the short-term suspension of a right. If the harm done can and will be repaired, suspension of the right so as to accommodate some other important consideration is more easily justified.

3. How *effective* is the protection that the right provides against these threats? Here we can distinguish between rights that are very effective as protections and those that are merely useful or sometimes effective.

Stated broadly as a single standard, these criteria suggest that one right is of greater importance than another if it is more essential to the protection of the core of a fundamental moral claim against substantial and regular threats.

Cost efficiency. This test suggests that in choosing among consistent cuts that save many of the most important rights one should preserve those rights with the lowest costs, where costs are understood in the broad terms explained in chapter 6. Once we are above a certain threshold of importance, those rights should be retained— assuming consistency—that have the highest ratio of importance to cost. One reason for giving costs such an important role here is that the situations in which this test applies are likely to be ones in which the ability to implement other rights effectively is restricted because of limited resources. In these situations, greater efficiency means greater ability to implement other rights.

Were Only the Weightiest Rights Included?

Our present concern is whether *all* and *only* the most important rights were held to be immune to derogation by the European Convention and the Covenant on Civil and Political Rights. In this section I search for rights present under false pretenses; in the next section I ask whether any of the weightiest rights were left out.

Rights Against Murder, Torture, and Slavery

In condemning without qualification acts of murder, torture, and slavery, the documents under discussion expressed some of the strongest and most widely shared moral attitudes of the human race. Further, we saw in chapter 5 that prohibitions of murder, torture, and slavery are central parts of people's moral claims to life and liberty. I will not belabor the obvious by providing arguments for the weight of rights that are so clearly important. However, a few remarks about the reasons for the weight of these rights will be useful as a demonstration of the standards that other rights must meet.

Consistency. This test asks whether axing or suspending rights against murder, torture, and slavery is practically consistent with retaining and effectively implementing other rights. Protections against murder, torture, and involuntary servitude are core parts of security, and thus Henry Shue's argument showing the importance of security to the enjoyment or implementation of other rights is applicable:

> No one can fully enjoy any right that is supposedly protected by society if someone can credibly threaten him or her with murder, rape, beating, etc., when he or she tries to enjoy the alleged right. Such threats to physical security are among the most serious and—in much of the world—the most widespread hindrances to the enjoyment of any right. If any right is to be exercised except at great risk, physical security must be protected.[3]

Shue may be mistaken in asserting that *no* other rights can be enjoyed or implemented if security is missing, but it is clear that most rights will be extremely difficult to implement effectively among a population that lives in terror of murder or torture. Thus the consistency test confirms the high weight of the rights against murder, torture, and enslavement.

Importance. A literal interpretation of rights against murder and torture would say that they protect people from the evils of death, excruciating pain, and total loss of freedom. It is obvious that basic moral claims of torture victims are at stake, but one can add that the rights against murder and torture protect not only against death and severe pain but also against the severe coercion that is exercised when these things are threatened. Murder and torture are the means of ruling through terror.

The second criterion of importance is also relevant. In almost every region of the world today we find numerous instances in which these crimes are committed by governments and individuals. Torture is common, and political murder during emergency situations is depressingly familiar. Enslavement in the sense of chattel slavery has become much less common in this century, but closely related phenomena can be found in the exploitation of the labor of political prisoners who have been neither tried nor convicted.

The third criterion of importance pertains to the effectiveness of rights against murder and torture. Here it is possible to say that these rights can be effective protections when implemented in con-

3. Ibid., 21.

stitutions and statutes and when backed by effective remedies and penalties. Law and morality do not rule the world, but they are not without influence in restraining governments faced with problems for which dirty means seem the easiest cure.

Cost. For a right to be of the highest weight it not only must be strongly supported by the consistency and importance tests, but it also must be of bearable cost. Suppose that a government is trying to cope with an internal insurrection, that the rebels have many inactive sympathizers among the population, and that the conflict is severely straining the resources of the government. Suppose further that the government is tempted to try to make some quick gains against the rebels and reduce their support among the population by using the methods of terror—killing and torturing some of those who are known to be silent supporters of the rebels.

The issue here is not whether government forces can kill rebel combatants during battles. Such killing is permitted by exceptions built into the right to life as it is defined in these documents. The issue is rather whether noncombatant sympathizers can be murdered and tortured. The kind of cost most relevant here is the cost of using weaker means. The issue raised by mentioning this kind of cost is whether ruling through terror is to be denied to governments as a means. If it is forbidden, more difficult and costly measures will sometimes have to be used. Implementation costs must also be considered, particularly if private armies or death squads are already torturing and killing noncombatants—should scarce financial and human resources be directed to restraining these groups? It is undeniable that substantial costs are sometimes associated with refraining from political torture and murder. These costs are not so large, however, as to be unbearable.

The most important thing to keep in mind here is the evil on the other side of the scale, namely, instituting coercive terror through repulsive and harmful means against a large group of innocent people. It is also important to realize that the tactics of terror will corrupt and undermine the political system whose salvation is usually the justification for these tactics and that terror, once unleashed, can seldom be constrained to cases where it is "necessary" or "useful." These sorts of considerations suggest that the costs of the rights against murder, torture, and enslavement are ones that governments should be expected to bear—even though they are often far from small.

The Right Against
Retroactive Criminal Laws

The fourth nonderogable right in the European Convention is the right to freedom from retroactive criminal laws. This right forbids retroactive modifications of a legal system's norms, evidential requirements, procedures, or statutes of limitations that make it possible to convict people of criminal offenses who would have been found innocent in the absence of these modifications. This is a due process right; its role is to strengthen protections of life and liberty by making it impossible for governments to kill or incarcerate their enemies by use of retroactive criminal laws. This right prevents a government from using legal tricks to kill and imprison its enemies and thus prevents violations of the fairness principle and contributes to security for life and liberty.

In addition to protecting very important interests, the right against retroactive laws is generally not very costly to comply with or implement. There are few cases in which the use of a retroactive criminal law is the only possible means to legitimate goals, and hence the cost of this right (as a cost of using weaker means) is not very high. It is easy to make a case for including it among the nonderogable rights.

One example that might counter this generalization about costs arises from the situation faced at the Nuremberg trials after World War II, where the problem was how to prosecute war criminals whose acts were not illegal under domestic law at the time they were committed. The European Convention dealt with this by saying that "no one shall be held guilty of any criminal offense on account of any act or omission which did not constitute a criminal offense under national *or international law* at the time when it was committed" (emphasis added). The International Covenant on Civil and Political Rights duplicates this exact language and adds the qualification: "Nothing in this article shall prejudice the trial and punishment of any person for any act or omission which, at the time it was committed, was criminal according to the general principles of law recognized by the community of nations." This qualification is so open-ended that one might worry that it will undercut the core of the right. The general point to be made here, however, is that this right would not preclude the prosecution of war criminals, and hence it is safe to say that it has very low costs in the sense of the costs of using weaker means.

Perhaps the most important thing about the right against retroactive criminal laws is that it raises the question of why other important due process rights were not made nonderogable as well. If the right against retroactive laws is needed to satisfy the fairness principle and to make life and liberty more secure against certain possible abuses of the criminal justice system, why are other due process rights not equally necessary?[4] This is a question to which I will return later.

The Right to Freedom of Conscience

The International Covenant on Civil and Political Rights, which was formulated after the European Convention, classifies as nonderogable all of the rights so labeled by the European Convention (life, and freedom from torture, slavery, and retroactive criminal laws) and adds to the list of nonderogable rights the following:

Article 4: A right against measures taken during national emergencies that discriminate solely on the ground of race, color, sex, language, religion, or social origin. This article was added to the nonderogation clause.

Article 7: The right to freedom from subjection without one's consent to medical or scientific experimentation. This was added to the right against torture.

Article 11: Immunity to imprisonment merely because of inability to fulfill contractual obligations.

Article 15: The right to recognition everywhere as a person before the law.

Article 18: The right to freedom of thought, conscience, and religion.

The most practically significant addition here is article 18, which reads as follows:

1. Everyone shall have the right to freedom of thought, conscience and religion. This right shall include freedom to have or to adopt a religion or belief of his choice, and freedom, either individually or in community with others and in public or private, to manifest his religion or belief in worship, observance, practice and teaching.

4. See Frank C. Newman, "Natural Justice, Due Process and the New International Covenants on Human Rights: Prospectus," *Public Law* (1967): 274–313.

2. No one shall be subject to coercion which would impair his freedom to have or to adopt a religion or belief of his choice.

3. Freedom to manifest one's religion or beliefs may be subject only to such limitations as are prescribed by law and are necessary to protect public safety, order, health, or morals or the fundamental rights and freedoms of others.

4. The States Parties to the present Covenant undertake to have respect for the liberty of parents and, when applicable, legal guardians to ensure the religious and moral education of their children in conformity with their own convictions.

It is important to note the limitations on this right. First, section 3 permits restrictions on actions taken to manifest religious beliefs. Second, freedom of expression is not included in this right, except insofar as it protects public teaching of religion. Freedom of expression is treated in article 19, and that article is derogable. And third, freedom of assembly is also separated from this right; it is treated in article 21, which is also derogable. Thus, what article 18 gives is a qualified but nonderogable right to religious belief and practice, where "religious belief" is understood in broad enough terms to include "thought" and "conscience."

Consistency.   To begin the application of the tests suggested earlier, we can ask whether compliance with or respect for other rights depends on enjoying freedom of conscience. So far as I can see, enjoying freedom of conscience requires enjoyment of many other rights but not vice versa. If this is correct, this right gains little support from the consistency test. One could ax or suspend this right and retain most others without involving oneself in a practical inconsistency—provided that the other rights were not defined in a way that discriminated against the beliefs or practices of any religious group. For example, one could enjoy the right to due process even if one's right to religious freedom were not respected or upheld. The question is not whether religious intolerance can weaken other rights—it clearly can—but whether some rights can be enjoyed by a religious minority in a largely intolerant society. The answer to this question is affirmative.

Importance.   The right to freedom of conscience is not essential to the enjoyment of other rights, so the case for it must stand on the importance of religious freedom itself. Here we must ask about the principles this right protects, the threats to those principles, and the efficacy of the right in responding to those threats. Freedom of belief and conscience is clearly a central rather than a marginal aspect of personal and social freedom. Because of the value we attach to having beliefs about God, the nature of the universe, and the place of human beings in it—beliefs that express our own personalities and commitments—freedom from coercion in these matters is likely to be one of our most valued freedoms. In many other areas we can let the majority decide for all. But here too much is at stake for the individual, and the issue is too intimately connected with personal identity and destiny, for collective decision making to be appropriate.

Second, threats to this freedom are common. Religious intolerance is probably a natural consequence of the great fervor with which religious beliefs are often held and the importance that people attach to having beliefs they deem correct. People who have made the "wrong" choice about a matter of such importance are often described as misguided and needing assistance for their own good, or they may be thought of as carriers of false beliefs that can, like harmful germs, infect others. Although conflicts involving religious intolerance have become less common in the last three centuries, they remain a severe problem all around the world.

Third, a number of societies have succeeded in creating a climate of religious tolerance and in building legal protections for religious freedom, and thus we can say that effective measures for upholding freedom of conscience are available. Government protection of freedom of conscience can be effective in helping unpopular religious minorities avoid persecution and harassment.

These three aspects of the importance of religious freedom seem to confirm the judgment that a right to freedom of conscience protects a central aspect of liberty against substantial and common threats.

Costs. The right to freedom of conscience as formulated in the Covenant on Civil and Political Rights permits governments to regulate religious practice and teaching to protect public order and safety and to protect the rights of others. This exception cuts out many of the costs that would be associated with a less limited right to religious belief and practice. As long as people can be prevented from manifesting their beliefs in harmful ways, the costs of their having those beliefs and passing them on to their children are not very high.

It may be thought that this right would have little relevance during emergencies, but here it is useful to remember the recent revolution in Iran, during which religious organizations were the center of a good deal of opposition to the shah. Although the right to freedom of conscience would not protect the revolutionary activities of religious people, it would prevent suppression of the religious practices and organizations of an entire religious group. Thus we must not suppose that freedom of conscience never imposes costs of using weaker means. In general, however, these costs are not very high; governments will usually be able to find other ways of dealing with their religiously based opponents. The right to freedom of conscience, as conceived in these documents, permits the regulation for purposes of public safety of all overt religious practices.

The right to freedom of conscience is of high priority because it protects freedoms of great value at a cost that is generally quite low. Its place among nonderogable rights makes sense—particularly in light of the qualifications it contains. In the next section we will address the question of whether its near relatives—freedom of expression and assembly—should also have been made immune to derogation during emergencies.

Were All of the Weightiest Rights Included?

The Demands of Emergency Situations

In a national emergency such as an armed foreign invasion or a disastrous earthquake, governments have the job of minimizing the damage to people and property, restoring order and security, and repairing the most disruptive damage. In order to do these things, certain emergency powers are often necessary.[5]

First, governments need powers to control the location and move-

5. See Michael Walzer, *Just and Unjust Wars* (New York: Basic Books, 1977), 127–137.

ment of people, to move them from the most dangerous areas and into areas where security and rudimentary services (food, shelter, and medical care) can be provided. Rights to freedom of movement and to choice of residence may be severely infringed during such emergencies.

Second, governments need powers to reestablish rudimentary services, which might involve commandeering public and private buildings and supplies to feed, house, or care for people and requiring that citizens, particularly those with special skills, assist in the provision of these services. Thus rights to property and against forced labor need to be qualified during emergencies.

Third, governments need powers to reestablish security. In a natural disaster this may be mainly a matter of preventing looting; in a war or insurrection it may also involve preparing defenses against additional attacks. To prepare such defense, people who are believed dangerous may be detained in circumstances where it is impossible to file charges or hold hearings quickly. Thus rights to due process need to be qualified during emergencies.

All the emergency powers just described are allowed to governments by the European Convention and the Covenant on Civil and Political Rights. Rights of movement, residence, property, freedom from forced labor, and due process are all subject to infringement or suspension during emergencies, provided that a necessity test can be satisfied. As we saw, the list of rights immune to suspension during emergencies is quite short. The question to be considered here is whether these documents give governments too much liberty to infringe and suspend rights. Should other rights be immune to suspension during emergencies?

Rights of Due Process

Here we are concerned with procedural safeguards that must be provided to people who are going to be deprived of their liberty or life. Article 6 of the European Convention, for example, requires that fair and public hearings be held within a reasonable time by an independent and impartial tribunal, that people accused of crimes be presumed innocent until proven guilty, and that people who are detained be informed of the charges against them, be given time to prepare a defense and assistance in doing so, and be able to cross-examine witnesses.

The importance of these safeguards of fairness to someone whose life or liberty is jeopardized is obvious, and it is further supported by the inclusion of the right against retroactive criminal laws among the nonderogable rights. But if the latter right is needed during emergencies to make life and liberty more secure against possible abuses of the criminal justice system, why are other due process rights not equally necessary?

The right of habeas corpus, which forces governments to file charges and produce evidence, does far more than the right against retroactive laws to keep governments from using their legal systems to kill or incarcerate their domestic enemies. Since the right of habeas corpus promotes fairness in a more effective way, why does it not have greater priority than the right against retroactive criminal laws? Similar questions can be asked about many due process rights.

The most plausible answer to these questions, I believe, lies in the high costs of complying with most due process rights during emergencies. As we saw earlier, a right that is less weighty in terms of consistency and importance may nevertheless have a higher priority than a right with much higher costs. Compare the right against retroactive criminal laws, which has low compliance costs, with the right of habeas corpus, which has high costs of compliance and implementation during emergencies.

The right of habeas corpus has a lower ratio of importance to cost than the right against retroactive criminal laws, which therefore has higher priority even though habeas corpus scores higher in terms of consistency and importance. This illustrates that it is possible to distinguish between these two rights in terms of cost and thus to provide a rationale for making the right against retroactive criminal laws nonderogable and the right of habeas corpus derogable. The difference in cost is found in the difficulty of filing charges quickly against all those detained during the stress and disorder of emergency situations.

But a third possibility should be explored, namely, making some aspects of due process nonderogable while incorporating exceptions that allow for faster and less formal procedures during emergencies. This possibility would have the advantage not only of providing clearer guidance but also of limiting the restrictions on due process that can be imposed in the name of national security.

Rights of Political Participation

A person who wanted to make political speeches or hold political rallies the day after a major earthquake or invasion could properly be told that the time for political discussion will come after the emergency is ended. Thus rights of freedom of speech and assembly might properly be suspended during a severe emergency, provided there were reason to believe that activities involving speech and assembly would do serious harm. But emergencies often continue for a long time, and important political issues must sometimes be decided during wars and insurrections.

The European Convention and the Covenant on Civil and Political Rights dealt with this matter simply by making rights of political participation derogable and subject to a necessity test. If it is plausible that restrictions on speech and assembly are necessary to deal effectively with the emergency, then such restrictions will be permissible as long as the necessity remains.

We should consider here not only rights of speech and assembly but also the lowlier right to petition government. The crude regulations and procedures characteristic of emergencies are likely to produce many legitimate requests for exceptions and remedies, and protection and provision for such petitions is highly desirable in terms of both importance and consistency. Further, such a right of petition does not seem unbearably expensive; indeed, it can be part of a useful feedback system for military and civilian commanders. Thus, if an emergency is to be extended, provision for freedom of petition seems to have both a high priority and a bearable cost. Such a right might include not only the freedom to file petitions but also a requirement that these petitions be given a reasonable amount of attention.

It is much harder to make a case for the nonderogability of speech and assembly, unless one qualifies them so severely that little is gained. Although these rights protect many of the same interests as freedom of conscience, they are more concerned with acting on one's beliefs. They protect people's coming together and voicing their views, and the consequences of these public and physical actions may be much greater, and potentially much more harmful, than those associated with merely holding certain beliefs. Thus it is not difficult to appeal to differences in costs to explain why freedom of conscience is, and freedoms of expression and assembly are not, appropriately made immune to derogation.

Overview

We have seen that the choice made by the authors of the European Convention and the International Covenant on Civil and Political Rights concerning which rights should be immune to derogation stands up fairly well to detailed philosophical investigation within this framework, provided one shares my willingness to give a substantial role to considerations of costs in determining the weight of a right. The major flaw discovered is the failure to give adequate protection during emergencies to rights of due process and the right to petition government.

9. Economic Rights

When economic rights are mentioned in the United States, liberals think of welfare rights and conservatives think of the rights of entrepreneurs. Each side is likely to deny the status of human right to what the other side takes as its paradigm. This polarity obviously makes meaningful dialogue between left and right on economic issues very difficult—in part because the broad and simplistic categories used in the debate tend to hide any common ground that might exist. This chapter offers a framework for economic rights that may facilitate more meaningful discussions of these issues. Questions about the affordability of welfare rights in less developed countries are also addressed.

One of the most important ways in which the list of human rights in the Universal Declaration of Human Rights differs from earlier lists is that it includes rights to economic benefits and services. The idea that all people have rights to provision for their physical needs has received widespread acceptance in this century. After World War II, liberals, democratic socialists, and communists all insisted that a concern for economic justice and progress should be part of the agenda of the United Nations Organization. The parties to the UN Charter (1945) committed themselves to promoting "higher standards of living, full employment, and conditions of economic and social progress and development." The Universal Declaration of Human Rights and the subsequent International Covenant on Social, Economic, and Cultural Rights asserted rights to an adequate standard of living, health services, education, support during disability and old age, employment and protection against unemployment, and limited working hours.[1]

1. Philosophical discussions of welfare rights include Peter G. Brown, Conrad Johnson, and Paul Vernier, eds., *Income Support: Conceptual and Policy Issues* (Totowa, N.J.: Rowman & Littlefield, 1981); Nicholas Rescher, *Welfare: The Social Issues in Philosophical Perspective* (Pittsburgh: University of Pittsburgh Press, 1972); and Carl Wellman, *Welfare Rights* (Totowa, N.J.: Rowman & Littlefield, 1982).

These rights to government-provided benefits were often rejected by conservatives who believed that the only genuine economic rights were rights to protections of property and the liberties involved in acquiring, holding, using, and transferring it. Advocates of this view often claimed that it made no sense to speak of human rights to supplies of economic goods.[2]

This chapter defends the view that some economic rights, including some welfare rights, are important moral or human rights. It also suggests that a plausible theory of economic rights requires two parts: one dealing with the production-related rights that conservatives emphasize and another dealing with the consumption-related rights, including welfare rights, that welfare-state liberals emphasize. I contend that a theory of economic rights cannot be plausible if it focuses entirely on the requirements of efficient production or—on the other side—entirely on the needs of those unable to provide for themselves.

An exclusive focus on production and property rights fails because not everyone can be productive and acquire property. There are always some people who because of age or disability are unable to engage effectively in production. An exclusive focus on welfare rights fails because not everyone can live on a supply that comes from others. Most people will need and want to provide for the physical needs of themselves and others by engaging in productive work.

The distinction between production-related and consumption-related rights is not the same as a distinction between negative and positive rights. Both production-related and consumption-related rights often require positive steps to make available goods needed for productive activity or consumption.

Human Rights and Economic Rights

To claim that any right is a human right is to assert that people have this right as persons rather than as citizens of a particular country, that this right exists and is valid as a weighty standard of moral criticism independently of its recognition or enforcement in

2. See, for example, Maurice Cranston, *What Are Human Rights?* (New York: Taplinger, 1973), 47–50, 65–72; Robert Nozick, *Anarchy, State, and Utopia* (New York: Basic Books, 1974), 26–42, 149–182.

particular countries, and that efforts to gain recognition for this right around the world are appropriate. The purpose of including economic rights among human rights is to identify areas within the economic sphere where powerful moral considerations provide fairly clear guidance for individual actions and social and political institutions. In these areas, basing economic decisions entirely on considerations of economic efficiency or personal gain is inappropriate. If common areas of this sort can be identified in all contemporary economic systems, we can formulate a set of international economic rights. When effectively implemented, economic rights also help to constitute a country's economic system.

Civil and political rights often have implications not only for political and legal practices but also for economic activities and arrangements. Rights against violence, torture, and murder, for example, restrain what one can do not only to gain or keep political office but also to gain possession of land or to obtain laborers. Many familiar rights not normally classified as economic rights have implications for what is permissible or required in the economic area. For example, the right to freedom of assembly would protect meetings to discuss plans for a new labor union, and a right to education is partly justified on the grounds that it contributes to the productivity necessary to satisfy human needs. But some rights are always primarily focused on economic matters, and my concern here will be with these.

Production-Related Rights

Production-related rights are directly concerned with people's access to production or with their roles, safety, and fair treatment in productive activities.

Rights to Liberty, Health, and Safety for People Engaged in Production

Workplaces have often been scenes of danger, cruelty, coercion, and unfair exploitation, and specific rights of workers have often been formulated in response to these conditions. For example, the International Covenant on Economic, Social, and Cultural Rights includes a right against discrimination, a right to free choice of employment, a right to education, a right to fair wages and equal pay for equal work, a right to safe and healthy working conditions, a right to reasonable limitations of working hours, and a right to form trade unions and engage in strikes. Because their justifications are fairly obvious, these sorts of economic rights tend to be among the least controversial. This is not to say, however, that there is no controversy about the proper scope of these rights, the role of consent in making risky jobs permissible, the methods of implementation, or the levels of enforcement.

Rights Needed for
Effective Production

Economic systems worldwide are as varied as political and legal systems, and economic rights should be formulated broadly enough to accommodate some of this variation. Just as due process rights allow some choice of methods for determining criminal guilt, economic rights should allow some choices among economic institutions. They should be stated in terms that would allow different kinds of economic systems to implement them in different ways. It may be helpful to begin by identifying, in broad terms, the activities and institutions required for production, some threats to them, and social and political means for responding to these threats. To find or make commodities with which to provision society, people must be able to

1. learn how to find or produce goods;

2. move in search of goods or the means to produce them;

3. plan and make arrangements for production, including arrangements for tools, materials, working groups, and labor supply (these arrangements may involve contracting, sharing, buying, borrowing, and renting);

4. engage individually or cooperatively in productive activities and associate with others for the purpose of doing so;

5. control the use and sale of resources and goods;

6. store resources and products to hedge against scarcity and famine; and

7. trade, sell, and ship goods.

All these are activities that people have usually managed to carry out to some degree; when survival is at stake, conditions do not have to be especially favorable for these activities to be possible.

One reason human rights exist in this area is that the ability to obtain the material necessities of life is part of each person's claim to life. Further, reasonable and workable economic arrangements are important from the perspective of human rights because of the role that national economies play in providing the resources and supporting the institutions needed to implement human rights.

Human actions or omissions can endanger practices essential to production in many ways. Such threats can come from both individuals and governments. They include theft and fraud; violations of agreements; conflicting claims to labor, resources, tools, and products; wasteful use of resources; and ignorance of effective production techniques. Threats from governments include all of the foregoing plus the use of government powers to enrich officials and their families, disruptive taxation and appropriations, and—from foreign governments—threats to capture or control rich territories and to divert their resources.

When implemented, production-related rights provide not only social guarantees for the availability of freedoms and benefits but also a fixed structure within which economic transactions—and thus markets—can arise. Economic rights prescribe who has the power and liberty to use, or sell, or give various items and thereby make possible actions central to economic activity. Production-related rights not only restrain and supplement market processes but also help to constitute those processes.

Property. Any economic system requires arrangements to assign the control and use of holdings and to protect these holdings against unauthorized appropriations. As Hobbes argued, a legally enforced system of property that includes protections against theft and methods for dealing with competing claims to goods is needed to make possible the productivity that civilization requires.[3] Some workable system of property arrangements is thus of great importance; to create and maintain it, both collective action and systems of rights are clearly necessary. Property rights of individuals or collectivities, along with associated rights to buy, sell, and contract, serve not only to distribute power and benefits but also to structure

---

3. Thomas Hobbes, *Leviathan* (1651), chap. 13. See also H. L. A. Hart, *The Concept of Law* (Oxford: Oxford University Press, 1961), 184–195.

the economic system by specifying which parties have the power
and liberty to sell or give away various items.

So far, the case for having some sort of system of property is not
very controversial; most disagreements arise when one considers
whether the inequalities that property often involves are morally acceptable and whether ownership of the means of production should
be individual or collective. The Universal Declaration sets out a
broad right to property; it says that everyone has the right to "own
property alone as well as in association with others" and forbids
arbitrary deprivations of property. No distinction is drawn between
personal and productive property. Neither the European Convention nor the Covenants contain clauses legitimating private property. Interestingly, however, both Covenants have identical clauses
protecting what might be called "national property rights," as article 1, Section 2—part of the self-determination sections—of each.
They state:

> All peoples may, for their own ends, freely dispose of their natural wealth
> and resources without prejudice to any obligations arising out of inter-
> national economic co-operation, based upon the principle of mutual
> benefit, and international law. In no case may a people be deprived of its
> own means of subsistence.

Personal property. By "personal property" I mean individual
ownership and control of possessions such as clothing, furniture,
food, writing materials, books, and artistic and religious objects.
Considerations of personal freedom provide strong reasons for instituting and protecting personal property. These reasons are related not to production but to the requirements of developing and
expressing one's own personality. Ownership of personal property is
a matter of personal liberty, not a production-related right. This personal right is clearly made more meaningful to the poor by welfare
rights; a minimum income ensures that people will have not merely
a right to hold personal property but also some property to hold.

Private productive property. The focus of controversies about
property is ownership of major means of production—land, facto-
ries, and equipment. A system of private ownership of land, fac-
tories, raw materials, and other goods used in production uses government power to confer on particular parties authority over the
use and disposition of some of these resources or goods and to make

others comply with that authority.[4] Private property serves to decentralize power by transferring a substantial measure of control over the use of productive resources from government to individuals or corporations.

When governments assign the control of productive resources to private owners, they typically enforce that control against unauthorized takeovers. It is clearly misleading to think of people with insufficient food as being "left alone" by a system of property. Such people are not left alone but rather are confronted by a system of property protections that prevents them from taking or using things needed for survival.[5]

There are many advantages to having a substantial private sector within a mixed national economy; it is not hard to make a case on utilitarian grounds for permitting regulated private ownership of productive resources. But I doubt whether a strong case can be made on grounds of basic liberty or fairness for a universal human right to own productive resources.

The claim to life, with its requirement that people have opportunities to obtain the necessities of life, does not necessarily require a right to ownership of productive property: socialist economies generally enable people to obtain the necessities of life. A country with a socialist economy may not reach the level of prosperity that some capitalist countries enjoy, but such a level is not necessary to satisfy basic rights. The right to life concerns results, not institutional specifics. The Universal Declaration sets out a right to "a standard of living adequate to . . . health and well-being" but does not specify the economic arrangements to make this possible. The Universal Declaration and its progeny prescribe neither capitalism nor socialism; they rather prescribe standards for what the economic system should do for people and not do *to* them.

4. On the concept of property and its moral status, see Lawrence C. Becker and Kenneth Kipnis, eds., *Property: Cases, Concepts, Critiques* (Englewood Cliffs, N.J.: Prentice-Hall, 1984); Lawrence C. Becker, *Property Rights* (London: Routledge & Kegan Paul, 1977); Adolf A. Berle, Jr., and Gardiner Means, *The Modern Corporation and Private Property* (New York: Harcourt Brace & World, 1968); Thomas C. Grey, "The Distintegration of Property," in *NOMOS XXII: Property* (New York: New York University Press, 1980), 69–85; Virginia Held, *Property, Profits, and Economic Justice* (Belmont, Calif.: Wadsworth, 1980); Charles A. Reich, "The New Property," *Yale Law Journal* 73 (1964): 733–787.

5. James Sterba, *The Demands of Justice* (Notre Dame, Ind.: Notre Dame University Press, 1980). See also introduction to Held, *Property, Profits, and Economic Justice*, 1–20.

Many believe that the liberty principle supports a human right to · own productive property. One might claim that freedoms to acquire, hold, and dispose of productive property are extremely valuable both intrinsically or instrumentally. The importance of these freedoms is presupposed by Nozick's claim that socialism is incompatible with freedom, that socialist societies would have to forbid capitalist acts between consenting adults.[6] It is certainly true that some forms of individual acquisition, ownership, and disposition of productive resources are generally prohibited by noncapitalist societies; the result is that individuals lack some freedoms they would have under capitalism. But merely pointing out this fact does not settle the matter, for one may have freedoms in noncapitalist societies that one lacks under capitalism. Private property gives individuals or corporations authority over resources, which can and typically will limit the freedom of nonowners to use the resource. In the case of land, nonowners are likely to be denied the liberty to enter, use, and occupy privately owned property. Nonowners are also likely to be denied the right to participate in decisions about the use of privately owned resources, even if these decisions affect them directly. Further, if most resources needed for production are privately owned, opportunities for self-employment are thereby restricted, and one may have to find employment with a property owner in order to have a means of life. This need for employment often gives employers power to restrict people's freedom.[7]

Capitalism and socialism, like all other forms of economic organization, allocate control over resources to some parties and hence reduce the liberty of others to use and benefit from those resources. The freedoms conferred by capitalism are not, in comparison with other alternatives, so obviously more important, or the restraints imposed so much less significant, that capitalism alone is compatible with people's claim to liberty.

An alternative line of argument here, which also seeks to show a connection between private ownership of productive resources and freedom, is based on the instrumental value of this freedom in preserving a system of freedoms and rights. It is often argued that it is

---

6. Nozick, *Anarchy, State, and Utopia,* 163.
7. On these points, see Cheyney C. Ryan, "Yours, Mine, and Ours: Property Rights and Individual Liberty," *Ethics* 87 (1977): 126–141; David Miller, "Constraints on Freedom," *Ethics* 94 (1983): 66–86; and Jeffrey H. Reiman, "The Fallacy of Libertarian Capitalism," *Ethics* 92 (1981): 85–95.

no accident that the highest levels of personal freedom and respect for rights are found in free-market economies that allow personal ownership of productive resources.[8] Spelled out in more detail, this argument asserts that private property in productive resources protects important freedoms against government tyranny by (1) decentralizing power and creating alternative sources of power and influence and (2) encouraging individual initiative in a way that supports self-government through democratic institutions.

A weak interpretation of this argument holds that private property in productive resources is a useful means to prevent some abuses of human rights. This claim is true enough, I think, but does not show that private property is an *essential* means—that we therefore *must* have it. Further, if private property is useful but not essential, then its costs can be considered in evaluating it. It is clear that the effects of private productive property on human rights are not entirely beneficial. For example, implementing democratic institutions may require curbing the ability of the wealthy to "buy" the political decisions they want.[9] Further, if a system of private property is justified on the grounds of promoting human rights, the property rights it creates cannot be absolute and unqualified. In order to finance the institutions needed to implement rights, national wealth has to be tapped through taxes or other means.

A strong interpretation holds that private ownership of many productive resources is an essential—that is, strictly necessary—means to a minimally acceptable level of respect for human rights. This interpretation suggests that without private property, sufficient decentralization of power and stimulation of private initiative cannot be obtained. This stronger version is much harder to defend. Alternative ways of decentralizing power—including economic power—are available. Control over many economic resources can be assigned to state and local governments or to organizations of workers. Institutions such as churches, labor unions, and consumer and professional organizations can be created or preserved as centers of nongovernmental power. Further, individual initiative can be stimulated by a variety of incentives for individual creativity and effort. Because these alternatives are available, I doubt whether one

8. See Milton Friedman, *Capitalism and Freedom* (Chicago: University of Chicago Press, 1962). For an attempt to evaluate this argument, see Charles Lindblom, *Politics and Markets* (New York: Basic Books, 1977).
9. See Lindblom, *Politics and Markets*, 161–233.

could show that private ownership of productive resources is an essential means of promoting respect for human rights.

An argument for a right to hold private productive property might also appeal to considerations of fairness, asserting that it is unfair to have people invest their energies in inventing or building a new productive resource only to have ownership of that resource taken over by a collectivity. However, this alleged unfairness can be avoided by a system that gives such people forms of compensation other than ownership of the product. Innovators might be given income, prizes, or other personal property as compensation for a valuable contribution. This argument and others that appeal to the fact that one has mixed one's labor with a product do not succeed in establishing an individual right to productive property.

The Right to Employment

In an urbanized and heavily populated world, most people cannot rely for subsistence on self-organized production that uses their own property. They must rather rely on employment in productive enterprises run by individuals, corporations, or government agencies. Claims to economic resources and rewards, which might once have been made as claims to land reform, are now often made as claims to employment. In most societies today there are sizable numbers of people who lack both access to productive resources and opportunities for employment. The economic systems of many countries persistently consign a significant percentage of the work force to unemployment.

Unemployment and underemployment are difficult problems for all societies, including socialist ones, but programs that help to deal with these problems are available. Large-scale work programs for young people that combine work experience and job training can be created. Tax and other incentives to hire more people can be given to industries. Economic policies designed to run the economy at a faster rate can be adopted. The most ambitious solution is for government to become the employer of last resort, guaranteeing a job to every person who is able to work, wants a job, and has been unable to find one.

Twentieth-century declarations of rights, unlike most of their eighteenth-century forebears, often include the right to employment, which contains not only a right against forced labor but also a right to be provided with a job. The parties to the Charter of the

United Nations committed themselves to promoting "higher standards of living, full employment, and conditions of economic and social progress and development." Article 23 of the Universal Declaration states that "everyone has the right to work, to free choice of employment, to just and favourable conditions of work and to protection against unemployment." Article 6 of the International Covenant on Economic, Social, and Cultural Rights defines some of the steps in realizing a right to employment: "The States Parties to the present Covenant recognize the right to work, which includes the right of everyone . . . to gain his living by work which he freely chooses or accepts, and will take appropriate steps to safeguard this right [including] technical and vocational guidance . . . programmes [and] policies and techniques to achieve steady economic, social and cultural development and full and productive employment."

Our understanding of the nature of a right to employment can be advanced by an analysis of employment. Three elements seem to be crucial here. First, one performs some activity, fulfills some responsibility, even if the responsibility is self-imposed. Second, this activity is believed to be productive, to make some contribution to the satisfaction of someone's desires. Third, the activity is performed in exchange for, or as a condition of getting, a significant amount of money or other goods. These three conditions distinguish employment from leisure activities and volunteer work, although the line of demarcation is not sharp.

A guarantee of employment is a guarantee of the availability of remunerative productive activity. What is at stake is the opportunity to participate in production and to share in its benefits. In a pre-agricultural society, the right to employment might cover permission to participate in hunting or gathering and to share in the resulting meals. As society and technology get more complicated, it becomes increasingly difficult for individuals to engage in production alone; modern production is apt to require cooperation within a large-scale enterprise. Hence in a modern society the main focus is on jobs that pay enough for a decent standard of living. A right to employment is not the same thing as a right to public assistance or to a minimum income. The availability of public assistance removes from the person who is unable to find a job the threat of starvation or of having to depend on friends or relatives for subsistence, but it does not generally provide the same financial and social benefits or support for self-respect that most jobs do. The assumption of those who emphasize the right to employment, socialists included, is that it is good for individuals and for society if people generally earn their own living through work. For this reason, employment is a production-related right rather than a consumption-related one.

The roots of the claim to employment. Remunerative work provides the most prevalent, reliable, and acceptable means of providing for one's survival needs, and most people have a strong interest in its availability. Many societies now provide subsistence payments to people independently of productive contribution, but unless the link between production and income is totally severed, productive work provides the main means of providing for one's survival and ability to carry out one's projects. The importance of the good of employment derives in part from its position as a central means to providing for one's fundamental interests.

A claim based on fairness may also be made. If unemployed people find that current economic arrangements allow them neither to appropriate property that will support their lives and liberty (because all valuable property is already owned by individuals or the state) nor to find paid employment, these economic arrangements in effect deny them the means of survival and self-development while providing access to those means to others who are similarly placed. A major burden is imposed on arbitrary grounds; in such circumstances the fairness principle will support a claim to employment.

I do not wish to preclude the possibility of future societies in which most work is done by automated machines and in which income is independent of work. If this sort of society emerges, and attitudes about what constitutes a meaningful existence change so that people's self-respect ceases to depend on remunerative employment, the case for a right to employment may lose its force.

Threats and the need for a right. Employment is often unavailable to those who want it badly; the availability of this basic good is often threatened by factors individuals cannot control. Employment is therefore something people have a claim to, but such a claim is not a political right; the justification of a right requires showing that this claim can be adequately satisfied only by a system that provides a guarantee of employment to every person who wants it, is unable to find it otherwise, and is able to work. In addition, such a guarantee must be affordable.

It has often been thought that people's claim to employment could be adequately satisfied through a policy of economic stimulation and full employment at the national level. Instead of controlling the economy so as to make jobs available or becoming the employer of last resort, a government may attempt to achieve full employment by choosing economic policies that cause the private sector to provide an adequate supply of jobs—stimulating the economy to make jobs plentiful. This method of dealing with unemployment, unlike the first, does not require that government control the economy. But it does require a substantial ability to influence it. Education and vocational guidance can be used to help fit people to the jobs available.

This is the approach that most nonsocialist countries have followed, but it has not been generally successful in eliminating unemployment or even in reducing it to a "frictional" level of four or five percent. In the United States, unemployment of blacks has often been in the vicinity of fifteen percent, and unemployment of young people in Europe is now recognized as a serious problem. When it is feasible, there is a strong case for a government-implemented right to employment that requires governments to become, if not the primary suppliers of jobs, at least the employers of last resort.

Feasibility.   Some Scandinavian countries have aggressively pursued full-employment policies and have been relatively successful in making jobs available to all who want them. Success has been accomplished without unbearable costs in economic disruption or inflation, and thus there are grounds for believing that the implementation of a political right to employment is now feasible in developed countries.[10] It may not be possible to eliminate unemployment to the last percentage point, but this no more defeats the right to employment than the impossibility of completely controlling crime defeats the right to security.

We should note, however, that increasing interdependence within the world economy now makes it more difficult, particularly in less developed countries, to insulate people from the effects of economic decisions made in other countries. Because of this interdependence, one who takes the right to employment—and other economic

10. See Bob Kuttner, "Sweden / Denmark: Trials of Two Welfare States," *The Atlantic* 252, no. 5 (November 1983): 14–22.

rights—seriously will need to consider international measures to re-structure and regulate the world economy.

Consumption-Related Rights

Economic rights are consumption-related if they serve to make possible the acquisition, use, and consumption of goods. The kinds of activities that may need protection here include shopping, purchasing, renting, borrowing, contracting, storing, using, sharing, giving, receiving, inhabiting, eating, and drinking. Those who dislike the images associated with the word "consumption" may prefer to think of these rights as use-related.

It is easy to think of ways in which these activities can be threatened. Supplies for consumption may be inadequate, or systems of distribution may be corrupt or otherwise inadequate, or people may lack money or other means to acquire needed goods. Knowledge of how to use available goods may also be lacking. Members of minority groups may be excluded from markets or sources of credit by systems of caste or discrimination.

One important role of welfare rights, in my opinion, is to ameliorate the disruptive effects of many modernizing economic activities and thus to make the imposition of desirable economic changes morally tolerable. In the absence of effective welfare rights, well-meant programs for economic development can be fatal to people whose subsistence depends on traditional economic arrangements if they cannot find a place within the new system.[11] An assurance of provision for the dislocated helps make morally tolerable the often disruptive adjustments that are needed to adapt production to social and technological changes. This is an important way in which production-related and consumption-related rights intertwine.

The International Covenant on Economic, Social, and Cultural Rights does not mention consumers, but it does formulate a number of norms in response to the threats mentioned. First, it roundly condemns discrimination in economic and other areas. Second, in article 11, it recognizes the importance of education not only in regard to production but also in regard to "disseminating knowledge of the principles of nutrition." Third, the same article addresses

11. See Henry Shue, *Basic Rights* (Princeton, N.J.: Princeton University Press, 1980), 35–64.

supplies of food by committing its signatories to improving "methods of production, conservation and distribution of food" and to "developing or reforming agrarian systems." And fourth, it responds to inadequate purchasing power by formulating a right of everyone to an adequate standard of living, as well as rights to social security, medical services, and education.

The Right to Adequate Nutrition

Consumption-related rights include welfare rights, that is, rights to the availability of goods needed for survival and a decent life. Although the human rights movement has declared a number of welfare rights, my focus here will be on just one, the right to adequate nutrition. I choose this right as my example because it is arguably the most important welfare right and because examination of it will raise issues about welfare rights generally.

Reflection on the idea of a right to adequate nutrition leads many people to ask whom it is addressed to and what it requires; they wonder whether it obligates them personally to feed the needy. The answer to these questions is that this right, like most others, has both individuals and governments as its addressees. Individuals have negative duties not to deprive people of needed food or of the liberty and means to grow or buy it. They have positive duties to make a contribution to society, to provide food for their children and other family members, and perhaps to engage in charitable endeavors to supply food to those in need.

Governments have the same negative duties as individuals, but their positive duties are stronger. They must provide protections against violations of the negative duties described above, arrange a system of food production and distribution that provides an adequate supply of food in all parts of the country, and ensure that all people have the ability to draw from this supply enough food to provide adequate nutrition. This ability can be conferred by remunerative employment, by income grants, price subsidies, or direct distributions of food.

A right to adequate nutrition does not require that governments nationalize and collectivize agriculture or that they become the main suppliers of food. It does require that governments regulate agricultural and economic systems so that enough food for all is grown or imported and so that all people can get what they need. The right to adequate nutrition both grounds and limits other economic rights. Where weather is a large variable in a country's ability to feed itself, stored food reserves may be necessary to prevent famine from crop failures or soaring prices. In the area of distribution, implementation of this right will require that food, or the money to buy it, be distributed in a manner that enables everyone to get the food they need. Most people, of course, will get their food, or the means to buy it, through work. But programs to provide food to those unable to find or perform remunerative work will also be needed; these might include meal programs for children and the elderly, food stamps, or guarantees of a minimum income.

One might think that the right to adequate nutrition could be rendered unnecessary if a right to employment or a right to a decent income were implemented. But a right to employment would not help people unable to work, and a right to a decent income, while solving the problem of purchasing power, would not necessarily solve problems of food production and distribution. Effective production often must be facilitated by land reform, water projects, and programs of agricultural research, development, and education. The right to adequate nutrition has both negative and positive elements. As with other economic rights, measures to implement it are likely to include noninvasion, protection, facilitation, and provision.

The claim to food and its basis. The first step in justifying a right to adequate nutrition is to show the great importance of what is at stake. This step is simple, as food is essential to people's ability to live, function, and flourish: without it, interests in life, health, and liberty are endangered and severe pain and death are inevitable. The connection is direct and obvious (something that is not always true with other rights), and thus there is no doubt that food is a basic good. When a good of such importance is at stake, people have a moral claim on others to refrain from depriving them of it and to render assistance when any are unable to obtain or protect the good by their own efforts.

Threats and the necessity of a right to food. The next step is to show that a political guarantee of the availability of food is necessary. Some very important goods, such as air, do not require social or political provision. But food is not like air; without one's own efforts and the help of others, it will often not be available. A number of threats to the production and consumption of food have already been identified, including inadequate supplies, inadequate purchasing power, and disruptions of traditional food systems by changing economic patterns. A political guarantee of adequate nutrition will have to cover more than the liberties to seek and consume food; even when these liberties are protected some people— the very young, the very old, the disabled, or the handicapped —will often have insufficient income to buy their own food.[12]

One might hold, however, that an adequate supply of food for all can be secured by a system that provides (1) government protections against actions by individuals or government officials that would deprive people of their own supplies of food, (2) government protections of the liberties needed to find and buy food, and (3) social rather than governmental provision for the needy. Social provision might include moral duties of family members to provide for each other, particularly for those unable to support themselves. It might also include moral duties of charity to provide food to people who are starving or malnourished, when one can do so without severe hardship to oneself or one's family. This duty might fall not only on individuals but also on community organizations. Such social guarantees are the traditional ways of providing for the nutritional needs of children, the ill, the handicapped, and the aged.

Even where there is a socially recognized moral duty to support family members and hungry neighbors, such a duty is often ignored, and social pressure often provides inadequate support for compliance. Duties of charity always give donors some discretion concerning their gifts—if not discretion about when or to whom they will give, then at least about how much they will give. Charity is likely to be ineffective in providing for people who do not happen to be in the vicinity of a suitable donor. Many of those who are unable to get food for themselves have no families, or no family members who are willing and able to fulfill their moral duties of support. Systems of charity tend to provide only spotty coverage; their capacities are generally insufficient to provide for everyone in need.

Because of these inadequacies of charitable and family support systems, there are strong reasons for developing government relief or welfare to supplement family support and charitable giving. Early measures of this sort involved poorhouses and other forms of

---

12. For a study of famines arguing that absolute shortages of food are seldom their cause, see Amartya Sen, *Poverty and Famines: An Essay on Entitlement and Deprivation* (Oxford: Clarendon Press, 1981).

public relief. When the welfare state emerged—with an income tax and other mechanisms to support it—it became possible for government to ensure adequate nutrition for all.

Feasibility. Government guarantees of adequate nutrition are clearly feasible in the developed countries; in fact, such guarantees are in force—with varying degrees of effectiveness and comprehensiveness—in all the developed countries. Feasibility in less developed countries is another matter.

Ranking Rights in Less Developed Countries

This section addresses the question of whether welfare rights are of high enough priority to merit implementation when a country's resources are very limited. One of the largest barriers to the acceptance of welfare rights as universal human rights is the belief that they are simply too expensive for many countries today. To simplify the discussion, I will continue to focus on just one of them, the right to food.

Suppose that the people of a less developed country are deciding which rights to respect and implement when it is clear that the resources the government has or can acquire without great disruption are insufficient to implement all the rights found in the Universal Declaration. Revolution or deep structural changes may offer a long-term solution, but in the shorter term such changes are usually disruptive to the economy and require major expenditures to fight those who would restore the old order. This is the situation, broadly speaking, that many countries are in today. These countries face severe limits not just of financial resources but also of trained personnel and of effective government institutions.

Respecting and implementing human rights is costly for governments, which must accept substantial restrictions on their resources of power and money. Rights that impose restraints on actions—such as a right against torture—often rule out tactics that are cheap and dirty and thus require more costly or difficult tactics to be used. Rights that require the provision of protections will necessitate an expensive police and legal system. Rights that ensure the availability of food or other benefits will obviously necessitate the creation of expensive service agencies and the distribution of scarce commodities.

Deliberation about the problem of implementing rights under scarcity can be thought of as a process of deciding which internationally recognized human rights should be included in a national constitution and implemented through legislation. If we think of the Universal Declaration as providing an international model for a constitutional bill of rights, we can imagine people arguing about which of the rights in the Declaration to include in or exclude from their own country's bill of rights. In considering such a decision we can use the three tests that were introduced in chapter 7.

The Consistency Test

This test asks whether the particular right (R1) whose weight is under discussion is practically necessary to upholding other rights. If other rights cannot be upheld without upholding R1, then R1 will acquire whatever weight the other rights have in addition to its own inherent importance. In the context of cutbacks in rights, the consistency test asks whether it is possible to cut R1 without undermining other rights.

The test can consider dependency relations both with rights that already exist and with future rights. In regard to future rights, one can ask whether implementing a particular right will over time enhance the ability to implement other important but currently unaffordable rights, and whether cutting a right will undermine over time the ability to implement those rights. Creating an effective right to education now, for example, may eventually lead to greater productivity and political awareness, which will in turn make it possible to implement other rights.

To officials who want to cut or trim some human rights to stay within their resources of power and money, the test of practical consistency is a mixed blessing. On the one hand it reduces the number of possible cuts and thus makes the task easier. On the other hand it may mean they cannot implement any rights at all unless they can implement a large set of them. Consistency sets a high threshold for creating a legal and political system that implements any rights at all. Some countries may therefore find that no system of rights for everyone is affordable—and thus that no rights can be implemented at present or at least that none can be implemented in all parts of the country. The inequalities involved in excluding altogether some regions or groups from the protections provided by rights may be unavoidable in many poor countries if the interdependencies between rights are very extensive.

The Importance Test

Once we have identified cuts that seem to leave systems of rights that are practically consistent, the next test is to rank the cuts by the importance of the rights they retain. This test judges the overall importance of a right according to the values it protects, the vulnerability of those values to frequent threats, and the effectiveness of the protections that rights provide. One right is of greater overall importance than another if it is more essential to the protection of central but vulnerable elements of life, freedom, or fairness.

Cost Efficiency

This criterion instructs that among consistent cuts that save many of the most important rights, one should choose to preserve those important rights with the lowest costs. Above a certain threshold of importance, rights should be chosen for retention—assuming consistency—in accordance with the ratio of importance to cost.

Before trying to apply these tests to welfare rights, two oversimplifications need to be corrected. One is the idea that rights are indivisible and must be either wholly cut or wholly kept. In fact, however, the exact elements that constitute an implemented right are appropriately variable in countries with different sorts of problems and different levels of resources. Under scarcity, a country has the option not only of axing rights but also of pruning them—that is, removing some of their more expensive elements while trying to retain enough of their substance to make them meaningful. For example, a right against violent crimes might continue to imply duties to refrain from these crimes and a few measures to punish violations of these duties, while losing some of its more expensive implementing measures, such as regular police patrols to prevent the occurrence of crimes.

The second oversimplification involves ignoring the possibility of shifting from political to social provision of benefits and protections. Under scarcity, people who are unable to provide for themselves may have to rely on their families and communities for provision of food and other necessities. This shift does not avoid the costs of provision—the expense is merely moved from government to families and communities—but it may avoid the overhead costs of the service institutions that systems of government provision require.

I now want to apply these criteria to two possible strategies for implementing human rights in very poor countries. Both strategies are moderate; there are other, more extreme, positions that I discard, one of which is the Nozickean view that all human rights and economic rights are merely side constraints.[13] In this view, the entire role of economic rights is to identify things that it is never permissible to do. Implementation merely requires a commitment to comply with negative duties; not even protection is required. This position would leave people in a Lockean state of nature—or a version of it involving all sorts of lingering inequalities and injustices—and thus exposed to all the inconveniences of such a state pointed out by Locke.

The other extreme position, taken by some communists and authoritarians, is that it is permissible to sacrifice virtually any civil and political right to promote economic rights or goals. I do not take this option seriously because I think that many civil and political rights, particularly those that protect life and security, are just as important as the right to food—certainly too important to ignore.

The first strategy that I want to discuss proposes to keep a full range of rights but to prune the provision of all benefits except protection. The only positive legal or political duties remaining would be duties to provide protection against violations of negative duties. Governments would comply with human rights in their actions and policies and provide protections through law for people's liberty and security against the main public and private threats to them. Such compliance would require the maintenance of legal and governmental institutions, the role of which would be restricted to protecting rights and maintaining a structure of liberty in which production and consumption could occur. Welfare rights against government would effectively be axed by this strategy, but rights to acquire, use, and consume property could be retained and protected. The axing of all forms of government welfare programs would mean that food programs and educational opportunities would not be available from government. Education, like other welfare benefits, would have to be paid for by oneself, one's family, or through charity.

This strategy strikes me as the most minimal approach that is plausible. It says that even under severe scarcity people still owe one

13. Nozick, *Anarchy, State, and Utopia*, 26–42, 149–183.

another respect for their rights and significant public protections for those rights. It may be that the poorest countries today cannot do any more to implement human rights than this strategy proposes—and will be lucky if they can do this much effectively. Further, this strategy will probably not attract much criticism from other countries. If a government has a good record of not invading people's rights, and if it provides rudimentary protections through law against invasions of rights, it is not likely to be criticized by human rights organizations—even if many of its people are going uneducated or hungry.

But this strategy does have some severe drawbacks. To see these clearly, it will be helpful to apply the three-test method. The first question to ask is whether this proposal results in a system of rights that is practically consistent. Are items missing whose absence will undermine the effective protection of items that are retained? For example, does the absence of programs to provide food, education, and economic opportunities to people who cannot otherwise get them mean that it will be impossible to protect their other human rights? Clearly such people can benefit from laws providing protections against crime and violence. That these protections may not be as valuable to them as to those who are better off does not mean that such protections will have no value whatever. Even the very poor can benefit from laws that deter invasions of their lives, liberties, and meager possessions. But this strategy allows ignorance and incapacities that seriously undermine some people's ability to know what they are permitted to do, when they are entitled to call for protection, when to take steps to protect themselves, and when to flee.

For example, an uneducated peasant whose labor and crops are seldom sufficient to provide adequate nutrition for himself and his family, and who is ignorant of the workings of the legal system, is unlikely to be able to use law to protect himself against fraud by those who purchase his products, or against extortion by local officials. This case illustrates how the absence of measures to make food and education available to all will partially undermine the possibility of fully protecting the rights of all—and will also possibly undermine or reduce the value of having other rights.

Another aspect of consistency is laying a foundation for implementation of rights in the future. A country that allows many of its children to be malnourished, and thus to suffer permanent physical and mental damage, will be handicapped in its efforts to promote productivity and to create effective political and legal institutions.

For these reasons, the strategy under discussion is clearly inconsistent in practice with the *full* protection of the human rights of all people both now and in the future.

The second test is concerned with whether the most inherently important rights have been preserved by this strategy. Here we need to ask whether all protections are more important than all provisions. They are not. The importance to a decent life of being generally able to procure necessities, and thus avoiding malnutrition and starvation, is surely as great as that of protection against severe crimes, and surely greater than that of protections against minor crimes.

The third test is that of cost efficiency. It may be argued that this test points in a different direction from the other two. One may allow that the availability of food is a matter of the highest importance to a person but claim that a right to a supply of food from government is so expensive to implement that many other rights will have higher priorities once cost is factored in. Suppose, for example, that protections of life and health against starvation and malnutrition have roughly the same intrinsic importance as protections against violence but that the former are much less expensive than the latter. The right to protection against violence would then be more cost-effective than the right to food and hence of higher priority in countries that cannot afford both.

Although this argument is logically valid, I doubt whether its premise about cost is true; that is, I doubt whether it is very much more expensive to create food programs to prevent starvation and malnutrition than it is to implement effective protections against violence. In order to do the latter one needs a system using police, lawmakers, judges, lawyers, and prisons, which is expensive to create, staff, and maintain. The exact level of expenditure will depend on, among other things, the degree of voluntary compliance with the law. The more crimes there are to block, prosecute, or punish, the higher the costs will be.

The situation in regard to government provision of food to those unable to get it for themselves or from their families is closely analogous. A welfare bureaucracy will need to be created and staff employed. Needy individuals will have to be identified and food delivered to them. The exact level of expenditure required will depend on how many people continue to rely on themselves or their families instead of turning to government for assistance.

The personnel costs of a food program of this rudimentary sort are probably a good deal lower than those of a criminal justice system, for it is far easier and cheaper to give people food than to provide, for example, a fair trial. The cost of supplies, however, will probably be higher for the food program. But overall, it is not obvious that a targeted program of nutritional assistance is much more expensive than a criminal justice system. In support of the proposition that a program of food subsidies is affordable for countries such as India or Pakistan, Amartya Sen has noted that Sri Lanka, which is at roughly the same economic level, has long had such programs and that they cost no more than five percent of its gross national product.[14]

These criticisms of the first strategy suggest an alternative: to devote less to protection against violence and provide a highly targeted program of nutritional assistance. This strategy will involve provision of food during emergency periods (e.g., famines or natural disasters) and to people who are routinely unable to provide for themselves and who have no family to aid them.

Although implementation of such a right is no substitute for effective programs of food self-sufficiency and economic development, it is also important to realize that such programs do not make this right unnecessary. I have tried to argue rather that it is both generally affordable and of highest priority. If I am right, there is at least one welfare right of sufficient priority to be operative in the entire world today.

Overview

My argument here has been that an adequate conception of economic life requires us to recognize two kinds of economic rights: production-related rights and consumption-related rights. Based on this argument, neither an account of property rights nor a theory of welfare rights alone can provide an adequate normative framework for economic policy. A more complex framework is needed, and this framework is already implicit in contemporary human rights documents.

14. Amartya Sen, "How Is India Doing?" *New York Review of Books* 29, no. 20 (December 16, 1982), 41–45.

10. Conclusion: Prospects for Human Rights

If the acceptance of human rights is to be maintained and increased around the world in the years ahead, the plausibility of the social and political vision they convey will be crucial. The Universal Declaration's vision of societies without oppression or unmet basic needs has proved attractive over the last several decades. The Declaration's rights are demanding, however, and they raise questions of coherence and feasibility. These rights can conflict with each other, and complying with all of them is a difficult matter in many countries. They both limit the freedom of governments to proceed as they wish and entail substantial implementation costs.

This book has argued that most of the content of the Universal Declaration is defensible and that it is not difficult to deal with the rest through axing and pruning. In general, I have not regarded the texts of the Universal Declaration and subsequent human rights documents as sacrosanct; it is unlikely that anyone today would agree with every clause of a document formulated almost forty years ago by a diverse group of international lawyers and diplomats. The Universal Declaration needs critical evaluation and interpretation. I submit, however, that abandoning it is not warranted. To summarize and bring together the various strands of my argument, I will respond to a number of critical questions about human rights.

Is Talk About Human Rights Just Empty Rhetoric?

Because rights are powerful considerations, the language of rights is attractive to people engaging in political argument. Many have worried that the extensive use of the concept of rights in exaggerated political rhetoric would soon destroy the concept's usefulness. But susceptibility to exaggeration and distortion is a frailty found in all normative concepts, not just the concept of rights. For example, repressive regimes on both the left and the right have frequently offered reinterpretations of the idea of democracy to support their practices. The concept of democracy, like most normative concepts, is vague, but it is far from useless. Vagueness is not emptiness, and it is possible to resist wholesale extensions of important concepts. Perhaps inflationary rights rhetoric has now passed its peak.[1]

Viewing human rights as protections of the minimal conditions of a decent life helps one resist exaggerations. A decent life is a modest standard; it does not require everything that could contribute to making people's lives good or excellent. Other concepts are available for talking about the requirements of excellence; the concept of human rights does not need to encompass every important dimension of social and political criticism.

Another way to resist exaggerated claims about rights is to view them as entitlements-plus. In this view, defending a right to something requires more than merely showing the great importance of people's having access to that thing; it also requires showing a feasible and morally acceptable way of imposing duties and constructing institutions that will make it possible to supply that thing— whether it is a protection, a service, or a provision—to everyone. A broad notion of feasibility must restrain the formulation and implementation of specific human rights. In estimating feasibility, not all existing economic relations need be taken as given; indeed, implementing human rights often requires changes in economic structures. When an internationally recognized human right is implemented at the national level, costs need to be considered in deciding how extensive the scope of the associated legal right should be and what sorts of enforcement or other forms of support should be provided for it. Implementing rights is usually not an all-or-nothing affair; when resources are scarce, pruning a right is often an attractive alternative to axing it.

Much talk about rights is empty rhetoric, but only a few clauses of the Universal Declaration are vulnerable to this charge. Its excesses can be dealt with by pruning a number of rights, axing a few, and recognizing that the scope of its rights will have to be adjusted at the implementation stage by reference to national resources.

1. See Philip Alston, "Conjuring Up New Human Rights: A Proposal for Quality Control," *American Journal of International Law* 78 (1984): 607–621.

Are Legal Rights
the Only Genuine Rights?

Rights are complex and high-priority norms with holders, addressees, conditions of possession, scopes, and weights. Because of their mandatory character, rights are the sorts of things that can be demanded or claimed by their holders and others. Fully specified rights are capable of giving very precise guidance to behavior; this capacity makes them very useful in law and well suited to legal enforcement.

Because of the importance of rights in law, many people take legal rights as their paradigms of rights. If legal rights provide the paradigm, moral rights may be thought of as phony rights—as lacking key features that real rights have. Prior to the implementation of human rights in international law, this view would have led to their rejection. Today, however, the recognition of human rights in international law, as well as in the constitutions and statutes of many countries, makes it possible for those who deny the existence of nonlegal rights to endorse human rights as rights.

This view allows one to explain the existence of human rights by saying that they exist as norms of domestic or international law. It does not, however, preserve the universality of human rights, because some countries have neither ratified international human rights treaties nor implemented human rights in domestic law. This problem is not merely academic; some of the countries who have refused to accept human rights treaties are currently engaged in serious violations of human rights. To account for the universality of human rights, I have suggested that we view them as existing— most fundamentally—as norms within justified moralities. This commits one not only to the view that rights can exist as moral norms but also to the view that there is such a thing as a justified morality.

We saw in chapter 2 that theorists have equated rights with entitlements, with entitlements plus duties, and with legally implemented entitlements. I argued that legal recognition and implementation mark an important difference among rights, but not a difference of such overwhelming importance as to require us to establish entirely different categories for legal and nonlegal norms. Important differences can exist within a single generic category without it being imperative to divide it into two or more distinct categories.

The claim that nonlegal rights are phony rights is a recommendation for a division, but such a division would obscure important similarities among rights of different kinds and restrict current usage to disadvantage people seeking to criticize oppressive governments.

Moral rights can exist either as norms of existing moralities or as norms of justified moralities. Epistemologically, the idea of a justified morality requires only that we admit a human capacity to recognize moral progress, that is, to know that there are good reasons for changing an existing morality (or for keeping something that is already part of an existing morality). Human rights are norms that we have good reasons for adding to, or retaining in, existing moralities. Human rights can exist, therefore, in actual and justified moralities and in national and international legal systems. Legal enforcement is often essential to the effectiveness of human rights, but such enforcement is not essential to their existence.

Can Human Rights Be Justified?

Today's specific human rights are descendents of, but different from, the broad natural rights of the eighteenth century. Not only are contemporary human rights international in scope; they are more egalitarian and less individualistic as well. They function as middle-level norms, derived from more basic and abstract moral and political considerations. They identify fairly specific areas in which powerful considerations demand of both individuals and social-political institutions that each person be assured at least a minimally good life.

Defending this conception of human rights requires at least two steps. One involves arguing that there are defensible abstract grounds for human rights. The second step involves showing that these abstract grounds support specific human rights such as the right to a fair trial or a right to freedom of assembly.

The first step was addressed in chapter 5, where I argued that human rights can be defended from several starting points. From the perspective of individual prudence, some protections for one's fundamental interests—such as life and liberty—are attractive if their costs are not too high. This mode of reasoning may not reach universal human rights, but it gets one somewhere in the vicinity. From the moral point of view, providing protections for each person's most fundamental interests is a central concern. Such protections are best provided, even at an abstract level, by an alternative to utilitarianism that gives each person firm moral claims to life, liberty, and fair treatment.

The second step—showing that these abstract considerations support specific human rights—was addressed in chapter 6. There I argued that the derivation of a specific political right required one to satisfy four tests. The first requires one to show that the specific right protects something of great importance. I interpreted this test by reference to abstract moral claims to life, liberty, and fair treatment. The next two tests involve showing that a specific political right, rather than some weaker norm, is necessary to the protection of the important interest against some substantial threat. The final test involves showing that a specific political right is feasible, compatible with other important moral principles, and affordable in most countries. In chapter 6 I illustrated how rights against torture, to a fair trial in criminal cases, and against discrimination can pass these four tests.

Do Human Rights Include Welfare Rights?

A distinctive and often controversial feature of the contemporary conception of human rights is that they include welfare or subsistence rights. The general idea, as I have interpreted it, is that people have a strong moral claim to assistance, when needed, in obtaining the material conditions of a decent life. I argued that welfare rights respond to powerful moral claims. The claim to have a life, which grounds the right to food, is the same claim that grounds the right against murder. I also showed that welfare rights are not unique in having large costs and in requiring substantial government activity for their implementation. Rights to due process in criminal proceedings or to protections against racial discrimination have similar costs.

Welfare rights are not the only economic rights. A conception of economic rights should include both production-related and consumption-related rights. Welfare rights alone fail to protect the productive activities that generate the resources needed to implement welfare and other rights, and production-related rights alone provide no response to the claims of those unable to produce.

Can Human Rights
Guide Behavior?

The language of rights is capable of giving precise guidance to addressees, but international human rights must be formulated broadly enough to cover different political and economic systems around the world. Because of this need, the rights of the Universal Declaration are not as specific as they could be. In particular, their weights in competition with each other and with other considerations were left unspecified.

The failure to assign weights to rights was partially remedied in the European Convention and the Covenant on Civil and Political Rights by provisions that make some rights immune to derogation during national emergencies. Investigation of this matter in chapter 8 revealed that the list of rights chosen for immunity could stand up to intellectual scrutiny. However, one important omission was found: rights to due process in criminal proceedings should also have been given this near-absolute status.

Another weakness of the Declaration is that it offers little guidance to very poor countries on how they should respond to specific human rights. Subsequent documents have not improved on this vagueness. In chapter 9, I suggested several tests that could be used in trying to decide which rights to cut or prune under extreme scarcity. First was the consistency test, which asks whether proposed cuts avoid undermining rights that are retained. The second test was importance, which asks whether proposed cuts will prune or eliminate rights that are less important than those being retained. One right is more important than another if it is more essential to the effective protection of core parts of fundamental moral claims. The third test was cost efficiency, which weighs importance against cost. If two rights are of equal importance, and the former is far less costly to comply with and to implement, then the former will have higher priority than the latter.

The scopes of human rights often provide fairly clear guidance to their addressees but usually do not specify what victims of violations may do to defend themselves, how persons other than the addressees should respond to violations, or how governments should respond to violations in other countries. In deciding what should be done in these instances, considerations about relevant rights play a central but partial role. These decisions require looking back to the abstract moral considerations that underlie specific human rights, sideways to moral considerations other than human rights, and forward to the likely consequences of actions and policies designed to promote respect for human rights. Human rights provide guidance to thoughtful policy deliberation, but they are not a substitute for it.

Will Human Rights Endure?

The concept of human rights came into widespread use around the world rather rapidly and could conceivably fade just as quickly. The question posed is whether attention to human rights within domestic and international politics is merely a transient phenomenon, a fad, without deep and enduring roots.

Human rights will be appealed to in criticizing governments if people accept human rights as appropriate standards for this purpose and if there is something in the behavior of governments that calls for criticism. In regard to this last condition, at least, we need not fear that the future will provide no role for human rights. Rising expectations, the difficulties of economic development, ethnic and religious conflicts, and corruption in government all increase the likelihood of rights violations and of the emergence of repressive regimes. But the continued—and increased—acceptance of human rights as reasonable standards for criticizing social and political institutions around the world is much more problematic.

A way of projecting continued international concern for human rights can be found in an examination of the forces that have propelled this concern to its current prominence. These forces or conditions are relatively stable and thus are likely to persist into the future.

The rise of human rights to international prominence would not have happened when it did without the defeat in World War II of those who stood for racial and ethnic inequality. The Allied victory led to the creation within the United Nations and the Council of Europe of international institutions to promote and protect human rights across international boundaries. Although the conflicts between the Allies that grew into the Cold War cannot be ignored in a discussion of the future of human rights, they should not lead us to forget that the victors in World War II believed broadly in human equality rather than in the innate inferiority of some groups.

A second factor in the rise of concern for human rights at the international level is greater public awareness of the horrors of modern war, genocide, and large-scale oppression. With contemporary weapons and modes of bureaucratic organization, most governments are capable of massive harm and destruction. People are aware of these horrors because of the great flow of information through the media. The atrocities of World War II, Korea, and Vietnam have forced us to recognize the awesome destruction that it is now possible for one country to inflict on another—and for a government to inflict on its people. The massacres in, for example, Indonesia, Chile, Uganda, and Cambodia carry the same message. In addition, people have higher expectations of what their lives will bring and thus are less inclined to accept the inevitability of war and oppression. The result has been an attempt to moralize politics in a new way by using international standards and institutions to prevent major wars and to restrain oppression.

Third, human rights have been institutionalized in international law through covenants accepted by countries in many parts of the world, thereby mitigating many of the problems of standards that exist only within natural law or justified moralities. International recognition of human rights has reduced the plausibility of the excuse, often given by rights violators, that they are merely Western ideas with little relevance elsewhere. Further, serious problems within a country are now more likely to be diagnosed in terms of human rights because human rights standards are available within international law and because human rights commissions and courts exist to investigate complaints and interpret these standards.

A fourth factor in the development of the human rights vocabulary is the emergence of groups who are professionally concerned to promote human rights, both in governmental organizations such as the United Nations and the Council of Europe and in nongovernmental organizations such as Amnesty International. For these people, human rights standards are professional tools for daily use. Their actions on behalf of human rights are relatively invulnerable to the fluctuations of public enthusiasm, and their uses of the rights vocabulary help provide it with a stable core.

All of these factors are likely to persist, and they therefore provide some basis for expecting the continued prominence of the idea of human rights in political discourse. This does not mean, however, that the task of developing human rights standards is finished. More theoretical work is needed, and standards should be reformulated in the light of this work. Beyond that, we need continued efforts to promote compliance with these standards. Making sense of human rights is just the beginning.

Appendix

UNIVERSAL DECLARATION OF HUMAN RIGHTS, 1948

Preamble

Whereas recognition of the inherent dignity and of the equal and inalienable rights of all members of the human family is the foundation of freedom, justice and peace in the world,

Whereas disregard and contempt for human rights have resulted in barbarous acts which have outraged the conscience of mankind, and the advent of a world in which human beings shall enjoy freedom of speech and belief and freedom from fear and want has been proclaimed as the highest aspiration of the common people,

Whereas it is essential, if man is not to be compelled to have recourse, as a last resort, to rebellion against tyranny and oppression, that human rights should be protected by the rule of law,

Whereas it is essential to promote the development of friendly relations between nations,

Whereas the peoples of the United Nations have in the Charter reaffirmed their faith in fundamental human rights, in the dignity and worth of the human person and in the equal rights of men and women and have determined to promote social progress and better standards of life in larger freedom,

Whereas Member States have pledged themselves to achieve, in cooperation with the United Nations, the promotion of universal respect for and observance of human rights and fundamental freedoms.

Whereas a common understanding of these rights and freedoms is of the greatest importance for the full realization of this pledge.

Now, Therefore,

The General Assembly

proclaims

This universal declaration of human rights as a common standard of achievement for all peoples and all nations, to the end that every individual and every organ of society, keeping this Declaration constantly in mind, shall strive by teaching and education to promote respect for these rights and freedoms and by progressive measures, national and international, to secure their universal and effective recognition and observance, both among the peoples of Member States themselves and among the peoples of territories under their jurisdiction.

ARTICLE 1

All human beings are born free and equal in dignity and rights. They are endowed with reason and conscience and should act towards one another in a spirit of brotherhood.

ARTICLE 2

Everyone is entitled to all the rights and freedoms set forth in this Declaration, without distinction of any kind, such as race, colour, sex, language, religion, political or other opinion, national or social origin, property, birth or other status.

Furthermore, no distinction shall be made on the basis of the political, jurisdictional or international status of the country or territory to which a person belongs, whether it be independent, trust, non-self-governing or under any other limitation of sovereignty.

ARTICLE 3

Everyone has the right to life, liberty and security of person.

ARTICLE 4

No one shall be held in slavery or servitude; slavery and the slave trade shall be prohibited in all their forms.

ARTICLE 5

No one shall be subjected to torture or to cruel, inhuman or degrading treatment or punishment.

ARTICLE 6

Everyone has the right to recognition everywhere as a person before the law.

ARTICLE 7

All are equal before the law and are entitled without any discrimination to equal protection of the law. All are entitled to equal protection against any discrimination in violation of this Declaration and against any incitement to such discrimination.

ARTICLE 8

Everyone has the right to an effective remedy by the competent national tribunals for acts violating the fundamental rights granted him by the constitution or by law.

ARTICLE 9

No one shall be subjected to arbitrary arrest, detention or exile.

ARTICLE 10

Everyone is entitled in full equality to a fair and public hearing by an independent and impartial tribunal, in the determination of his rights and obligations and of any criminal charge against him.

ARTICLE 11

1. Everyone charged with a penal offence has the right to be presumed innocent until proved guilty according to law in a public trial at which he has had all the guarantees necessary for his defence.

2. No one shall be held guilty of any penal offence on account of any act or omission which did not constitute a penal offence, under national or international law, at the time when it was committed. Nor shall a heavier penalty be imposed than the one that was applicable at the time the penal offence was committed.

ARTICLE 12

No one shall be subjected to arbitrary interference with his privacy, family, home or correspondence, nor to attacks upon his honour and reputation. Everyone has the right to the protection of the law against such interference or attacks.

ARTICLE 13

1. Everyone has the right to freedom of movement and residence within the borders of each state.

2. Everyone has the right to leave any country, including his own, and to return to his country.

ARTICLE 14

1. Everyone has the right to seek and to enjoy in other countries asylum from persecution.

2. This right may not be invoked in the case of prosecutions genuinely arising from non-political crimes or from acts contrary to the purposes and principles of the United Nations.

ARTICLE 15

1. Everyone has the right to a nationality.

2. No one shall be arbitrarily deprived of his nationality nor denied the right to change his nationality.

ARTICLE 16

1. Men and women of full age, without any limitation due to race, nationality or religion, have the right to marry and to found a family. They are entitled to equal rights as to marriage, during marriage and at its dissolution.

2. Marriage shall be entered into only with the free and full consent of the intending spouses.

3. The family is the natural and fundamental group unit of society and is entitled to protection by society and the State.

ARTICLE 17

1. Everyone has the right to own property alone as well as in association with others.

2. No one shall be arbitrarily deprived of his property.

ARTICLE 18

Everyone has the right to freedom of thought, conscience and religion; this right includes freedom to change his religion or belief, and freedom, either alone or in community with others and in public or private, to manifest his religion or belief in teaching, practice, worship and observance.

ARTICLE 19

Everyone has the right to freedom of opinion and expression; this right includes freedom to hold opinions without interference and to seek, receive and impart information and ideas through any media and regardless of frontiers.

ARTICLE 20

1. Everyone has the right to freedom of peaceful assembly and association.

2. No one may be compelled to belong to an association.

ARTICLE 21

1. Everyone has the right to take part in the government of his country, directly or through freely chosen representatives.

2. Everyone has the right of equal access to public service in his country.

3. The will of the people shall be the basis of the authority of government; this will shall be expressed in periodic and genuine elections which shall be by universal and equal suffrage and shall be held by secret vote or by equivalent free voting procedures.

ARTICLE 22

Everyone, as a member of society, has the right to social security and is entitled to realization, through national effort and international co-operation and in accordance with the organization and resources of each State, of the economic, social and cultural rights indispensable for his dignity and the free development of his personality.

ARTICLE 23

1. Everyone has the right to work, to free choice of employment, to just and favourable conditions of work and to protection against unemployment.

2. Everyone, without any discrimination, has the right to equal pay for equal work.

3. Everyone who works has the right to just and favourable remuneration ensuring for himself and his family an existence worthy of human dignity, and supplemented, if necessary, by other means of social protection.

4. Everyone has the right to form and to join trade unions for the protection of his interests.

ARTICLE 24

Everyone has the right to rest and leisure, including reasonable limitation of working hours and periodic holidays with pay.

ARTICLE 25

1. Everyone has the right to a standard of living adequate for the health and well-being of himself and of his family, including food, clothing, housing and medical care and necessary social services, and the right to security in the event of unemployment, sickness, disability, widowhood, old age or other lack of livelihood in circumstances beyond his control.

2. Motherhood and childhood are entitled to special care and assistance. All children, whether born in or out of wedlock, shall enjoy the same social protection.

ARTICLE 26

1. Everyone has the right to education. Education shall be free, at least in the elementary and fundamental stages. Elementary education shall be compulsory. Technical and professional education shall be made generally available and higher education shall be equally accessible to all on the basis of merit.

2. Education shall be directed to the full development of the human personality and to the strengthening of respect for human rights and fundamental freedoms. It shall promote understanding, tolerance and friendship among all nations, racial or religious groups, and shall further the activities of the United Nations for the maintenance of peace.

3. Parents have a prior right to choose the kind of education that shall be given to their children.

ARTICLE 27

1. Everyone has the right freely to participate in the cultural life of the community, to enjoy the arts and to share in scientific advancement and its benefits.

2. Everyone has the right to the protection of the moral and material interests resulting from any scientific, literary or artistic production of which he is the author.

ARTICLE 28

Everyone is entitled to a social and international order in which the rights and freedoms set forth in this Declaration can be fully realized.

ARTICLE 29

1. Everyone has duties to the community in which alone the free and full development of his personality is possible.

2. In the exercise of his rights and freedoms, everyone shall be subject only to such limitations as are determined by law solely for the purpose of securing due recognition and respect for the rights and freedoms of others and of meeting the just requirements of morality, public order and the general welfare in a democratic society.

3. These rights and freedoms may in no case be exercised contrary to the purposes and principles of the United Nations.

ARTICLE 30

Nothing in this Declaration may be interpreted as implying for any State, group or person any right to engage in any activity or to perform any act aimed at the destruction of any of the rights and freedoms set forth herein.

THE EUROPEAN CONVENTION
ON HUMAN RIGHTS

TEXT

The Governments signatory hereto, being Members of the Council of Europe,

Considering the Universal Declaration of Human Rights proclaimed by the General Assembly of the United Nations on 10 December 1948;

Considering that this Declaration aims at securing the universal and effective recognition and observance of the Rights therein declared;

Considering that the aim of the Council of Europe is the achievement of greater unity between its Members and that one of the methods by which that aim is to be pursued is the maintenance and further realization of Human Rights and Fundamental Freedoms;

Reaffirming their profound belief in those Fundamental Freedoms which are the foundation of justice and peace in the world and are best maintained on the one hand by an effective political democracy and on the other by a common understanding and observance of the Human Rights upon which they depend;

Being resolved, as the Governments of European countries which are likeminded and have a common heritage of political traditions, ideals, freedom and the rule of law to take the first steps for the collective enforcement of certain of the Rights stated in the Universal Declaration;

Have agreed as follows:

ARTICLE 1

The High Contracting Parties shall secure to everyone within their jurisdiction the rights and freedoms defined in Section 1 of this Convention.

Section I

ARTICLE 2

1. Everyone's right to life shall be protected by law. No one shall be deprived of his life intentionally save in the execution of a sentence of a court following his conviction of a crime for which this penalty is provided by law.

2. Deprivation of life shall not be regarded as inflicted in contravention of this Article when it results from the use of force which is no more than absolutely necessary:

(*a*) in defence of any person from unlawful violence;

(*b*) in order to effect a lawful arrest or to prevent the escape of a person lawfully detained;

(*c*) in action lawfully taken for the purpose of quelling a riot or insurrection.

ARTICLE 3

No one shall be subjected to torture or to inhuman or degrading treatment or punishment.

ARTICLE 4

1. No one shall be held in slavery or servitude.

2. No one shall be required to perform forced or compulsory labour.

3. For the purpose of this Article the term 'forced or compulsory labour' shall not include:

(*a*) any work required to be done in the ordinary course of detention imposed according to the provisions of Article 5 of this Convention or during conditional release from such detention;

(*b*) any service of a military character or, in case of conscientious objectors in countries where they are recognized, service exacted instead of compulsory military service;

(*c*) any service exacted in case of an emergency or calamity threatening the life or well-being of the community;

(*d*) any work or service which forms part of normal civic obligations.

ARTICLE 5

1. Everyone has the right to liberty and security of person.

No one shall be deprived of his liberty save in the following cases and in accordance with a procedure prescribed by law;

(*a*) the lawful detention of a person after conviction by a competent court;

(*b*) the lawful arrest or detention of a person for non-compliance with the lawful order of a court or in order to secure the fulfilment of any obligation prescribed by law;

(*c*) the lawful arrest or detention of a person effected for the purpose of bringing him before the competent legal authority on reasonable suspicion of having committed an offence or when it is reasonably considered necessary to prevent his committing an offence or fleeing after having done so;

(*d*) the detention of a minor by lawful order for the purpose of educational supervision or his lawful detention for the purpose of bringing him before the competent legal authority;

(*e*) the lawful detention of persons for the prevention of the spreading of infectious diseases, of persons of unsound mind, alcoholics or drug addicts, or vagrants;

(*f*) the lawful arrest or detention of a person to prevent his effecting an unauthorized entry into the country or of a person against whom action is being taken with a view to deportation or extradition.

2. Everyone who is arrested shall be informed promptly, in a language which he understands, of the reasons for his arrest and of any charge against him.

3. Everyone arrested or detained in accordance with the provisions of paragraph 1 (*c*) of this Article shall be brought promptly before a judge or other officer authorized by law to exercise judicial power and shall be entitled to trial within a reasonable time or to release pending trial. Release may be conditioned by guarantees to appear for trial.

4. Everyone who is deprived of his liberty by arrest or detention shall be entitled to take proceedings by which the lawfulness of his detention shall be decided speedily by a court and his release ordered if the detention is not lawful.

5. Everyone who has been the victim of arrest or detention in contravention of the provisions of this Article shall have an enforceable right to compensation.

ARTICLE 6

1. In the determination of his civil rights and obligations or of any criminal charge against him, everyone is entitled to a fair and public hearing within a reasonable time by an independent and impartial tribunal established by law. Judgment shall be pronounced publicly but the press and public may be excluded from all or part of the trial in the interest of morals, public order or national security in a democratic society, where the interests of juveniles or the protection of the private life of the parties so require, or to the extent strictly necessary in the opinion of the court in special circumstances where publicity would prejudice the interests of justice.

2. Everyone charged with a criminal offence shall be presumed innocent until proved guilty according to law.

3. Everyone charged with a criminal offence has the following minimum rights:

(*a*) to be informed promptly, in a language which he understands and in detail, of the nature and cause of the accusation against him;

(*b*) to have adequate time and facilities for the preparation of his defence;

(*c*) to defend himself in person or through legal assistance of his own choosing or, if he has not sufficient means to pay for legal assistance, to be given it free when the interests of justice so require;

(*d*) to examine or have examined witnesses against him and to obtain the attendance and examination of witnesses on his behalf under the same conditions as witnesses against him;

(*e*) to have the free assistance of an interpreter if he cannot understand or speak the language used in court.

ARTICLE 7

1. No one shall be held guilty of any criminal offence on account of any act or omission which did not constitute a criminal offence under national or international law at the time when it was committed. Nor shall a heavier penalty be imposed than the one that was applicable at the time the criminal offence was committed.

2. This Article shall not prejudice the trial and punishment of any person for any act or omission which, at the time when it was committed, was criminal according to the general principles of law recognized by civilized nations.

ARTICLE 8

1. Everyone has the right to respect for his private and family life, his home and his correspondence.

2. There shall be no interference by a public authority with the exercise of this right except such as is in accordance with the law and is necessary in a democratic society in the interests of national security, public safety or the economic well-being of the country, for the prevention of disorder or crime, for the protection of health or morals, or for the protection of the rights and freedoms of others.

ARTICLE 9

1. Everyone has the right to freedom of thought, conscience and religion; this right includes freedom to change his religion or belief, and freedom, either alone or in community with others and in public or private, to manifest his religion or belief, in worship, teaching, practice and observance.

2. Freedom to manifest one's religion or beliefs shall be subject only to such limitations as are prescribed by law and are necessary in a democratic society in the interests of public safety, for the protection of public order, health or morals, or for the protection of the rights and freedoms of others.

ARTICLE 10

1. Everyone has the right to freedom of expression. This right shall include freedom to hold opinions and to receive and impart information and ideas without interference by public authority and regardless of frontiers. This Article shall not prevent States from requiring the licensing of broadcasting, television or cinema enterprises.

2. The exercise of these freedoms, since it carries with it duties and responsibilities, may be subject to such formalities, conditions, restrictions or penalties as are prescribed by law and are necessary in a democratic society, in the interests of national security, territorial integrity or public safety, for the prevention of disorder or crime, for the protection of health or morals, for the protection of the reputation or rights of others, for preventing the disclosure of information received in confidence, or for maintaining the authority and impartiality of the judiciary.

ARTICLE 11

1. Everyone has the right to freedom of peaceful assembly and to freedom of association with others, including the right to form and to join trade unions for the protection of his interests.

2. No restrictions shall be placed on the exercise of these rights other than such as are prescribed by law and are necessary in a democratic society in the interests of national security or public safety, for the prevention of disorder or crime, for the protection of health or morals or for the protection of the rights and freedoms of others. This Article shall not prevent the imposition of lawful restrictions on the exercise of these rights by members of the armed forces, of the police or of the administration of the State.

ARTICLE 12

Men and women of marriageable age have the right to marry and to found a family, according to the national laws governing the exercise of this right.

ARTICLE 13

Everyone whose rights and freedoms as set forth in this Convention are violated shall have an effective remedy before a national authority notwithstanding that the violation has been committed by persons acting in an official capacity.

ARTICLE 14

The enjoyment of the rights and freedoms set forth in this Convention shall be secured without discrimination on any ground such as sex, race, colour, language, religion, political or other opinion, national or social origin, association with a national minority, property, birth or other status.

ARTICLE 15

1. In time of war or other public emergency threatening the life of the nation any High Contracting Party may take measures derogating from its obligations under this Convention to the extent strictly required by the exigencies of the situation, provided that such measures are not inconsistent with its other obligations under international law.

2. No derogation from Article 2, except in respect of deaths resulting from lawful acts of war, or from Article 3, 4 (paragraph 1) and 7 shall be made under this provision.

3. Any High Contracting Party availing itself of this right of derogation shall keep the Secretary-General of the Council of Europe fully informed of the measures which it has taken and the reasons therefor. It shall also inform the Secretary-General of the Council of Europe when such measures have ceased to operate and the provisions of the Convention are again being fully executed.

ARTICLE 16

Nothing in Articles 10, 11, and 14 shall be regarded as preventing the High Contracting Parties from imposing restrictions on the political activity of aliens.

ARTICLE 17

Nothing in this Convention may be interpreted as implying for any State, group or person any right to engage in any activity or perform any act aimed at the destruction of any of the rights and freedoms set forth herein or at their limitation to a greater extent than is provided for in the Convention.

ARTICLE 18

The restrictions permitted under this Convention to the said rights and freedoms shall not be applied for any purpose other than those for which they have been prescribed.

Section II
ARTICLE 19

To ensure the observance of the engagements undertaken by the High Contracting Parties in the present Convention, there shall be set up:

1. A European Commission of Human Rights hereinafter referred to as 'the Commission';

2. A European Court of Human Rights, hereinafter referred to as 'the Court'.

Section III
ARTICLE 20

The Commission shall consist of a number of members equal to that of the High Contracting Parties. No two members of the Commission may be nationals of the same State.

ARTICLE 21

1. The members of the Commission shall be elected by the Committee of Ministers by an absolute majority of votes, from a list of names drawn up by the Bureau of the Consultative Assembly; each group of the Representatives of the High Contracting Parties in the Consultative Assembly shall put forward three candidates, of whom two at least shall be its nationals.

2. As far as applicable, the same procedure shall be followed to complete the Commission in the event of other States subsequently becoming Parties to this Convention, and in filling casual vacancies.

ARTICLE 22

1. The members of the Commission shall be elected for a period of six years. They may be re-elected. However, of the members elected at the first election, the terms of seven members shall expire at the end of three years.

2. The members whose terms are to expire at the end of the initial period of three years shall be chosen by lot by the Secretary-General of the Council of Europe immediately after the first election has been completed.

3. A member of the Commission elected to replace a member whose term of office has not expired shall hold office for the remainder of his predecessor's term.

4. The members of the Commission shall hold office until replaced. After having been replaced, they shall continue to deal with such cases as they already have under consideration.

ARTICLE 23

The members of the Commission shall sit on the Commission in their individual capacity.

ARTICLE 24

Any High Contracting Party may refer to the Commission through the Secretary-General of the Council of Europe, any alleged breach of the provisions of the Convention by another High Contracting Party.

ARTICLE 25

1. The Commission may receive petitions addressed to the Secretary-General of the Council of Europe from any person, non-governmental organization or group of individuals claiming to be the victim of a violation by one of the High Contracting Parties of the rights set forth in this Convention, provided that the High Contracting Party against which the complaint has been lodged has declared that it recognizes the competence of the Commission to receive such petitions. Those of the High Contracting Par-

ties who have made such a declaration undertake not to hinder in any way the effective exercise of this right.

2. Such declarations may be made for a specific period.

3. The declarations shall be deposited with the Secretary-General of the Council of Europe who shall transmit copies thereof to the High Contracting Parties and publish them.

4. The Commission shall only exercise the powers provided for in this Article when at least six High Contracting Parties are bound by declarations made in accordance with the preceding paragraphs.

ARTICLE 26

The Commission may only deal with the matter after all domestic remedies have been exhausted, according to the generally recognized rules of international law, and within a period of six months from the date on which the final decision was taken.

ARTICLE 27

1. The Commission shall not deal with any petition submitted under Article 25 which

(*a*) is anonymous, or

(*b*) is substantially the same as a matter which has already been examined by the Commission or has already been submitted to another procedure of international investigation or settlement and if it contains no relevant new information.

2. The Commission shall consider inadmissible any petition submitted under Article 25 which it considers incompatible with the provisions of the present Convention, manifestly illfounded, or an abuse of the right of petition.

3. The Commission shall reject any petition referred to it which it considers inadmissible under Article 26.

ARTICLE 28

In the event of the Commission accepting a petition referred to it:

(*a*) it shall, with a view to ascertaining the facts undertake together with the representatives of the parties an examination of the petition and, if need be, an investigation, for the effective conduct of which the States concerned shall furnish all necessary facilities, after an exchange of views with the Commission:

(*b*) it shall place itself at the disposal of the parties concerned with a view to securing a friendly settlement of the matter on the basis of respect for Human Rights as defined in this Convention.

ARTICLE 29

1. The Commission shall perform the functions set out in Article 28 by means of a Sub-Commission consisting of seven members of the Commission.

2. Each of the parties concerned may appoint as members of this Sub-Commission a person of its choice.

3. The remaining members shall be chosen by lot in accordance with arrangements prescribed in the Rules of Procedure of the Commission.

ARTICLE 30

If the Sub-Commission succeeds in effecting a friendly settlement in accordance with Article 28, it shall draw up a Report which shall be sent to the States concerned, to the Committee of Ministers and to the Secretary-General of the Council of Europe for publication. This Report shall be confined to a brief statement of the facts and of the solution reached.

ARTICLE 31

1. If a solution is not reached, the Commission shall draw up a Report on the facts and state its opinion as to whether the facts found disclose a breach by the State concerned of its obligations under the Convention. The opinions of all the members of the Commission on this point may be stated in the Report.

2. The Report shall be transmitted to the Committee of Ministers. It shall also be transmitted to the States concerned, who shall not be at liberty to publish it.

3. In transmitting the Report to the Committee of Ministers the Commission may make such proposals as it thinks fit.

ARTICLE 32

1. If the question is not referred to the Court in accordance with Article 48 of this Convention within a period of three months from the date of the transmission of the Report to the Committee of Ministers, the Committee of Ministers shall decide by a majority of two-thirds of the members entitled to sit on the Committee whether there has been a violation of the Convention.

2. In the affirmative case the Committee of Ministers shall prescribe a period during which the Contracting Party concerned must take the measures required by the decision of the Committee of Ministers.

3. If the High Contracting Party concerned has not taken satisfactory measures within the prescribed period, the Committee of Ministers shall decide by the majority provided for in paragraph 1 above what effect shall be given to its original decision and shall publish the Report.

4. The High Contracting Parties undertake to regard as binding on them any decision which the Committee of Ministers may take in application of the preceding paragraphs.

ARTICLE 33

The Commission shall meet *in camera*.

ARTICLE 34

The Commission shall take its decisions by a majority of the Members present and voting; the Sub-Commission shall take its decisions by a majority of its members.

ARTICLE 35

The Commission shall meet as the circumstances require. The meetings shall be convened by the Secretary-General of the Council of Europe.

ARTICLE 36

The Commission shall draw up its own rules of procedure.

ARTICLE 37

The secretariat of the Commission shall be provided by the Secretary-General of the Council of Europe.

Section IV

ARTICLE 38

The European Court of Human Rights shall consist of a number of judges equal to that of the Members of the Council of Europe. No two judges may be nationals of the same State.

ARTICLE 39

1. The members of the Court shall be elected by the Consultative Assembly by a majority of the votes cast from a list of persons nominated by the Members of the Council of Europe; each Member shall nominate three candidates, of whom two at least shall be its nationals.

2. As far as applicable, the same procedure shall be followed to complete the Court in the event of the admission of new members of the Council of Europe, and in filling casual vacancies.

3. The candidates shall be of high moral character and must either possess the qualifications required for appointment to high judicial office or be jurisconsults of recognized competence.

ARTICLE 40

1. The members of the Court shall be elected for a period of nine years. They may be re-elected. However, of the members elected at the first election the terms of four members shall expire at the end of three years, and the terms of four more members shall expire at the end of six years.

2. The members whose terms are to expire at the end of the initial periods of three and six years shall be chosen by lot by the Secretary-General immediately after the first election has been completed.

3. A member of the Court elected to replace a member whose term of office has not expired shall hold office for the remainder of his predecessor's term.

4. The members of the Court shall hold office until replaced. After having been replaced, they shall continue to deal with such cases as they already have under consideration.

ARTICLE 41

The Court shall elect its President and Vice-President for a period of three years. They may be re-elected.

ARTICLE 42

The members of the Court shall receive for each day of duty a compensation to be determined by the Committee of Ministers.

ARTICLE 43

For the consideration of each case brought before it the Court shall consist of a Chamber composed of seven judges. There shall sit as an *ex officio* member of the Chamber the judge who is a national of any State party concerned, or, if there is none, a person of its choice who shall sit in the capacity of judge; the names of the other judges shall be chosen by lot by the President before the opening of the case.

ARTICLE 44

Only the High Contracting Parties and the Commission shall have the right to bring a case before the Court.

ARTICLE 45

The jurisdiction of the Court shall extend to all cases concerning the interpretation and application of the present Convention which the High Contracting Parties or the Commission shall refer to it in accordance with Article 48.

ARTICLE 46

1. Any of the High Contracting Parties may at any time declare that it recognizes as compulsory *ipso facto* and without special agreement the jurisdiction of the Court in all matters concerning the interpretation and application of the present Convention.

2. The declarations referred to above may be made unconditionally or on condition of reciprocity on the part of several or certain other High Contracting Parties or for a specified period.

3. These declarations shall be deposited with the Secretary-General of the Council of Europe who shall transmit copies thereof to the High Contracting Parties.

ARTICLE 47

The Court may only deal with a case after the Commission has acknowledged the failure of efforts for a friendly settlement and within the period of three months provided for in Article 32.

ARTICLE 48

The following may bring a case before the Court, provided that the High Contracting Party concerned, if there is only one, or the High Contracting Parties concerned, if there is more than one, are subject to the compulsory jurisdiction of the Court or, failing that, with the consent of the High Contracting Party concerned, if there is only one, or of the High Contracting Parties concerned if there is more than one:

(*a*) the Commission;
(*b*) a High Contracting Party whose national is alleged to be a victim;
(*c*) a High Contracting Party which referred the case to the Commission;
(*d*) a High Contracting Party against which the complaint has been lodged.

ARTICLE 49

In the event of dispute as to whether the Court has jurisdiction, the matter shall be settled by the decision of the Court.

ARTICLE 50

If the Court finds that a decision or a measure taken by a legal authority or any other authority of a High Contracting Party, is completely or partially in conflict with the obligations arising from the present Convention, and if the internal law of the said Party allows only partial reparation to be made for the consequences of this decision or measure, the decision of the Court shall, if necessary, afford just satisfaction to the injured party.

ARTICLE 51

1. Reasons shall be given for the judgment of the Court.

2. If the judgment does not represent in whole or in part the unanimous opinion of the judges, any judge shall be entitled to deliver a separate opinion.

ARTICLE 52

The judgment of the Court shall be final.

ARTICLE 53

The High Contracting Parties undertake to abide by the decision of the Court in any case to which they are parties.

ARTICLE 54

The judgment of the Court shall be transmitted to the Committee of Ministers which shall supervise its execution.

ARTICLE 55

The Court shall draw up its own rules and shall determine its own procedure.

ARTICLE 56

1. The first election of the members of the Court shall take place after the declarations by the High Contracting Parties mentioned in Article 46 have reached a total of eight.

2. No case can be brought before the Court before this election.

Section V

ARTICLE 57

On receipt of a request from the Secretary-General of the Council of Europe any High Contracting Party shall furnish an explanation of the manner in which its internal law ensures the effective implementation of any of the provisions of this Convention.

ARTICLE 58

The expenses of the Commission and the Court shall be borne by the Council of Europe.

ARTICLE 59

The members of the Commission and of the Court shall be entitled, during the discharge of their functions, to the privileges and immunities provided for in Article 40 of the Statute of the Council of Europe and in the agreements made thereunder.

ARTICLE 60

Nothing in this Convention shall be construed as limiting or derogating from any of the human rights and fundamental freedoms which may be ensured under the laws of any High Contracting Party or under any other agreement to which it is a Party.

ARTICLE 61

Nothing in this Convention shall prejudice the powers conferred on the Committee of Ministers by the Statute of the Council of Europe.

ARTICLE 62

The High Contracting Parties agree that, except by special agreement, they will not avail themselves of treaties, conventions or declarations in force between them for the purpose of submitting, by way of petition, a dispute arising out of the interpretation or application of this Convention to a means of settlement other than those provided for in this Convention.

ARTICLE 63

1. Any State may at the time of its ratification or at any time thereafter declare by notification addressed to the Secretary-General of the Council of Europe that the present Convention shall extend to all or any of the territories for whose international relations it is responsible.

2. The Convention shall extend to the territory or territories named in the notification as from the thirtieth day after the receipt of this notification by the Secretary-General of the Council of Europe.

3. The provisions of this Convention shall be applied in such territories with due regard, however, to local requirements.

4. Any State which has made a declaration in accordance with paragraph 1 of this Article may at any time thereafter declare on behalf of one or more of the territories to which the declaration relates that it accepts the competence of the Commission to receive petitions from individuals, non-governmental organizations or groups of individuals in accordance with Article 25 of the present Convention.

ARTICLE 64

1. Any State may, when signing this Convention or when depositing its instrument of ratification, make a reservation in respect of any particular provision of the Convention to the extent that any law then in force in its

territory is not in conformity with the provision. Reservations of a general character shall not be permitted under this Article.

2. Any reservation made under this Article shall contain a brief statement of the law concerned.

ARTICLE 65

1. A High Contracting Party may denounce the present Convention only after the expiry of five years from the date on which it became a Party to it and after six months' notice contained in a notification addressed to the Secretary-General of the Council of Europe, who shall inform the other High Contracting Parties.

2. Such a denunciation shall not have the effect of releasing the High Contracting Party concerned from its obligations under this Convention in respect of any act which, being capable of constituting a violation of such obligations, may have been performed by it before the date at which the denunciation became effective.

3. Any High Contracting Party which shall cease to be a Member of the Council of Europe shall cease to be a Party to this Convention under the same conditions.

4. The Convention may be denounced in accordance with the provisions of the preceding paragraphs in respect of any territory to which it has been declared to extend under the terms of Article 63.

ARTICLE 66

1. This Convention shall be open to the signature of the Members of the Council of Europe. It shall be ratified. Ratifications shall be deposited with the Secretary-General of the Council of Europe.

2. The present Convention shall come into force after the deposit of ten instruments of ratification.

3. As regards any signatory ratifying subsequently, the Convention shall come into force at the date of the deposit of its instrument of ratification.

4. The Secretary-General of the Council of Europe shall notify all the Members of the Council of Europe of the entry into force of the Convention, the names of the High Contracting Parties who have ratified it, and the deposit of all instruments of ratification which may be effected subsequently.

Done at Rome this 4th day of November, 1950, in English and French, both texts being equally authentic, in a single copy which shall remain deposited in the archives of the Council of Europe. The Secretary-General shall transmit certified copies to each of the signatories.

Protocols

1. *Enforcement of certain Rights and Freedoms not included in Section I of the Convention*

The Governments signatory hereto, being Members of the Council of Europe,

Being resolved to take steps to ensure the collective enforcement of certain rights and freedoms other than those already included in Section I of the Convention for the Protection of Human Rights and Fundamental Freedoms signed at Rome on 4th November, 1950 (hereinafter referred to as 'the Convention'),

Have agreed as follows:

ARTICLE 1

Every natural or legal person is entitled to the peaceful enjoyment of his possessions. No one shall be deprived of his possessions except in the public interest and subject to the conditions provided for by law and by the general principles of international law.

The preceding provisions shall not, however, in any way impair the right of a State to enforce such laws as it deems necessary to control the use of property in accordance with the general interest or to secure the payment of taxes or other contributions or penalties.

ARTICLE 2

No person shall be denied the right to education. In the exercise of any functions which it assumes in relation to education and to teaching, the State shall respect the right of parents to ensure such education and teaching in conformity with their own religious and philosophical convictions.

ARTICLE 3

The High Contracting Parties undertake to hold free elections at reasonable intervals by secret ballot, under conditions which will ensure the free expression of the opinion of the people in the choice of the legislature.

ARTICLE 4

Any High Contracting Party may at the time of signature or ratification or at any time thereafter communicate to the Secretary-General of the Council of Europe a declaration stating the extent to which it undertakes that the provisions of the present Protocol shall apply to such of the territories for the international relations of which it is responsible as are named therein.

Any High Contracting Party which has communicated a declaration in virtue of the preceding paragraph may from time to time communicate a further declaration modifying the terms of any former declaration or terminating the application of the provisions of this Protocol in respect of any territory.

A declaration made in accordance with this Article shall be deemed to have been made in accordance with paragraph 1 of Article 63 of the Convention.

ARTICLE 5

As between the High Contracting Parties the provisions of Articles 1, 2, 3 and 4 of this Protocol shall be regarded as additional Articles to the Convention and all the provisions of the Convention shall apply accordingly.

ARTICLE 6

This Protocol shall be open for signature by the Members of the Council of Europe, who are the signatories of the Convention; it shall be ratified at the same time as or after the ratification of the Convention. It shall enter into force after the deposit of ten instruments of ratification. As regards any signatory ratifying subsequently, the Protocol shall enter into force at the date of the deposit of its instrument of ratification.

The instruments of ratification shall be deposited with the Secretary-General of the Council of Europe, who will notify all Members of the names of those who have ratified.

Done at Paris on the 20th day of March 1952, in English and French, both texts being equally authentic, in a single copy which shall remain deposited in the archives of the Council of Europe. The Secretary-General shall transmit certified copies to each of the signatory Governments.

2. *Conferring upon the European Court*
of Human Rights Competence to give
Advisory Opinions

The member States of the Council of Europe signatory hereto:

Having regard to the provisions of the Convention for the Protection of Human Rights and Fundamental Freedoms signed at Rome on 4 November 1950 (hereinafter referred to as 'the Convention'), and in particular Article 19 instituting, among other bodies, a European Court of Human Rights (hereinafter referred to as 'the Court');

Considering that it is expedient to confer upon the Court competence to give advisory opinions subject to certain conditions;

Have agreed as follows:

ARTICLE 1

1. The Court may, at the request of the Committee of Ministers, give advisory opinions on legal questions concerning the interpretation of the Convention and the Protocols thereto.

2. Such opinions shall not deal with any question relating to the content or scope of the rights or freedoms defined in Section 1 of the Convention and in the Protocols thereto, or with any other question which the Commission, the Court, or the Committee of Ministers might have to consider in consequence of any such proceedings as could be instituted in accordance with the Convention.

3. Decisions of the Committee of Ministers to request an advisory opinion of the Court shall require a two-thirds majority vote of the representatives entitled to sit on the Committee.

ARTICLE 2

The Court shall decide whether a request for an advisory opinion submitted by the Committee of Ministers is within its consultative competence as defined in Article 1 of this Protocol.

ARTICLE 3

1. For the consideration of requests for an advisory opinion, the Court shall sit in plenary session.

2. Reasons shall be given for advisory opinions of the Court.

3. If the advisory opinion does not represent in whole or in part the unanimous opinion of the judges, any judge shall be entitled to deliver a separate opinion.

4. Advisory opinions of the Court shall be communicated to the Committee of Ministers.

ARTICLE 4

The powers of the Court under Article 55 of the Convention shall extend to the drawing up of such rules and the determination of such procedure as the Court may think necessary for the purposes of this Protocol.

ARTICLE 5

1. This Protocol shall be open to signature by Member States of the Council of Europe, signatories to the Convention, who may become Parties to it by:

   (*a*) signature without reservation in respect of ratification or acceptance;
   (*b*) signature with reservation in respect of ratification or acceptance, followed by ratification or acceptance. Instruments of ratification or acceptance shall be deposited with the Secretary-General of the Council of Europe.

2. This Protocol shall enter into force as soon as all the States Parties to the Convention shall have become Parties to the Protocol in accordance with the Provisions of paragraph 1 of this Article.

3. From the date of the entry into force of this Protocol, Articles 1 to 4 shall be considered an integral part of the Convention.

4. The Secretary-General of the Council of Europe shall notify the Member States of the Council of:

(a) any signature without reservation in respect of ratification or acceptance;

(b) any signature with reservation in respect of ratification or acceptance;

(c) the deposit of any instrument of ratification or acceptance;

(d) the date of entry into force of this Protocol in accordance with paragraph 2 of this Article.

In witness whereof the undersigned, being duly authorized thereto, have signed this Protocol.

Done at Strasbourg, this 6th day of May 1963, in English and in French, both texts being equally authoritative, in a single copy which shall remain deposited in the archives of the Council of Europe. The Secretary-General shall transmit certified copies to each of the signatory States.

3. Amending Articles 29, 30, and 94 of the Convention

The member States of the Council of Europe, signatories to this Protocol,

Considering that it is advisable to amend certain provisions of the Convention for the Protection of Human Rights and Fundamental Freedoms signed at Rome on 4 November 1960 (hereinafter referred to as 'the Convention') concerning the procedure of the European Commission of Human Rights,

Have agreed as follows:

ARTICLE I

1. Article 29 of the Convention is deleted.

2. The following provision shall be inserted in the Convention:
'Article 29

After it has accepted a petition submitted under Article 25, the Commission may nevertheless decide unanimously to reject the petition if, in the course of its examination, it finds that the existence of one of the grounds for non-acceptance provided for in Article 27 has been established.

In such a case, the decision shall be communicated to the parties.'

ARTICLE 2

In Article 30 of the Convention, the word 'Sub-Commission' shall be replaced by the word 'Commission'.

ARTICLE 3

1. At the beginning of Article 34 of the Convention, the following shall be inserted:

'Subject to the provisions of Article 29. . . .'

2. At the end of the same Article, the sentence 'the Sub-commission shall take its decisions by a majority of its members' shall be deleted.

ARTICLE 4

1. The Protocol shall be open to signature by the member States of the Council of Europe, who may become Parties to it either by:

(*a*) signature without reservation in respect of ratification or acceptance, or

(*b*) signature with reservation in respect of ratification or acceptance, followed by ratification or acceptance. Instruments of ratification or acceptance shall be deposited with the Secretary-General of the Council of Europe.

2. This Protocol shall enter into force as soon as all States Parties to the Convention shall have become Parties to the Protocol, in accordance with the provisions of paragraph 1 of this Article.

3. The Secretary-General of the Council of Europe shall notify the Member States of the Council of:

(*a*) any signature without reservation in respect of ratification or acceptance;

(*b*) any signature with reservation in respect of ratification or acceptance;

(*c*) the deposit of any instrument of ratification or acceptance;

(*d*) the date of entry into force of this Protocol in accordance with paragraph 2 of this Article.

In witness whereof the undersigned, being duly authorized thereto, have signed this Protocol.

Done at Strasbourg, this 6th day of May 1963, in English and in French, both texts being equally authoritative, in a single copy which shall remain deposited in the archives of the Council of Europe. The Secretary-General shall transmit certified copies to each of the signatory States.

4. *Protecting certain Additional Rights*

The Governments signatory hereto, being Members of the Council of Europe,

Being resolved to take steps to ensure the collective enforcement of certain rights and freedoms other than those already included in Section I of the Convention for the Protection of Human Rights and Fundamental

Freedoms signed at Rome on 4 November 1950 (hereinafter referred to as 'the Convention') and in Articles 1 to 3 of the First Protocol to the Convention, signed at Paris on 20 March 1952,

Have agreed as follows:

ARTICLE 1

No one shall be deprived of his liberty merely on the ground of inability to fulfil a contractual obligation.

ARTICLE 2

1. Everyone lawfully within the territory of a State shall, within that territory, have the right to liberty of movement and freedom to choose his residence.

2. Everyone shall be free to leave any country, including his own.

3. No restrictions shall be placed on the exercise of these rights other than such as are in accordance with law and are necessary in a democratic society in the interests of national security or public safety for the maintenance of 'ordre public', for the prevention of crime, for the protection of the rights and freedoms of others.

4. The rights set forth in paragraph 1 may also be subject, in particular areas, to restrictions imposed in accordance with law and justified by the public interest in a democratic society.

ARTICLE 3

1. No one shall be expelled, by means either of an individual or of a collective measure, from the territory of the State of which he is a national.

2. No one shall be deprived of the right to enter the territory of the State of which he is a national.

ARTICLE 4

Collective expulsion of aliens is prohibited.

ARTICLE 5

1. Any High Contracting Party may, at the time of signature or ratification of this Protocol, or at any time thereafter, communicate to the Secretary-General of the Council of Europe a declaration stating the extent to which it undertakes that the provisions of this Protocol shall apply to such of the territories for the international relations of which it is responsible as are named therein.

2. Any High Contracting Party which has communicated a declaration in virtue of the preceding paragraph may, from time to time, communicate a

further declaration modifying the terms of any former declaration or terminating the application of the provisions of this Protocol in respect of any territory.

3. A declaration made in accordance with this Article shall be deemed to have been made in accordance with paragraph 1 of Article 63 of the Convention.

4. The territory of any State to which this Protocol applies by virtue of ratification or acceptance by that State, and each territory to which this Protocol is applied by virtue of a declaration by that State under this Article, shall be treated as separate territories for the purpose of the references in Articles 2 and 3 to the territory of a State.

ARTICLE 6

1. As between the High Contracting Parties the provisions of Articles 1 to 5 of this Protocol shall be regarded as additional articles to the Convention, and all the provisions of the Convention shall apply accordingly.

2. Nevertheless, the right of individual recourse recognized by a declaration made under Article 25 of the Convention, or the accceptance of the compulsory jurisdiction of the Court by a declaration made under Article 46 of the Convention, shall not be effective in relation to this Protocol unless the High Contracting Party concerned has made a statement recognizing such right, or accepting such jurisdiction, in respect of all or any of Articles 1 to 4 of the Protocol.

ARTICLE 7

1. This Protocol shall be open for signature by the members of the Council of Europe who are the signatories of the Convention; it shall be ratified at the same time as or after the ratification of the Convention. It shall enter into force after the deposit of five instruments of ratification. As regards any signatory ratifying subsequently, the Protocol shall enter into force at the date of the deposit of its instrument of ratification.

2. The instruments of ratification shall be deposited with the Secretary-General of the Council of Europe, who will notify all members of the names of those who have ratified.

In witness whereof, the undersigned, being duly authorized thereto, have signed this Protocol.

Done at Strasbourg, this 16th day of September 1963, in English and in French, both texts being equally authoritative, in a single copy which shall remain deposited in the archives of the Council of Europe. The Secretary-General shall transmit certified copies to each of the signatory States.

5. *Amending Articles 22 and 40 of*
   the Convention

The Governments signatory hereto, being Members of the Council of Europe,

Considering that certain inconveniences have arisen in the application of the provisions of Articles 22 and 40 of the Convention for the Protection of Human Rights and Fundamental Freedoms signed at Rome on 4th November 1950 (hereinafter referred to as 'the Convention') relating to the length of the terms of office of the members of the European Commission of Human Rights (hereinafter referred to as 'the Commission') and of the European Court of Human Rights (hereinafter referred to as 'the Court');

Considering that it is desirable to ensure as far as possible an election every three years of one half of the members of the Commission and of one third of the members of the Court;

Considering therefore that it is desirable to amend certain provisions of the Convention,

Have agreed as follows:

ARTICLE I

In Article 22 of the Convention, the following two paragraphs shall be inserted after paragraph (2):

'(3) In order to ensure that, as far as possible, one half of the membership of the Commission shall be renewed every three years, the Committee of Ministers may decide, before proceeding to any subsequent election, that the term or terms of office of one or more members to be elected shall be for a period other than six years but not more than nine and not less than three years.

(4) In cases where more than one term of office is involved and the Committee of Ministers applies the preceding paragraph, the allocation of the terms of office shall be effected by the drawing of lots by the Secretary-General, immediately after the election.'

ARTICLE 2

In Article 22 of the Convention, the former paragraphs (3) and (4) shall become respectively paragraphs (5) and (6).

ARTICLE 3

In Article 40 of the Convention, the following two paragraphs shall be inserted after paragraph (2):

'(3) In order to ensure that, as far as possible, one third of the membership of the Court shall be renewed every three years, the Consultative Assembly may decide, before proceeding to any subsequent election, that the term or terms of office of one or more members to be elected shall be for a period other than nine years but not more than twelve and not less than six years.

(4) In cases where more than one term of office is involved and the Consultative Assembly applies the preceding paragraph, the allocation of the terms of office shall be effected by the drawing of lots by the Secretary-General immediately after the election.'

ARTICLE 4

In Article 40 of the Convention, the former paragraphs (3) and (4) shall become respectively paragraphs (5) and (6).

ARTICLE 5

1. This Protocol shall be open to signature by Members of the Council of Europe, signatories to the Convention, who may become Parties to it by:

   (a) signature without reservation in respect of ratification or acceptance;
   (b) signature with reservation in respect of ratification or acceptance, followed by ratification or acceptance.

Instruments of ratification or acceptance shall be deposited with the Secretary-General of the Council of Europe.

2. This Protocol shall enter into force as soon as all Contracting Parties to the Convention shall have become Parties to the Protocol, in accordance with the provisions of paragraph 1 of this Article.

3. The Secretary-General of the Council of Europe shall notify the Members of the Council of:

   (a) any signature without reservation in respect of ratification or acceptance;
   (b) any signature with reservation in respect of ratification or acceptance;
   (c) the deposit of any instrument of ratification or acceptance;
   (d) the date of entry into force of this Protocol in accordance with paragraph 2 of this Article.

In witness whereof the undersigned, being duly authorized thereto, have signed this Protocol.

Done at Strasbourg, this 20th day of January 1966, in English and in French, both texts being equally authoritative, in a single copy which shall remain deposited in the archives of the Council of Europe. The Secretary-General shall transmit certified copies to each of the signatory Governments.

INTERNATIONAL COVENANT ON CIVIL AND POLITICAL RIGHTS, 1966

TEXT

Preamble

The States Parties to the present Covenant,

Considering that, in accordance with the principles proclaimed in the Charter of the United Nations, recognition of the inherent dignity and of the equal and inalienable rights of all members of the human family is the foundation of freedom, justice and peace in the world,

Recognizing that these rights derive from the inherent dignity of the human person,

Recognizing that, in accordance with the Universal Declaration of Human Rights, the ideal of free human beings enjoying civil and political freedom and freedom from fear and want can only be achieved if conditions are created whereby everyone may enjoy his civil and political rights, as well as his economic, social and cultural rights,

Considering the obligation of States under the Charter of the United Nations to promote universal respect for, and observance of, human rights and freedoms,

Realizing that the individual, having duties to other individuals and to the community to which he belongs, is under a responsibility to strive for the promotion and observance of the rights recognized in the present Covenant,

Agree upon the following articles:

Part I

ARTICLE I

1. All peoples have the right of self-determination. By virtue of that right they freely determine their political status and freely pursue their economic, social and cultural development.

2. All peoples may, for their own ends, freely dispose of their natural wealth and resources without prejudice to any obligations arising out of international economic co-operation, based upon the principle of mutual benefit, and international law. In no case may a people be deprived of its own means of subsistence.

3. The States Parties to the present Covenant, including those having responsibility for the administration of Non-Self-Governing and Trust Territories, shall promote the realization of the right of self-determination, and shall respect that right, in conformity with the provisions of the Charter of the United Nations.

Part II

ARTICLE 2

1. Each State Party to the present Covenant undertakes to respect and to ensure to all individuals within its territory and subject to its jurisdiction the rights recognized in the present Covenant, without distinction of any kind, such as race, colour, sex, language, religion, political or other opinion, national or social origin, property, birth or other status.

2. Where not already provided for by existing legislative or other measures, each State Party to the present Covenant undertakes to take the necessary steps, in accordance with its constitutional processes and with the provisions of the present Covenant, to adopt such legislative or other measures as may be necessary to give effect to the rights recognized in the present Covenant.

3. Each State Party to the present Covenant undertakes:

(*a*) To ensure that any person whose rights or freedoms as herein recognized are violated shall have an effective remedy, notwithstanding that the violation has been committed by persons acting in an official capacity;

(*b*) To ensure that any person claiming such a remedy shall have his right thereto determined by competent judicial, administrative or legislative authorities, or by any other competent authority provided for by the legal system of the State, and to develop the possibilities of judicial remedy;

(*c*) To ensure that the competent authorities shall enforce such remedies when granted.

ARTICLE 3

The States Parties to the present Covenant undertake to ensure the equal right of men and women to the enjoyment of all civil and political rights set forth in the present Covenant.

ARTICLE 4

1. In time of public emergency which threatens the life of the nation and the existence of which is officially proclaimed, the State Parties to the present Covenant may take measures derogating from their obligations

under the present Covenant to the extent strictly required by the exigencies of the situation, provided that such measures are not inconsistent with their other obligations under international law and do not involve discrimination solely on the ground of race, colour, sex, language, religion or social origin.

2. No derogation from Articles 6, 7, 8 (paragraphs 1 and 2), 11, 15, 16 and 18 may be made under this provision.

3. Any State Party to the present Covenant availing itself of the right of derogation shall immediately inform the other States Parties to the present Covenant, through the intermediary of the Secretary-General of the United Nations of the provisions from which it has derogated and of the reasons by which it was actuated. A further communication shall be made, through the same intermediary on the date on which it terminates such derogation.

ARTICLE 5

1. Nothing in the present Covenant may be interpreted as implying for any State, group or person any right to engage in any activity or perform any act aimed at the destruction of any of the rights and freedoms recognized herein or at their limitation to a greater extent than is provided for in the present Covenant.

2. There shall be no restriction upon or derogation from any of the fundamental human rights recognized or existing in any State Party to the present Covenant pursuant to law, conventions, regulations or custom on the pretext that the present Covenant does not recognize such rights or that it recognizes them to a lesser extent.

Part III

ARTICLE 6

1. Every human being has the inherent right to life. This right shall be protected by law. No one shall be arbitrarily deprived of his life.

2. In countries which have not abolished the death penalty, sentence of death may be imposed only for the most serious crimes in accordance with the law in force at the time of the commission of the crime and not contrary to the provisions of the present Covenant and to the Convention on the Prevention and Punishment of the Crime of Genocide. This penalty can only be carried out pursuant to a final judgement rendered by a competent court.

3. When deprivation of life constitutes the crime of genocide, it is understood that nothing in this article shall authorize any State Party to the present Covenant to derogate in any way from any obligation assumed under the provisions of the Convention on the Prevention and Punishment of the Crime of Genocide.

4. Anyone sentenced to death shall have the right to seek pardon or commutation of the sentence. Amnesty, pardon or commutation of the sentence of death may be granted in all cases.

5. Sentence of death shall not be imposed for crimes committed by persons below eighteen years of age and shall not be carried out on pregnant women.

6. Nothing in this article shall be invoked to delay or to prevent the abolition of capital punishment by any State Party to the present Covenant.

ARTICLE 7

No one shall be subjected to torture or to cruel, inhuman or degrading treatment or punishment. In particular, no one shall be subjected without his free consent to medical or scientific experimentation.

ARTICLE 8

1. No one shall be held in slavery; slavery and the slave-trade in all their forms shall be prohibited.

2. No one shall be held in servitude.

3. (a) No one shall be required to perform forced or compulsory labour;
   (b) Paragraph 3 (a) shall not be held to preclude, in countries where imprisonment with hard labour may be imposed as a punishment for a crime, the performance of hard labour in pursuance of a sentence to such punishment by a competent court;
   (c) For the purpose of this paragraph the term 'forced or compulsory labour' shall not include:
      (i) Any work or service, not referred to in sub-paragraph (b), normally required of a person who is under detention in consequence of a lawful order of a court, or of a person during conditional release from such detention;
      (ii) Any service of a military character and, in countries where conscientious objection is recognized, any national service required by law of conscientious objectors;
      (iii) Any service exacted in cases of emergency or calamity threatening the life or well-being of the community;
      (iv) Any work or service which forms part of normal civil obligations.

ARTICLE 9

1. Everyone has the right to liberty and security of person. No one shall be subjected to arbitrary arrest or detention. No one shall be deprived of his liberty except on such grounds and in accordance with such procedure as are established by law.

2. Anyone who is arrested shall be informed, at the time of arrest, of the reasons for his arrest and shall be promptly informed of any charges against him.

3. Anyone arrested or detained on a criminal charge shall be brought promptly before a judge or other officer authorized by law to exercise judicial power and shall be entitled to trial within a reasonable time or to release. It shall not be the general rule that persons awaiting trial shall be detained in custody, but release may be subject to guarantees to appear for trial, at any other stage of the judicial proceedings, and, should occasion arise, for execution of the judgement.

4. Anyone who is deprived of his liberty by arrest or detention shall be entitled to take proceedings before a court, in order that that court may decide without delay on the lawfulness of his detention and order his release if the detention is not lawful.

5. Anyone who has been the victim of unlawful arrest or detention shall have an enforceable right to compensation.

ARTICLE 10

1. All persons deprived of their liberty shall be treated with humanity and with respect for the inherent dignity of the human person.

2. (*a*) Accused persons shall, save in exceptional circumstances, be segregated from convicted persons and shall be subject to separate treatment appropriate to their status as unconvicted persons;

(*b*) Accused juvenile persons shall be separated from adults and brought as speedily as possible for adjudication.

3. The penitentiary system shall comprise treatment of prisoners the essential aim of which shall be their reformation and social rehabilitation. Juvenile offenders shall be segregated from adults and be accorded treatment appropriate to their age and legal status.

ARTICLE 11

No one shall be imprisoned merely on the ground of inability to fulfil a contractual obligation.

ARTICLE 12

1. Everyone lawfully within the territory of a State shall, within that territory, have the right to liberty of movement and freedom to choose his residence.

2. Everyone shall be free to leave any country, including his own.

3. The above-mentioned rights shall not be subject to any restrictions except those which are provided by law, are necessary to protect national se-

curity, public order (*ordre public*), public health or morals or the rights and freedoms of others, and are consistent with the other rights recognized in the present Convenant.

4. No one shall be arbitrarily deprived of the right to enter his own country.

ARTICLE 13

An alien lawfully in the territory of a State Party to the present Covenant may be expelled therefrom only in pursuance of a decision reached in accordance with law and shall, except where compelling reasons of national security otherwise require, be allowed to submit the reasons against his expulsion and to have his case reviewed by, and be represented for the purpose before, the competent authority or a person or persons especially designated by the competent authority.

ARTICLE 14

1. All persons shall be equal before the courts and tribunals. In the determination of any criminal charge against him, or of his rights and obligations in a suit at law, everyone shall be entitled to a fair and public hearing by a competent, independent and impartial tribunal established by law. The Press and the public may be excluded from all or part of a trial for reasons of morals, public order (*ordre public*) or national security in a democratic society, or when the interest of the private lives of the parties so requires, or to the extent strictly necessary in the opinion of the court in special circumstances where publicity would prejudice the interests of justice; but any judgement rendered in a criminal case or in a suit at law shall be made public except where the interest of juvenile persons otherwise requires or the proceedings concern matrimonial disputes or the guardianship of children.

2. Everyone charged with a criminal offence shall have the right to be presumed innocent until proved guilty according to law.

3. In the determination of any criminal charge against him, everyone shall be entitled to the following minimum guarantees, in full equality:

> (*a*) To be informed promptly and in detail in a language which he understands of the nature and cause of the charge against him;
> (*b*) To have adequate time and facilities for the preparation of his defence and to communicate with counsel of his own choosing;
> (*c*) To be tried without undue delay;
> (*d*) To be tried in his presence, and to defend himself in person or through legal assistance of his own choosing; to be informed, if he does not have legal assistance, of this right; and to have legal assistance assigned to him, in any case where the interests of justice so require, and without payment by him in any such case if he does not have sufficient means to pay for it;

(*e*) To examine, or have examined, the witnesses against him and to obtain the attendance and examination of witnesses on his behalf under the same conditions as witnesses against him;

(*f*) To have the free assistance of an interpreter if he cannot understand or speak the language used in court;

(*g*) Not to be compelled to testify against himself or to confess guilt.

4. In the case of juvenile persons, the procedure shall be such as will take account of their age and the desirability of promoting their rehabilitation.

5. Everyone convicted of a crime shall have the right to his conviction and sentence being reviewed by a higher tribunal according to law.

6. When a person has by a final decision been convicted of a criminal offence and when subsequently his conviction has been reversed or he has been pardoned on the ground that a new or newly discovered fact shows conclusively that there has been a miscarriage of justice, the person who has suffered punishment as a result of such conviction shall be compensated according to law, unless it is proved that the nondisclosure of the unknown fact in time is wholly or partly attributable to him.

7. No one shall be liable to be tried or punished again for an offence for which he has already been finally convicted or acquitted in accordance with the law and penal procedure of each country.

ARTICLE 15

1. No one shall be held guilty of any criminal offence on account of any act or omission which did not constitute a criminal offence, under national or international law, at the time when it was committed. Nor shall a heavier penalty be imposed than the one that was applicable at the time when the criminal offence was committed. If, subsequent to the commission of the offence, provision is made by law for the imposition of a lighter penalty, the offender shall benefit thereby.

2. Nothing in this article shall prejudice the trial and punishment of any person for any act or omission which, at the time when it was committed, was criminal according to the general principles of law recognized by the community of nations.

ARTICLE 16

Everyone shall have the right to recognition everywhere as a person before the law.

ARTICLE 17

1. No one shall be subjected to arbitrary or unlawful interference with his privacy, family, home or correspondence, nor to unlawful attacks on his honour and reputation.

2. Everyone has the right to the protection of the law against such interference or attacks.

ARTICLE 18

1. Everyone shall have the right to freedom of thought, conscience and religion. This right shall include freedom to have or to adopt a religion or belief of his choice, and freedom, either individually or in community with others and in public or private, to manifest his religion or belief in worship, observance, practice and teaching.

2. No one shall be subject to coercion which would impair his freedom to have or to adopt a religion or belief of his choice.

3. Freedom to manifest one's religion or beliefs may be subject only to such limitations as are prescribed by law and are necessary to protect public safety, order, health, or morals or the fundamental rights and freedoms of others.

4. The States Parties to the present Covenant undertake to have respect for the liberty of parents and, when applicable, legal guardians to ensure the religious and moral education of their children in conformity with their own convictions.

ARTICLE 19

1. Everyone shall have the right to hold opinions without interference.

2. Everyone shall have the right to freedom of expression; this right shall include freedom to seek, receive and impart information and ideas of all kinds, regardless of frontiers, either orally, in writing or in print, in the form of art, or through any other media of his choice.

3. The exercise of the rights provided for in paragraph 2 of this Article carries with it special duties and responsibilities. It may therefore be subject to certain restrictions, but these shall only be such as are provided by law and are necessary:

    (*a*) For respect of the rights or reputations of others;
    (*b*) For the protection of national security or of public order (*ordre public*), or of public health or morals.

ARTICLE 20

1. Any propaganda for war shall be prohibited by law.

2. Any advocacy of national, racial or religious hatred that constitutes incitement to discrimination, hostility or violence shall be prohibited by law.

ARTICLE 21

The right of peaceful assembly shall be recognized. No restrictions may be placed on the exercise of this right other than those imposed in conformity with the law and which are necessary in a democratic society in the interests of national security or public safety, public order (*ordre public*), the protection of public health or morals or the protection of the rights and freedoms of others.

ARTICLE 22

1. Everyone shall have the right to freedom of association with others, including the right to form and join trade unions for the protection of his interests.

2. No restrictions may be placed on the exercise of this right other than those which are prescribed by law and which are necessary in a democratic society in the interests of national security or public safety, public order (*ordre public*), the protection of public health or morals or the protection of the rights and freedoms of others. This Article shall not prevent the imposition of lawful restrictions on members of the armed forces and of the police in their exercise of this right.

3. Nothing in this article shall authorize States Parties to the International Labour Organization Convention of 1948 concerning Freedom of Association and Protection of the Right to Organize to take legislative measures which would prejudice, or to apply the law in such a manner as to prejudice, the guarantees provided for in that Convention.

ARTICLE 23

1. The family is the natural and fundamental group unit of society and is entitled to protection by society and the State.

2. The right of men and women of marriageable age to marry and to found a family shall be recognized.

3. No marriage shall be entered into without the free and full consent of the intending spouses.

4. States Parties to the present Covenant shall take appropriate steps to ensure equality of rights and responsibilities of spouses as to marriage, during marriage and at its dissolution. In the case of dissolution, provision shall be made for the necessary protection of any children.

ARTICLE 24

1. Every child shall have, without any discrimination as to race, colour, sex, language, religion, national or social origin, property or birth, the right to such measures of protection as are required by his status as a minor, on the part of his family, society and the State.

2. Every child shall be registered immediately after birth and shall have a name.

3. Every child has the right to acquire a nationality.

ARTICLE 25

Every citizen shall have the right and the opportunity, without any of the distinctions mentioned in Article 2 and without unreasonable restrictions:

(*a*) To take part in the conduct of public affairs, directly or through freely chosen representatives;

(*b*) To vote and to be elected at genuine periodic elections which shall be by universal and equal suffrage and shall be held by secret ballot, guaranteeing the free expression of the will of the electors;

(*c*) To have access, on general terms of equality, to public service in his country.

ARTICLE 26

All persons are equal before the law and are entitled without any discrimination to the equal protection of the law. In this respect, the law shall prohibit any discrimination and guarantee to all persons equal and effective protection against discrimination on any ground such as race, colour, sex, language, religion, political or other opinion, national or social origin, property, birth or other status.

ARTICLE 27

In those States in which ethnic, religious or linguistic minorities exist, persons belonging to such minorities shall not be denied the right, in community with the other members of their group, to enjoy their own culture, to profess and practise their own religion, or to use their own language.

Part IV

ARTICLE 28

1. There shall be established a Human Rights Committee (hereafter referred to in the present Covenant as the Committee). It shall consist of eighteen members and shall carry out the functions hereinafter provided.

2. The Committee shall be composed of nationals of the States Parties to the present Covenant who shall be persons of high moral character and recognized competence in the field of human rights, consideration being given to the usefulness of the participation of some persons having legal experience.

3. The members of the Committee shall be elected and shall serve in their personal capacity.

ARTICLE 29

1. The members of the Committee shall be elected by secret ballot from a list of persons possessing the qualifications prescribed in Article 28 and nominated for the purpose by the States Parties to the present Covenant.

2. Each State Party to the present Covenant may nominate not more than two persons. These persons shall be nationals of the nominating State.

3. A person shall be eligible for renomination.

ARTICLE 30

1. The initial election shall be held no later than six months after the date of the entry into force of the present Covenant.

2. At least four months before the date of each election to the Committee, other than an election to fill a vacancy declared in accordance with Article 34, the Secretary-General of the United Nations shall address a written invitation to the States Parties to the present Covenant to submit their nominations for membership of the Committee within three months.

3. The Secretary-General of the United Nations shall prepare a list in alphabetical order of all the persons thus nominated, with an indication of the States Parties which have nominated them, and shall submit it to the States Parties to the present Covenant no later than one month before the date of each election.

4. Elections of the members of the Committee shall be held at a meeting of the States Parties to the present Covenant convened by the Secretary-General of the United Nations at the Headquarters of the United Nations. At that meeting, for which two thirds of the States Parties to the present Covenant shall constitute a quorum, the persons elected to the Committee shall be those nominees who obtain the largest number of votes and an absolute majority of the votes of the representatives of States Parties present and voting.

ARTICLE 31

1. The Committee may not include more than one national of the same State.

2. In the election of the Committee, consideration shall be given to equitable geographical distribution of membership and to the representation of the different forms of civilization and of the principal legal systems.

ARTICLE 32

1. The members of the Committee shall be elected for a term of four years. They shall be eligible for re-election if renominated. However, the terms of nine of the members elected at the first election shall expire at the end of two years; immediately after the first election, the names of these nine members shall be chosen by lot by the Chairman of the meeting referred to in Article 30, paragraph 4.

2. Elections at the expiry of office shall be held in accordance with the preceding articles of this part of the present Covenant.

ARTICLE 33

1. If, in the unanimous opinion of the other members, a member of the Committee has ceased to carry out his functions for any cause other than absence of a temporary character, the Chairman of the Committee shall notify the Secretary-General of the United Nations, who shall then declare the seat of that member to be vacant.

2. In the event of the death or the resignation of a member of the Committee, the Chairman shall immediately notify the Secretary-General of the United Nations, who shall declare the seat vacant from the date of death or the date on which the resignation takes effect.

ARTICLE 34

1. When a vacancy is declared in accordance with Article 33 and if the term of office of the member to be replaced does not expire within six months of the declaration of the vacancy, the Secretary-General of the United Nations shall notify each of the States Parties to the present Covenant, which may within two months submit nominations in accordance with Article 29 for the purpose of filling the vacancy.

2. The Secretary-General of the United Nations shall prepare a list in alphabetical order of the persons thus nominated and shall submit it to the States Parties to the present Covenant. The election to fill the vacancy shall then take place in accordance with the relevant provisions of this part of the present Covenant.

3. A member of the Committee elected to fill a vacancy declared in accordance with Article 33 shall hold office for the remainder of the term of the member who vacated the seat on the Committee under the provisions of that Article.

ARTICLE 35

The members of the Committee shall, with the approval of the General Assembly of the United Nations, receive emoluments from United Nations resources on such terms and conditions as the General Assembly may decide, having regard to the importance of the Committee's responsibilities.

ARTICLE 36

The Secretary-General of the United Nations shall provide the necessary staff and facilities for the effective performance of the functions of the Committee under the present Covenant.

ARTICLE 37

1. The Secretary-General of the United Nations shall convene the initial meeting of the Committee at the Headquarters of the United Nations.

2. After its initial meeting, the Committee shall meet at such times as shall be provided in its rules of procedure.

3. The Committee shall normally meet at the Headquarters of the United Nations or at the United Nations Office at Geneva.

ARTICLE 38

Every member of the Committee shall, before taking up his duties, make a solemn declaration in open committee that he will perform his functions impartially and conscientiously.

ARTICLE 39

1. The Committee shall elect its officers for a term of two years. They may be re-elected.

2. The Committee shall establish its own rules of procedure, but these rules shall provide, *inter alia,* that:

    (*a*) Twelve members shall constitute a quorum;

    (*b*) Decisions of the Committee shall be made by a majority vote of the members present.

ARTICLE 40

1. The States Parties to the present Covenant undertake to submit reports on the measures they have adopted which give effect to the rights recognized herein and on the progress made in the enjoyment of those rights:

    (*a*) Within one year of the entry into force of the present Covenant for the States Parties concerned;

    (*b*) Thereafter whenever the Committee so requests.

2. All reports shall be submitted to the Secretary-General of the United Nations, who shall transmit them to the Committee for consideration. Reports shall indicate the factors and difficulties, if any, affecting the implementation of the present Covenant.

3. The Secretary-General of the United Nations may, after consultation with the Committee, transmit to the specialized agencies concerned copies of such parts of the reports as may fall within their field of competence.

4. The Committee shall study the reports submitted by the States Parties to the present Covenant. It shall transmit its reports, and such general comments as it may consider appropriate, to the States Parties. The Committee may also transmit to the Economic and Social Council these comments along with the copies of the reports it has received from States Parties to the present Covenant.

5. The States Parties to the present Covenant may submit to the Committee observations on any comments that may be made in accordance with paragraph 4 of this Article.

ARTICLE 41

1. A State Party to the present Covenant may at any time declare under this article that it recognizes the competence of the Committee to receive and consider communications to the effect that a State Party claims that another State Party is not fulfilling its obligations under the present Covenant. Communications under this Article may be received and considered only if submitted by a State Party which has made a declaration recognizing in regard to itself the competence of the Committee. No communication shall be received by the Committee if it concerns a State Party which has not made such a declaration. Communications received under this article shall be dealt with in accordance with the following procedure:

(*a*) If a State Party to the present Covenant considers that another State Party is not giving effect to the provisions of the present Covenant, it may, by written communication, bring the matter to the attention of that State Party. Within three months after the receipt of the communication, the receiving State shall afford the State which sent the communication an explanation or any other statement in writing clarifying the matter, which should include, to the extent possible and pertinent, reference to domestic procedures and remedies taken, pending, or available in the matter.

(*b*) If the matter is not adjusted to the satisfaction of both States Parties concerned within six months after the receipt by the receiving State of the initial communication, either State shall have the right to refer the matter to the Committee, by notice given to the Committee and to the other State.

(*c*) The Committee shall deal with a matter referred to it only after it has ascertained that all available domestic remedies have been invoked and exhausted in the matter, in conformity with the generally recognized principles of international law. This shall not be the rule where the application of the remedies is unreasonably prolonged.

(*d*) The Committee shall hold closed meetings when examining communications under this Article.

(*e*) Subject to the provisions of sub-paragraph (*c*), the Committee shall make available its good offices to the States Parties concerned with a view to a friendly solution of the matter on the basis of respect for human rights and fundamental freedoms as recognized in the present Covenant.

(*f*) In any matter referred to it, the Committee may call upon the States Parties concerned, referred to in sub-paragraph (*b*), to supply any relevant information.

(*g*) The States Parties concerned, referred to in sub-paragraph (*b*), shall have the right to be represented when the matter is being considered in the Committee and to make submissions orally and/or in writing.

(*h*) The Committee shall, within twelve months after the date of receipt of notice under sub-paragraph (*b*), submit a report:

   (i) If a solution within the terms of sub-paragraph (*e*) is reached, the Committee shall confine its report to a brief statement of the facts and of the solution reached;

   (ii) If a solution within the terms of sub-paragraph (*e*) is not reached, the Committee shall confine its report to a brief statement of the facts; the written submissions and record of the oral submissions made by the States Parties concerned shall be attached to the report.

In every matter, the report shall be communicated to the States Parties concerned.

2. The provisions of this article shall come into force when ten States Parties to the present Covenant have made declarations under paragraph 1 of this article. Such declarations shall be deposited by the States Parties with the Secretary-General of the United Nations, who shall transmit copies thereof to the other States Parties. A declaration may be withdrawn at any time by notification to the Secretary-General. Such a withdrawal shall not prejudice the consideration of any matter which is the subject of a communication already transmitted under this Article; no further communication by any State Party shall be received after the notification of withdrawal of the declaration has been received by the Secretary-General, unless the State Party concerned has made a new declaration.

ARTICLE 42

1. (*a*) If a matter referred to the Committee in accordance with Article 41 is not resolved to the satisfaction of the States Parties concerned, the Committee may, with the prior consent of the States Parties concerned, appoint an *ad hoc* Conciliation Commission (hereinafter referred to as the Commission). The good offices of the Commission shall be made available to the States Parties concerned with a view to an amicable solution of the matter on the basis of respect for the present Covenant;

   (*b*) The Commission shall consist of five persons acceptable to the States Parties concerned. If the States Parties concerned fail to reach agreement within three months on all or part of the composition of the Commission the members of the Commission concerning whom no agreement has been reached shall be elected by secret ballot by a two-thirds majority vote of the Committee from among its members.

2. The members of the Commission shall serve in their personal capacity. They shall not be nationals of the States Parties concerned, or of a State not party to the present Covenant, or of a State Party which has not made a declaration under Article 41.

3. The Commission shall elect its own Chairman and adopt its own rules of procedure.

4. The meetings of the Commission shall normally be held at the Headquarters of the United Nations or at the United Nations Office at Geneva. However, they may be held at such other convenient places as the Commission may determine in consultation with the Secretary-General of the United Nations and the States Parties concerned.

5. The secretariat provided in accordance with Article 36 shall also service the commissions appointed under this Article.

6. The information received and collated by the Committee shall be made available to the Commission and the Commission may call upon the States Parties concerned to supply any other relevant information.

7. When the Commission has fully considered the matter, but in any event not later than twelve months after having been seized of the matter, it shall submit to the Chairman of the Committee a report for communication to the States Parties concerned.

(*a*) If the Commission is unable to complete its consideration of the matter within twelve months, it shall confine its report to a brief statement of the status of its consideration of the matter.

(*b*) If an amicable solution to the matter on the basis of respect for human rights as recognized in the present Covenant is reached, the Commission shall confine its report to a brief statement of the facts and of the solution reached.

(*c*) If a solution within the terms of sub-paragraph (*b*) is not reached, the Commission's report shall embody its findings on all questions of fact relevant to the issues between the States Parties concerned, and its views on the possibilities of an amicable solution of the matter. This report shall also contain the written submissions and a record of the oral submissions made by the States Parties concerned.

(*d*) If the Commission's report is submitted under sub-paragraph (*c*), the States Parties concerned shall, within three months of the receipt of the report, notify the Chairman of the Committee whether or not they accept the contents of the report of the Commission.

8. The provisions of this Article are without prejudice to the responsibilities of the Committee under Article 41.

9. The States Parties concerned shall share equally all the expenses of the members of the Commission in accordance with estimates to be provided by the Secretary-General of the United Nations.

10. The Secretary-General of the United Nations shall be empowered to pay the expenses of the members of the Commission, if necessary, before reimbursement by the States Parties concerned, in accordance with paragraph 9 of this Article.

ARTICLE 43

The members of the Committee, and of the *ad hoc* conciliation commissions which may be appointed under Article 42, shall be entitled to the facilities, privileges and immunities of experts on mission for the United Nations as laid down in the relevant sections of the Convention on the Privileges and Immunities of the United Nations.

ARTICLE 44

The provisions for the implementation of the present Covenant shall apply without prejudice to the procedures prescribed in the field of human rights by or under the constituent instruments and the conventions of the United Nations and of the specialized agencies and shall not prevent the States Parties to the present Covenant from having recourse to other procedures for settling a dispute in accordance with general or special international agreements in force between them.

ARTICLE 45

The Committee shall submit to the General Assembly of the United Nations through the Economic and Social Council, an annual report on its activities.

Part V

ARTICLE 46

Nothing in the present Covenant shall be interpreted as impairing the provisions of the Charter of the United Nations and of the constitutions of the specialized agencies which define the respective responsibilities of the various organs of the United Nations and of the specialized agencies in regard to the matters dealt with in the present Covenant.

ARTICLE 47

Nothing in the present Covenant shall be interpreted as impairing the inherent right of all peoples to enjoy and utilize fully and freely their natural wealth and resources.

Part VI

ARTICLE 48

1. The present Covenant is open for signature by any State Member of the United Nations or member of any of its specialized agencies, by any State Party to the Statute of the International Court of Justice, and by any other State which has been invited by the General Assembly of the United Nations to become a party to the present Covenant.

2. The present Covenant is subject to ratification. Instruments of ratification shall be deposited with the Secretary-General of the United Nations.

3. The present Covenant shall be open to accession by any State referred to in paragraph 1 of this Article.

4. Accession shall be effected by the deposit of an instrument of accession with the Secretary-General of the United Nations.

5. The Secretary-General of the United Nations shall inform all States which have signed this Covenant or acceded to it of the deposit of each instrument of ratification or accession.

ARTICLE 49

1. The present Covenant shall enter into force three months after the date of the deposit with the Secretary-General of the United Nations of the thirty-fifth instrument of ratification or instrument of accession.

2. For each State ratifying the present Covenant or acceding to it after the deposit of the thirty-fifth instrument of ratification or instrument of accession, the present Covenant shall enter into force three months after the date of the deposit of its own instrument of ratification or instrument of accession.

ARTICLE 50

The provisions of the present Covenant shall extend to all parts of federal States without any limitations or exceptions.

ARTICLE 51

1. Any State Party to the present Covenant may propose an amendment and file it with the Secretary-General of the United Nations. The Secretary-General of the United Nations shall thereupon communicate any proposed amendments to the States Parties to the present Covenant with a request that they notify him whether they favour a conference of States Parties for the purpose of considering and voting upon the proposals. In the event that at least one third of the States Parties favours such a conference, the Secretary-General shall convene the conference under the auspices of the United Nations. Any amendment adopted by a majority of the States Parties present and voting at the conference shall be submitted to the General Assembly of the United Nations for approval.

2. Amendments shall come into force when they have been approved by the General Assembly of the United Nations and accepted by a two-thirds majority of the States Parties to the present Covenant in accordance with their respective constitutional processes.

3. When amendments come into force, they shall be binding on those States Parties which have accepted them, other States Parties still being bound by the provisions of the present Covenant and any earlier amendment which they have accepted.

ARTICLE 52

Irrespective of the notifications made under Article 48, paragraph 5, the Secretary-General of the United Nations shall inform all States referred to in paragraph 1 of the same article of the following particulars:

(*a*) Signatures, ratifications and accessions under Article 48;

(*b*) The date of the entry into force of the present Covenant under Article 49 and the date of the entry into force of any amendments under Article 51.

ARTICLE 53

1. The present Covenant, of which the Chinese, English, French, Russian and Spanish texts are equally authentic, shall be deposited in the archives of the United Nations.

2. The Secretary-General of the United Nations shall transmit certified copies of the present Covenant to all States referred to in Article 48.

INTERNATIONAL COVENANT ON ECONOMIC, SOCIAL, AND CULTURAL RIGHTS, 1966

TEXT

Preamble

The States Parties to the present Covenant,

Considering that, in accordance with the principles proclaimed in the Charter of the United Nations, recognition of the inherent dignity and of the equal and inalienable rights of all members of the human family is the foundation of freedom, justice and peace in the world,

Recognizing that these rights derive from the inherent dignity of the human person,

Recognizing that, in accordance with the Universal Declaration of Human Rights, the ideal of free human beings enjoying freedom from fear and want can only be achieved if conditions are created whereby everyone may enjoy his economic, social and cultural rights, as well as his civil and political rights,

Considering the obligation of States under the Charter of the United Nations to promote universal respect for, and observance of, human rights and freedoms,

Realizing that the individual, having duties to other individuals and to the community to which he belongs, is under a responsibility to strive for the promotion and observance of the rights recognized in the present Covenant,

Agree upon the following articles:

Part I

ARTICLE I

1. All peoples have the right of self-determination. By virtue of that right they freely determine their political status and freely pursue their economic, social and cultural development.

2. All peoples may, for their own ends, freely dispose of their natural wealth and resources without prejudice to any obligations arising out of international economic co-operation, based upon the principle of mutual benefit, and international law. In no case may a people be deprived of its own means of subsistence.

3. The States Parties to the present Covenant, including those having responsibility for the administration of Non-Self-Governing and Trust Territories, shall promote the realization of the right of self-determination, and shall respect that right, in conformity with the provisions of the Charter of the United Nations.

Part II

ARTICLE 2

1. Each State Party to the present Covenant undertakes to take steps, individually and through international assistance and co-operation, especially economic and technical, to the maximum of its available resources, with a view to achieving progressively the full realization of the rights recognized in the present Covenant by all appropriate means, including particularly the adoption of legislative measures.

2. The States Parties to the present Covenant undertake to guarantee that the rights enunciated in the present Covenant will be exercised without discrimination of any kind as to race, colour, sex, language, religion, political or other opinion, national or social origin, property, birth or other status.

3. Developing countries, with due regard to human rights and their national economy, may determine to what extent they would guarantee the economic rights recognized in the present Covenant to non-nationals.

ARTICLE 3

The States Parties to the present Covenant undertake to ensure the equal right of men and women to the enjoyment of all economic, social and cultural rights set forth in the present Covenant.

ARTICLE 4

The States Parties to the present Covenant recognize that, in the enjoyment of those rights provided by the State in conformity with the present Covenant, the State may subject such rights only to such limitations as are determined by law only in so far as this may be compatible with the nature of these rights and solely for the purpose of promoting the general welfare in a democratic society.

ARTICLE 5

1. Nothing in the present Covenant may be interpreted as implying for any State, group or person any right to engage in any activity or to perform any act aimed at the destruction of any of the rights or freedoms recognized herein, or at their limitation to a greater extent than is provided for in the present Covenant.

2. No restriction upon or derogation from any of the fundamental human rights recognized or existing in any country in virtue of law, conventions, regulations or custom shall be admitted on the pretext that the present Covenant does not recognize such rights or that it recognizes them to a lesser extent.

Part III

ARTICLE 6

1. The States Parties to the present Covenant recognize the right to work, which includes the right of everyone to the opportunity to gain his living by work which he freely chooses or accepts, and will take appropriate steps to safeguard this right.

2. The steps to be taken by a State Party to the present Covenant to achieve the full realization of this right shall include technical and vocational guidance and training programmes, policies and techniques to achieve steady economic, social and cultural development and full and productive employment under conditions safeguarding fundamental political and economic freedoms to the individual.

ARTICLE 7

The States Parties to the present Covenant recognize the right of everyone to the enjoyment of just and favourable conditions of work, which ensure, in particular:

(*a*) Remuneration which provides all workers, as a minimum with:

(i) Fair wages and equal remuneration for work of equal value without distinction of any kind, in particular women being guaranteed conditions of work not inferior to those enjoyed by men, with equal pay for equal work;

(ii) A decent living for themselves and their families in accordance with the provisions of the present Covenant;

(*b*) Safe and healthy working conditions;

(*c*) Equal opportunity for everyone to be promoted in his employment to an appropriate higher level, subject to no considerations other than those of seniority and competence;

(*d*) Rest, leisure and reasonable limitation of working hours and periodic holidays with pay, as well as remuneration for public holidays.

ARTICLE 8

1. The States Parties to the present Covenant undertake to ensure:

(*a*) The right of everyone to form trade unions and join the trade union of his choice, subject only to the rules of the organization concerned, for the promotion and protection of his economic and social interests. No restrictions may be placed on the exercise of this right other than those prescribed by law and which are necessary in a democratic society in the interests of national security or public order or for the protection of the rights and freedoms of others;

(*b*) The right of trade unions to establish national federations or confederations and the right of the latter to form or join international trade union organizations;

(*c*) The right of trade unions to function freely subject to no limitations other than those prescribed by law and which are necessary in a democratic society in the interests of national security or public order or for the protection of the rights and freedoms of others;

(*d*) The right to strike, provided that it is exercised in conformity with the laws of the particular country.

2. This article shall not prevent the imposition of lawful restrictions on the exercise of these rights by members of the armed forces or of the police or of the administration of the State.

3. Nothing in this article shall authorize States Parties to the International Labour Organization Convention of 1948 concerning Freedom of Association and Protection of the Right to Organize to take legislative measures which would prejudice, or apply the law in such a manner as would prejudice, the guarantees provided for in that Convention.

ARTICLE 9

The States Parties to the present Covenant recognize the right of everyone to social security, including social insurance.

ARTICLE 10

The States Parties to the present Covenant recognize that:

1. The widest possible protection and assistance should be accorded to the family, which is the natural and fundamental group unit of society, particularly for its establishment and while it is responsible for the care and education of dependent children. Marriage must be entered into with the free consent of the intending spouses.

2. Special protection should be accorded to mothers during a reasonable period before and after childbirth. During such period working mothers should be accorded paid leave or leave with adequate social security benefits.

3. Special measures of protection and assistance should be taken on behalf of all children and young persons without any discrimination for reasons of parentage or other conditions. Children and young persons should be protected from economic and social exploitation. Their employment in work harmful to their morals or health or dangerous to life or likely to hamper

their normal development should be punishable by law. States should also set age limits below which the paid employment of child labour should be prohibited and punishable by law.

ARTICLE 11

1. The States Parties to the present Covenant recognize the right of everyone to an adequate standard of living for himself and his family, including adequate food, clothing and housing, and to the continuous improvement of living conditions. The States Parties will take appropriate steps to ensure the realization of this right, recognizing to this effect the essential importance of international co-operation based on free consent.

2. The States Parties to the present Covenant, recognizing the fundamental right of everyone to be free from hunger, shall take, individually and through international co-operation, the measures, including specific programmes, which are needed:

    (*a*) To improve methods of production, conservation and distribution of food by making full use of technical and scientific knowledge, by disseminating knowledge of the principles of nutrition and by developing or reforming agrarian systems in such a way as to achieve the most efficient development and utilization of natural resources;

    (*b*) Taking into account the problems of both food-importing and food-exporting countries, to ensure an equitable distribution of world food supplies in relation to need.

ARTICLE 12

1. The States Parties to the present Covenant recognize the right of everyone to the enjoyment of the highest attainable standard of physical and mental health.

2. The steps to be taken by the States Parties to the present Covenant to achieve the full realization of this right shall include those necessary for:

    (*a*) The provision for the reduction of the stillbirth-rate and of infant mortality and for the healthy development of the child;

    (*b*) The improvement of all aspects of environmental and industrial hygiene;

    (*c*) The prevention, treatment and control of epidemic, endemic, occupational and other diseases;

    (*d*) The creation of conditions which would assure to all medical service and medical attention in the event of sickness.

ARTICLE 13

1. The States Parties to the present Covenant recognize the right of everyone to education. They agree that education shall be directed to the full development of the human personality and the sense of its dignity, and shall

strengthen the respect for human rights and fundamental freedoms. They further agree that education shall enable all persons to participate effectively in a free society, promote understanding, tolerance and friendship among all nations and all racial, ethnic or religious groups, and further the activities of the United Nations for the maintenance of peace.

2. The States Parties to the present Covenant recognize that, with a view to achieving the full realization of this right:

(a) Primary education shall be compulsory and available free to all;

(b) Secondary education in its different forms, including technical and vocational secondary education, shall be made generally available and accessible to all by every appropriate means, and in particular by the progressive introduction of free education;

(c) Higher education shall be made equally accessible to all, on the basis of capacity, by every appropriate means, and in particular by the progressive introduction of free education;

(d) Fundamental education shall be encouraged or intensified as far as possible for those persons who have not received or completed the whole period of their primary education;

(e) The development of a system of schools at all levels shall be actively pursued, an adequate fellowship system shall be established, and the material conditions of teaching staff shall be continuously improved.

3. The States Parties to the present Covenant undertake to have respect for the liberty of parents and, when applicable, legal guardians, to choose for their children schools, other than those established by the public authorities, which conform to such minimum educational standards as may be laid down or approved by the State and to ensure the religious and moral education of their children in conformity with their own convictions.

4. No part of this article shall be construed so as to interfere with the liberty of individuals and bodies to establish and direct educational institutions, subject always to the observance of the principles set forth in paragraph 1 of this Article and to the requirement that the education given in such institutions shall conform to such minimum standards as may be laid down by the State.

ARTICLE 14

Each State Party to the present Covenant which, at the time of becoming a Party, has not been able to secure in its metropolitan territory or other territories under its jurisdiction compulsory primary education, free of charge, undertakes, within two years, to work out and adopt a detailed plan of action for the progressive implementation, within a reasonable number of years, to be fixed in the plan, of the principle of compulsory education free of charge for all.

ARTICLE 15

1. The States Parties to the present Covenant recognize the right of everyone:

   (*a*) To take part in cultural life;

   (*b*) To enjoy the benefits of scientific progress and its applications;

   (*c*) To benefit from the protection of the moral and material interests resulting from any scientific, literary or artistic production of which he is the author.

2. The steps to be taken by the States Parties to the present Covenant to achieve the full realization of this right shall include those necessary for the conservation, the development and the diffusion of science and culture.

3. The States Parties to the present Covenant undertake to respect the freedom indispensable for scientific research and creative activity.

4. The States Parties to the present Covenant recognize the benefits to be derived from the encouragement and development of international contacts and co-operation in the scientific and cultural fields.

Part IV

ARTICLE 16

1. The States Parties to the present Covenant undertake to submit in conformity with this part of the Covenant reports on the measures which they have adopted and the progress made in achieving the observance of the rights recognized herein.

2. (*a*) All reports shall be submitted to the Secretary-General of the United Nations, who shall transmit copies to the Economic and Social Council for consideration in accordance with the provisions of the present Covenant.

   (*b*) The Secretary-General of the United Nations shall also transmit to the specialized agencies copies of the reports, or any relevant parts therefrom, from States Parties to the present Covenant which are also members of these specialized agencies in so far as these reports, or parts therefrom, relate to any matters which fall within the responsibilities of the said agencies in accordance with their constitutional instruments.

ARTICLE 17

1. The States Parties to the present Covenant shall furnish their reports in stages, in accordance with a programme to be established by the Economic and Social Council within one year of the entry into force of the present Covenant after consultation with the States Parties and the specialized agencies concerned.

2. Reports may indicate factors and difficulties affecting the degree of fulfilment of obligations under the present Covenant.

3. Where relevant information has previously been furnished to the United Nations or to any specialized agency by any State Party to the present Covenant, it will not be necessary to reproduce that information, but a precise reference to the information so furnished will suffice.

ARTICLE 18

Pursuant to its responsibilities under the Charter of the United Nations in the field of human rights and fundamental freedoms, the Economic and Social Council may make arrangements with the specialized agencies in respect of their reporting to it on the progress made in achieving the observance of the provisions of the present Covenant falling within the scope of their activities. These reports may include particulars of decisions and recommendations on such implementation adopted by their competent organs.

ARTICLE 19

The Economic and Social Council may transmit to the Commission on Human Rights for study and general recommendation or as appropriate for information the reports concerning human rights submitted by States in accordance with Articles 16 and 17, and those concerning human rights submitted by the specialized agencies in accordance with Article 18.

ARTICLE 20

The States Parties to the present Covenant and the specialized agencies concerned may submit comments to the Economic and Social Council on any general recommendation under Article 19 or reference to such general recommendation in any report of the Commission on Human Rights or any documentation referred to therein.

ARTICLE 21

The Economic and Social Council may submit from time to time to the General Assembly reports with recommendations of a general nature and a summary of the information received from the States Parties to the present Covenant and the specialized agencies on the measures taken and the progress made in achieving general observance of the rights recognized in the present Covenant.

ARTICLE 22

The Economic and Social Council may bring to the attention of other organs of the United Nations, their subsidiary organs and specialized agencies concerned with furnishing technical assistance any matters arising out of the reports referred to in this part of the present Covenant which may assist such bodies in deciding, each within its field of competence, on the advisability of international measures likely to contribute to the effective progressive implementation of the present Covenant.

ARTICLE 23

The States Parties to the present Covenant agree that international action for the achievement of the rights recognized in the present Covenant includes such methods as the conclusion of conventions, the adoption of recommendations, the furnishing of technical assistance and the holding of regional meetings and technical meetings for the purpose of consultation and study organized in conjunction with the Governments concerned.

ARTICLE 24

Nothing in the present Covenant shall be interpreted as impairing the provisions of the Charter of the United Nations and of the constitutions of the specialized agencies which define the respective responsibilities of the various organs of the United Nations and of the specialized agencies in regard to the matters dealt with in the present Covenant.

ARTICLE 25

Nothing in the present Covenant shall be interpreted as impairing the inherent right of all peoples to enjoy and utilize fully and freely their natural wealth and resources.

Part V

ARTICLE 26

1. The present Covenant is open for signature by any State Member of the United Nations or member of any of its specialized agencies, by any State Party to the Statute of the International Court of Justice, and by any other State which has been invited by the General Assembly of the United Nations to become a party to the present Covenant.

2. The present Covenant is subject to ratification. Instruments of ratification shall be deposited with the Secretary-General of the United Nations.

3. The present Covenant shall be open to accession by any State referred to in paragraph 1 of this Article.

4. Accession shall be effected by the deposit of an instrument of accession with the Secretary-General of the United Nations.

5. The Secretary-General of the United Nations shall inform all States which have signed the present Covenant or acceded to it of the deposit of each instrument of ratification or accession.

ARTICLE 27

1. The present Covenant shall enter into force three months after the date of the deposit with the Secretary-General of the United Nations of the thirty-fifth instrument of ratification or instrument of accession.

2. For each State ratifying the present Covenant or acceding to it after the deposit of the thirty-fifth instrument of ratification or instrument of accession, the present Covenant shall enter into force three months after the date of the deposit of its own instrument of ratification or instrument of accession.

ARTICLE 28

The provisions of the present Covenant shall extend to all parts of federal States without any limitations or exceptions.

ARTICLE 29

1. Any State Party to the present Covenant may propose an amendment and file it with the Secretary-General of the United Nations. The Secretary-General shall thereupon communicate any proposed amendments to the States Parties to the present Covenant with a request that they notify him whether they favour a conference of States Parties for the purpose of considering and voting upon the proposals. In the event that at least one third of the States Parties favours such a conference, the Secretary-General shall convene the conference under the auspices of the United Nations. Any amendment adopted by a majority of the States Parties present and voting at the conference shall be submitted to the General Assembly of the United Nations for approval.

2. Amendments shall come into force when they have been approved by the General Assembly of the United Nations and accepted by a two-thirds majority of the States Parties to the present Covenant in accordance with their respective constitutional processes.

3. When amendments come into force they shall be binding on those States Parties which have accepted them, other States Parties still being bound by the provisions of the present Covenant and any earlier amendment which they have accepted.

ARTICLE 30

Irrespective of the notifications made under Article 26, paragraph 5, the Secretary-General of the United Nations shall inform all States referred to in paragraph 1 of the same article of the following particulars:

(*a*) Signatures, ratifications and accessions under Article 26;
(*b*) The date of the entry into force of the present Covenant under Ar-

ticle 27 and the date of the entry into force of any amendments under Article 29.

ARTICLE 31

1. The present Covenant, of which the Chinese, English, French, Russian and Spanish texts are equally authentic, shall be deposited in the archives of the United Nations.

2. The Secretary-General of the United Nations shall transmit certified copies of the present Covenant to all States referred to in Article 26.

Index

Absolute human rights, 50, 59; relative to exceptions and weight of rights, 132–133

Absolute moral norms, 74

Abstract rights, 15; compared with specific rights, 19, 20, 107, 108; in entitlements-plus theory, 32; and transition to specific rights, 107, 108; universality and inalienability of, 47

Abundance strategy, 116

Acceptance of rights: and behavior guidance, 53–54; and evaluation of Universal Declaration, 171; in justified vs. accepted moralities, 39; vs. existence of rights, 37

Accuracy, as criterion for analyzing rights, 29; applied to entitlements-plus theory, 32; applied to legally implemented entitlements theory, 35

Addressees of human rights, 41–43; defined, 14; in entitlements-plus theory, 28, 30–31, 32, 33; governments as, 41–42, 161; individuals as, 42–43, 161; normative burdens of, 28, 32, 33, 35, 41

Affordability of rights, xii; assessment of, 123–124; in Universal Declaration, 127–130; and welfare rights in less developed countries, 147, 164–170

African Charter on Human and Peoples' Rights, 12

African nations, and International Covenants, 6, 67. See also Less developed countries; Organization of African Unity; Third World

Aliens, rights of, 45–46; and stateless persons, 5, 6 n

American Anthropological Association, 68, 69

American Convention on Human Rights, 11–12

Amnesty International, 66 n.5

Analysis of rights, 29–35, 39–40; criteria for, 29

Animals, moral status of, 45 n

Anthropologists, 68–71

Arbitrary arrest, freedom from, 7; interpretation of, 76

Asian countries, 12, 67. See also Less developed countries; Third World

Assembly, freedom of, 4, 105; as derogable right during emergencies, 140, 145; and economic rights, 149; implementation of, 101; and positive duties of governments, 14

Association, freedom of, 4, 8

Asylum, right to, 104

Austin, John, 27 n

Authority: conferring of, 19–23; for international enforcement of human rights, 10

Autonomy, in contemporary concept of human rights, 8

Axing of rights, 171, 172; and consistency test for weight of rights, 133, 135–136; for cost reduction, 125; defined, 125; and governmental welfare programs, 167

Bargaining power, 90

Basic interests, 92. See also Fundamental interests